Chauncey Crafts Hotchkiss

In Defiance of the King

A Romance of the American Revolution

Chauncey Crafts Hotchkiss

In Defiance of the King
A Romance of the American Revolution

ISBN/EAN: 9783744673389

Printed in Europe, USA, Canada, Australia, Japan

Cover: Foto ©Thomas Meinert / pixelio.de

More available books at **www.hansebooks.com**

IN DEFIANCE OF THE KING

THE KING

*A ROMANCE OF
THE AMERICAN REVOLUTION*

BY
CHAUNCEY C. HOTCHKISS

NEW YORK
D. APPLETON AND COMPANY
1895

TO

CAPTAIN SAMUEL PEARL CRAFTS,

OF NEW HAVEN, CONN.,

THIS BOOK IS AFFECTIONATELY DEDICATED

BY HIS NEPHEW.

CONTENTS.

IN DEFIANCE OF THE KING.

CHAPTER I.

"THE REGULARS ARE OUT."

"THERE, now! There's the king's shilling to bind you, for you are booked; 'tis according to usage and runs with my commission."

The speaker tossed a silver piece onto the table, only to see it picked up and thrown violently across the room by the party addressed.

"D——n the king's shilling and your commission, and you too, for the matter o' that!" was the angry retort.

The sergeant clapped his leathern book together, placed it in his pocket, and deliberately buttoned his scarlet coat over his broad chest as he arose and answered:

"'Tis too late, my young buck. You may d——n your fill. No doubt you'll cut up and make matters worse for yourself, but you now belong to His Majesty, and I'll see that he gets you. You signed your name and have fingered the coin; so there you are. You may chafe at the outset—most of you do; and now, will you follow along quietly, or must you be forced?"

"I'll not go nor be taken!" came the firm reply. "You enlisted me by a fraud. I but asked for the forms out of curiosity, and now you tell me I have joined. I have no mind to become a soldier, least of all, to serve the king. Your cursed horde have worked mischief enough in

Boston, without trying to beguile unsuspecting men. Nay, I'll not go—I'll fight first."

"Well! But you be a plucky rascal. As for fighting, I might take you, but it would be with a broken head—and 'tis far to barracks. But go you shall! I've but to wait here for those I know will soon come; and I'll see that you wait with me. Settle down, now, and nurse your wrath as best you may; but no tricks, mind you, for I've a heavy hand."

It was the momentous night of the 18th of April, 1775, and the coffee room in the Sign of the White Horse at Cambridge was tenanted by but three people when I entered. The two who were engaged in the foregoing dispute, and a man, asleep or apparently so, stretched on the settle near the fire; for though the day had been unusually warm for the season, there was the chill of spring in the night.

I had expected to find more of a gathering at the White Horse. The times were such that the sober, early-retiring provincials were agog with a mixture of fear and expectation, for there had been flying rumors during the day that General Gage was to send out the "regulars" to search for and destroy the colonial stores gathered at Concord and Lexington by the Committees of Safety and Supplies. But rumor in various shapes had long been rife and failed to stir the blood, though on this day at noon a party of British officers had dined at the White Horse, and later ridden in the direction of Menotomy* where the Committees were in session, and the event was looked upon as an harbinger of coming activity among the British.

I had known of the movement of the officers, and knew, as everyone did, of the stores hidden in the neighborhood of Concord. I felt the tension of the times. My prowlings for further news had kept me from college until long

* Now West Cambridge.

after "hours," and I had applied for admission in vain. The doors were shut and the verger deaf, so that my only resource for a bed was at the tavern, where I had been greeted with the opening episode as I advanced into the room.

It took but little penetration to catch the situation. A recruiting sergeant and his victim, who had been caught through his ignorance, only waking to his blunder when bound. The tactics used differed but little from the old press gang method, which consisted in bodily seizing a man and hurrying him aboard ship. Now, with the provincials in a temper to resent the slightest violation of their rights, such a course would have led to a popular uprising; therefore, the newer plan had been to beguile the prey into a blind form which was none the less binding though repudiated when understood. This latest example of recruiting by fraud was a young man about my own age, slight, yet well knit, but his general appearance led me to think him a stranger in these parts; his being so easily trapped proclaiming it as loudly as his dress.

As I closed the door behind me and dropped into a chair, he at once appealed to me in an impassioned manner, the soldier looking on with a frown, but making no move to interrupt him.

I glanced at the sleeper on the settle as I cast the chances of help at a rescue; for it took me but few minutes to pass my sympathies to the young fellow, my hatred for things British being a sentiment ever ready to leap to the surface, and the manifest injustice of the whole proceeding making it stronger. But if the recumbent figure was awake, he gave no sign of it. His back was toward me, and I saw from his iron gray hair that he was past middle age. Probably a tired farmer, who would have to be "worked up" to become hot enough to act, so I gave over hoping for help from that direction.

The hour was late; the Dutch clock showing past

eleven, and the possibility of the arrival of a belated college mate to aid an escape small. On the other hand, the sergeant had hinted of re-enforcement which might appear at any moment, so if action was to be taken it should be at once. The reckless blood of my twenty years mounted into my brain as I rose to my feet, walked to the door and threw it wide.

"There's your chance, lad; jump for it!" I shouted, whisking a table in front of the sergeant as he sprang to his feet. The young fellow was up in a flash and out into the night before his guard could get around the obstruction; while I slammed the door and braced my back against it.

I was well aware that I had got myself into a pretty mess, for physically I was no match for the soldier. He was twice my years and broader and heavier, and though I had some idea of my own powers, I feared I was bound to come out hardly in an encounter with him, for an encounter seemed inevitable. My heart beat fast at the prospect as he made a plunge at me, using an oath as he came, while I sprang aside and behind the settle. It was to be no child's play at fight, as the gleam in the eye of my adversary showed how thoroughly he was in earnest; but help came from an unhoped-for quarter. As the redcoat passed in front of the settle to head me off, the foot of the sleeper shot out, and catching the runner's legs, tripped him and brought him to the floor with a crash; while the sleeper himself, now as wide awake as was ever any man, leaped or fell onto the prostrate form.

"'Tis time I took a hand," said he, as he settled his weight on the sergeant. "The game is played, an' ye had better get to cover. Slide out, lad, like the fellow before ye, an' never fear for me; I'll hold this lobster-back until ye be well clear. I love the spirit ye showed, but ye are fat for the provost marshal if ye linger. Belay yer thanks an' go."

I hesitated an instant, for it seemed unfair to desert my rescuer. I had caught but a glimpse of his face. His powerful frame made him a match for my late antagonist, who was now beginning to struggle under him, and I cast a glance about the room; at the two on the floor, the overturned table and chairs, the low, black rafters of the ceiling, and the shining pewter ranged over the bar. The next moment I was out in the clear moonlight and speeding up the road. It was my last view of the Sign of the White Horse.

The episode had been sharp and short, and it had placed me in an awkward predicament. For the future I was a marked man, and no longer durst venture into Boston for fear of recognition, and must be careful whenever out of the college grounds, even in Cambridge. The lesser affair of being deprived of lodgings for the night at the White Horse was a small matter. I might try for Wetherby's at Menotomy, or the Sign of the Sun at Charlestown; either some four miles in opposite directions, and as a bed for the night was a necessity, I halted on the moonlit road, took a shilling from my pocket and tossed for choice. It fell for Charlestown, and I started off, thinking little of the way ahead, my brain working over my late experience and the probable penalty I would incur on the morrow for being out of grounds all night.

To-morrow! Little I knew that on the morrow (and it was then lacking but few minutes of midnight), a nation would be born. Little I dreamed that an hour before Paul Revere had rowed across the harbor; that Dawes was then well on his way to Lexington, bearing fateful news, and that on the very instant the Mystic River was black with the enemy's boats, which were landing a force at Phipp's Farms and within two miles of where I was walking.

The night seemed too pure and beautiful for aught but a lover's romance, but being no lover, I trudged at a swinging gait, for the chill was growing with the late hour, whistling the while for companionship, or stopping to fill myself with the novel feeling of being on a lonely road at midnight. The highway lay clear and white before me; the fields stretching broadly on either hand, the fences cleanly marked, and an occasional tree throwing its black shadow athwart the road. There had been no sound save my whistle and my footsteps, the air being too quiet to hum in the ears.

I had walked perhaps two-thirds of the distance to Charlestown Neck and was nearing a turn in the way, when through the surrounding silence I caught a note that brought me to a halt in an instant. It was the clinking of metal and the tramp of a body of men. Quietly and guardedly they must have advanced, for the head of a column of scarlet-coated infantry came around the turn before I had fairly gathered the import of the sound.

I knew it all, and all at once. Rumor had been right at last. The long looked for order had been given. *The "regulars" were out.*

Fortunately for me, perhaps, I had stopped under a tree, else I had been marked; for a squirrel could have been seen against the white roadway an hundred paces off. Dropping into the shadow of the wall that bounded the highway, I sped backward and crawled through the bars of a pasture gate, throwing myself along the ground with my head in position to command the opening. I was more excited then than in the heat of the action at the tavern. Over me rushed the sense of the importance of this movement of the enemy, for I well knew the temper and determination of my countrymen and the result of a collision with the infantry. The question was: Would the patriots be taken unawares?

The column came on quickly and quietly for so large a body, led by an officer on horseback. I heard no word spoken as they passed. Possibly there were eight hundred men, all told, and in full fighting order, for the rear was brought up with a field-piece. As their footsteps died low in the distance and the clouds of dust raised had begun to dissipate, I was up and following. I had little need of extra care, the dust making an effectual screen; but care I took lest a detachment might return, and so kept near the edge of the road that I might leap a fence or dodge into a shadow if it became necessary.

So stunned and impressed was I by what I had seen, that I followed on without thought of action. House after house was passed, but no light was shown or indications made that the inmates had been disturbed by the passage of an army. Presently the tramp ahead ceased, and I knew there was a halt. Through the night air came the sound of a bell far in the distance; then the barking of a dog, and suddenly the clatter of a horse at full speed coming from the enemy ahead. I had barely time to leap the fence before it passed, and I have now reason to believe it was the dispatch for re-enforcements, sent back when it was discovered that even at that early hour the raid had been anticipated. I could plainly hear the bell now—rung vigorously, and it was soon followed by another further north and fainter. Ahead there was no movement forward, and the delay chafed me and determined me to act. Cutting straight across the fields, I flanked the body of soldiery by a wide détour, and in twenty minutes came out on the road a quarter of a mile ahead of them. The road forked here, the north going toward Lexington, and on that I guessed they would march. Taking the south fork, therefore, I sped on for nearly a mile before I came to the first house. Picking up a stone from the road, I ran to the door and began hammering on the panel. In a moment a man appeared from around an angle of the building, bearing a gun.

"What's up?" he demanded.

"For God's sake saddle and get to Lexington," I panted. "The 'regulars' are out."

"Out?"

"Aye, and within half a mile of the fork. I have followed them from Charlestown. Hark! Do you hear the bell?"

"You're right," he answered. "Dawes rode through here four hours or more agone, and warned the district; but there has been no sign till now, or I have been nodding. What's your name, friend?"

"Anthony Gresham of Groton, Connecticut; a Cambridge student."

"Aye? Mine's Bacon. Well, ye have done a good deed in coming. Ye be well blown. Wait an' I'll hitch up an' give ye a lift along. Why! ye be wet through."

Wet I certainly was. The dew on the fields was like rain, and I had met with two falls in my passage over them, beside lying in the soaked grass while the troops passed. The water had penetrated clothing, stockings and shoes; but I cared little for that.

"Have you any arms?" I asked, as I followed him to the barn in the rear and hurriedly helped him hitch his horse to a farm wagon.

"None but my own musket, I am sorry to say. If ye be going to Lexington ye may find provision there, though I fancy they are scarce to be had. The British will miss their aim this time."

"What aim?"

"The arms and stores at Concord. Jump in an' we'll be off. How many did you say there were?"

"Some eight hundred."

"Well, by Jehovah! they may all go forward, but 'twill be strange if they all get back," said he, as he cut the horse.

The rattle and jolt of the wagon made further talk impossible. At the first house we came to, he stopped, ran to the door, gave a thundering kick with his heavy boot, and with the shout of "the reg'lars are out," jumped into the wagon again, and was off.

At house after house we halted and roused the inmates, I doing my best at shouting while he hammered on the doors. But ere long, as we approached Lexington, it became useless, for the ringing of bells and discharge of firearms showed the country was fully aroused. The minutemen had wakened, and the bridge at Lexington was about to be contested.

CHAPTER II.

HAVING taken a back road to Lexington and being delayed by frequent stops, it was after three in the morning when we drove into the village.

Save for a huge fire that had been kindled on the common, around which were grouped a number of men, there was no sign of preparation. Lights burned in every house, and that the townsmen were fully alive to the approach of the British was evident; but no force was then marshaled to oppose them, and at this I wondered.

On our entering Beckwith's Tavern we found it crowded with minutemen, and there learned that a horseman had been sent forward to meet the oncoming force and ride back to give timely warning of its advance.

The cold of the early morning, coupled with my damp clothing, struck a chill to my very marrow, and I hugged the fire as I listened to the talk going on around me. There was little brag. Elderly men mingled with those but shortly past boyhood, and what surprised me most was the lack of arms among them. Diligent effort made by my companion failed to procure me a gun, and to this is due the fact that I took no part in the fight.

There was a constant passing in and out, and I became the center of a silent group of men, who listened with anxious faces to the tale I told of the numbers on the way to destroy the stores.

Time sped under the suppressed excitement, and many a dram I swallowed during that gray hour betwixt darkness and dawn; partly to save me from chill, and partly from

10

the good-fellowship of those who needed something to give them courage to meet the fearful British, and that at an hour when human vitality is at its lowest.

Suddenly there was a distant shout, followed by several nearer, and upon the green hard by a drum sounded the assembly. Presently a horseman pulled up at the door, and without dismounting, shouted:

"Fall in, fall in! they are coming; they are less than three miles back."

The room was emptied in an instant, and what had been confusion a moment before became excited riot for the while. I could not make out who was commanding, and the difference betwixt rank and file, if it ever existed, was unrecognizable. After many orders and counter-orders, a space was cleared on the green, and some seventy men and boys, all armed, fell into line with a semblance of military form, and soon after marched down the dim road.

A crowd followed, I among them, until we arrived at the bridge that crossed the little river, and at once the planks of the structure were torn up and placed in a pile *on the side nearest the enemy.* This one act showed me how totally ignorant of military strategy were the brave men who were to oppose the march of England's veterans.

Knowing that I was to play the part of a spectator only, I left the crowd, crossed the bridge on its timbers, and took my station on a knoll commanding the field of action, where I was soon after joined by a number of others.

The wait was not long, though it seemed endless. The east was a broad field of light when I caught the first glimpse of the redcoats, and to my surprise there were not more than two hundred in the force. It was evidently a detachment sent ahead to clear the way. The crowd near the bridge scattered as they came in sight, and the few patriots who had determined to oppose its passage recrossed the structure and took their stand on the side toward Lexington.

The troops advanced to within fifty paces of the stream, halted and swung into line across the road, and the tragedy opened.   I could hear no words from where I was standing, but suddenly there came the flash of a firearm, and then a volley from the "regulars."   I marked the single mounted officer go down with his horse and then stagger to his feet as the fire was returned, and for a brief space of time the fusillade was general.   Flash followed flash and report followed report at irregular intervals. Soon I saw the little band break and retreat, firing as it went, until it melted away, and the "Battle of Lexington" was over.   It had taken less than ten minutes.

An impotent fury shook me as I witnessed this high-handed act of military despotism.   Groans issued from the lips of those about me, and I cursed the invaders from the bottom of my soul.   So unreasoning was my rage that I stooped to grasp a stone to hurl at them, though they were a good musket-shot away; but the paroxysm passed, and as the soldiers relaid the planking of the bridge and crossed it, I ran with the rest to the scene of the recent conflict, the action of which had hardly assumed the dignity of a skirmish.

History has given the details of the fight in a manner I am unable to do.   Though it was now broad day, all that happened after the troops passed the bridge was lost to me, partly from the confusion that reigned, and partly because my attention was diverted from their further movements.

I know there was no more firing, but whether or no there were outrages committed I had no means of telling, for I was soon engaged heart and hand among those who had fallen at the bridge.

Among the first of the heroes I came upon was my late companion Bacon.   He lay on his face by the side of the road, and for a space I thought him dead, but soon discovered that his wound was comparatively slight, a ball having passed through the fleshy part of his hip, and he had fainted from loss of blood.

My studies had been directed toward medicine (the profession I was destined to follow), but I then knew little or nothing of its practice, and was no better than a bungler as I attempted to bind up the gap from which the blood was flowing. There was no lack of assistance in caring for the dead and maimed, and Bacon was carried to the tavern, where his wound was dressed. He was a plucky fellow, and his first desire on recovering his senses was to be up; but I soon convinced him of the importance of quiet, and leaving him, went to prepare the wagon for his immediate removal home.

I had more than one motive for leaving Lexington as soon as possible, and getting on my way toward Cambridge. The main body of the British was yet to arrive, and now that blood had been shed I feared more violence would ensue, which fear was justified by later events. Six months previous to this time I had joined a company of thirty of my college mates, who were to march in defense of colonial rights; and now that those rights had been deliberately outraged, I had little doubt that we should be called to act in the general retaliation which I felt sure was bound to follow.

Another motive was to get Bacon under the care of his own family and away from the danger of further violence; while yet another though lesser consideration was that possibly the sergeant with whom I had interfered the night before might have joined the main body of troops, enter the village, and recognize me.

I had some little difficulty in placing the wounded man in his wagon, but he was at last comfortably installed on a bed of hay, and I drove slowly from the spot which proved to be the field of the opening of the Revolution, taking the back road that I might not meet the British.

We had started none too soon, for as I ascended a hill

a mile from town, I saw the scarlet column marching into the village.

I shall not detail the minor events of the day, as they have no bearing on my story; nor, so far as my actions are concerned, would they be interesting to the reader.

The journey of ten or twelve miles, with the horse never driven faster than a walk, was longer than I anticipated. Enough to say that it was nearly nine at night before I had finally disposed of the wounded man, rested and refreshed myself, and entered the town of Cambridge.

Who does not now know the harrowing events of the 19th of April, 1775? The mixture of rage, sorrow, and triumph that possessed the town is beyond my description. The tragedy was over when I arrived, and the remnant of the redcoats safe past Charlestown Neck. I had heard the whole story by the time I reached college, and I started for my room to prepare for the morrow, toward which each man now looked with both dread and longing. I might have thought my cup was full, but I was destined to receive yet another shock and of a personal nature.

As I opened the door I saw the room was tenanted. A well-guttered candle burned upon the table, and among the books and papers that littered it, with his head thrown forward and resting on his crossed arms, sat a man, sound asleep. Stepping forward, I laid my hand on his shoulder, and, as he raised himself and blinked at me in sleepy-eyed wonder, I recognized Hal Bailey, the close friend of my boyhood, and the son of our nearest neighbor at home; the one person in the world, next my father or sister, I most wished to see.

The emotions of the moment confused my thoughts. My prevailing idea was that he had come to join the general uprising, while an instant's reflection might have told me that the people of Connecticut could have hardly yet heard the momentous news of Concord and Lexington.

"How could you have gotten here so quickly, Hal?

Why, you could not have heard of the fight! or were you here at the time?" I asked, as the situation dawned slowly upon me.

"Nay, Tony," he replied, "I knew naught of it until I was well-nigh into it. I have not come to stay, though much I wish I might. It is to hurry you home I am here. Your father has been stricken down, and I have a letter for you—I will give you the details later on the road. 'Tis bad enough—God grant it may not be worse."

I can even now recollect, or perhaps better to express it, *feel* the way I drew from and stupidly looked at him. I still remember the terrible pressure on the top of my skull, the sickness that struck my stomach, and the distressing oppression of breath as I tore loose the seal of the letter he gave me, and saw a strange handwriting.

It was from my Aunt Jane, and to the effect that my father's present condition was precarious. It contained a trite moral in the fervent hope that his fate would stand as a warning to me to follow the straight and narrow path of righteousness and virtue, and ended by saying that I was to take the horse she had sent by Mr. Bailey and ride home as quickly as possible, making sure to bring back all my belongings with me, foremost my linen, as it would save carrier's expense.

The indignation aroused in me by the last few words did more to awaken me from the stunning effects of the tidings than aught else could have done.

Torn betwixt my duty to my only remaining parent, whom I both loved and revered, and the present condition of political affairs, for a moment I knew not how to act. I was bound in honor not to shirk my agreement with my fellow-students to risk my life on the morrow should it prove necessary, and to desert them at this critical time would be a reflection on my patriotism or bravery. Nevertheless, I determined to obey the call from home.

I at once took steps to keep my character clear, and having done so, prepared for the journey. While packing, and putting in order the many matters that seemed to throw themselves athwart my notice, as is common when we are most hurried, I obtained from Bailey the particulars of my father's illness.

The old gentleman had been in New London superintending the finishing of a new boat to take the place of the ancient *Gloosecap*, which had outlived its usefulness. He had descended from the deck to the "ways" on which the vessel rested prior to launching, when his foot slipped and he fell. The blow completely stunned him, but he recovered sufficiently to mount his horse and ride home, and had fallen on his arrival there. Being carried into the house, a doctor was summoned from New London, and immediately pronounced him suffering from a paralytic stroke.

Undoubtedly the blow received in the fall occasioned the attack, and though at the time Bailey left New London he was conscious, it was an open question whether he was liable to another and more severe shock, or would linger in hopeless helplessness.

CHAPTER III.

WE started from the university town in the gray of the morning shortly after the setting of the moon. My anxiety and lack of rest, coupled with the penetrating chill of the early hour, reduced my spirits to their lowest ebb. With cloaks closely drawn, we put our horses to a good pace, the rapidity of the movement somewhat relieving the extreme tension of my nerves, but conversation between us was impossible. The fog from the nostrils of our animals drove backward in clouds, and the road slid beneath us like a ribbon in the uncertain light.

Spring came that year unusually early. The hillsides were covered with grass; the young grain, well grown, moved like a green sea; fruit trees were in blossom, and the woods were hazy with foliage advanced a month before its time.

The noise of rushing water was through all the air, and to this day, the tumble of a torrent brings a quick, fleeting flash of recollection of that spring morning and the lowness of my spirits.

The sky was cloudless and gave promise of a perfect day. It was the hour when the world begins to open its eyes, but a considerable portion of it seemed to have been awake long before; for we constantly met upon the road, singly and in groups of five or six, individuals armed and unarmed, who were bound for the scene of the recent conflict, and made anxious inquiries for news we were unable to give. Such had been my absorption in my own misfortunes that I had made no effort to learn if aught had

17

occurred during the night, and could only listen with
wonder to the varied reports given us, but which we were
unable to corroborate or deny.

I heard the British, exasperated by their defeat and
losses on the road from Concord, had fired Boston and
Charlestown, and then retired to their ships, from which
they were pouring a constant cannonade upon the flying
and defenseless inhabitants. Another report was that the
people of Boston, with the help of the yeomen of the surrounding country, had attacked the fortifications on Boston
Neck at front and rear, and after carrying them, turned
their attention to the demoralized redcoats in the city, and
had driven them into the bay. That Gage was a prisoner;
and Pitcairn, who had opened hostilities in Lexington
with a pistol shot, and who was an object of special hatred
to the mob, had been captured and hung out of hand,
while riot ruled the city.

I knew enough of the prodigious growth of rumor to be
aware of its exaggeration, and reports so widely differing
confirmed me in the belief that nothing of moment had
occurred since the British escaped across Charlestown
Neck, but that Boston would soon be the scene of tragedy
I nowise doubted.

The brilliant light of a lovely spring morning, the quick
action of the ride, the constantly recurring stoppages on
the road, and conversations with the excited farmers, and
perhaps more than all, the perfect beauty of the surrounding country, did much for me. With no process of
reasoning for so doing, I felt better in spirits; and hope,
born of no argument, seemed to be a tangible thing that
swelled within me.

We drove forward in all haste through the fair country
and beneath a bright sky, in hopes of reaching a farmhouse
by dusk, where Bailey had stopped on the way out, thought-
fully making arrangements for our halt for the night. As
the sun went low in the west our pace became a walk, both

horses and riders being thoroughly beaten out, and we arrived as the red glow faded in the sky and the frogs boomed out the setting in of night.

We breakfasted betimes the next morning, being again on the road long before its freshness had worn itself away, and at noon stopped to rest at the ford of a river. Here we planned to remain an hour to wind and bait the horses, and while there, my companion, who had been rather silent, turned toward me and said:

"Tony, I have a word to say if you won't take it amiss, a thing you may easily do, since it bears on a relative."

"Who?" said I wonderingly.

"Your Aunt Jane—none other. I have had a year's experience with her, while you have known her barely two months."

This was true. At the death of my mother two years before, my father had invited Aunt Jane (my late uncle's widow) to make her home with us, further the education of my sister Charlotte, and attend to the household affairs at "Hardscrabble," the name of our estate. This rescued my sister from the neglect and influence of our black servants, and gave my father, who was deeply interested in the political aspect of the colonies, more leisure to devote to the cause. I soon after went to college, but my two months' acquaintance with my aunt had not ripened into more than a show of respect. She was a soft-spoken woman of middle age, with a smile I never liked (albeit it generally made an agreeable impression on strangers), and whose ostentatious piety savored strongly of hypocrisy. Her parsimony was extreme, and as it extended beyond herself to everything she influenced, she administered the household affairs economically and kept the help in order. It was soon seen that she was incapable of even assisting Charlotte at her studies, and latterly my father's letters had referred to her in a semi-sarcastic humor, and I readily guessed she was a source of irritation to him. She comes to me now like a picture. I see her silent glide; her smile that was ever ready and meant nothing. I hear her soft, yet thin and high-pitched, voice. She rarely volunteered a remark, but repeated the last words used by others, as though they expressed the opinion she had held all along, which habit went far to make those as ignorant as herself think she held a vast sum of hidden wisdom.

"Well, what of her?" I asked, as he hesitated.

"I may as well out with it," he began, "and then you will be as wise as I. Did your father write you that Squire Beauchamp's wife was dead?"

"Why, yes; six months ago."

"Then mark what I say. Your aunt is hoping to fill her shoes. That is as plain as the ford yonder, and I have reason to know that Squire Beauchamp, despite his smoothness, is a Tory of the sneaking kind. I know he has an income from someone in England, and is kindred, in a roundabout way, with the aristocracy there, and though he bleats Whigism, he will stab it in the back when he can. The captain, your father, told me that much. The squire comes to see your aunt. He is a man of more than common schooling. He knows what the times are like to be; and knows, too, the need of such a person as your aunt to fetch and carry news. He's no fool if your Aunt Jane is. She tunes up on the divine right of the king; as though George III. had aught that was godly about him. She is a rank Tory, Tony, and might be up to much mischief if this trouble with the king keeps on growing, as it bids fair to do. Charlotte hates her like the devil, or as much as she is capable of hating anyone. I speak by the mark, lad."

"Sorry am I," said I, "for the lack of unity in the family. As I have been living near the spring of this agitation," I continued, with considerable importance, "I have seen enough to venture to predict that England has but slight hold on her colonies here, and the trouble is sure to advance apace since blood has been shed, but I fancy my aunt will have small part in the broil. I remember father saying that the squire was lukewarm in politics, but a man can't be damned for that. As to my aunt's opinions —what do they matter? So say no more about it."

The subject dropped here, and we arose to saddle and be off. I had just mounted and was waiting for Harry to gain his seat, when over the hill from the south came a rider in hot haste. Down the stony slope he advanced with a rush, without a turn of the rein; his horse white with lather, while the noise of its breathing could be heard above the clatter of its hoofs as they scattered the loose pebbles.

Both horse and rider seemed to have no eyes but for the road in front of them. As they dashed into the ford, a halt of an instant was made while the animal bent his neck for a mouthful from the clear, shallow stream.

They had just crossed when the rider caught sight of us and reined up. He was a man of fifty or more, short in stature and compactly built. His dress was plain homespun, with coarse woolen stockings, and his heavy shoes were covered with dried soil. His face was homely and strong, being particularly firm about the mouth and chin. The long, iron-gray hair having lost the ribbon that confined it, streamed over his shoulders. At his hip hung a heavy sword in a tarnished scabbard, and he sat his horse with an air that showed him to be something more than the common farmer he appeared. In a voice that had a full, rich ring, he sung out:

"Whither bound, young gentlemen? This is no time to rest. Are ye deaf to the news?"

"The news we have, sir, is two days old. What's afoot? You are from the south—what news could have overreached us?" I said, as I noted the glitter of his keen eyes.

"Have ye not met many on the road? There has been no lack of tongues, I take it, to give ye enough to act on. Where be ye from?"

"We have met none," I answered, "as well informed as ourselves about what has passed, though we have seen many afoot and riding, bound for Boston. We are from Cambridge, and on the way home to New London."

With a sudden straightening of his heavy brows, he returned harshly:

"An' is it seemly that ye should be *from* Boston at such a time as this? For shame, young gentleman! Have ye been picnicing here while the dead of Lexington are yet unburied? By the God above me! ye lead easy lives to be going home when ye should have your faces set to the north. Were ye arrant Tories ye were better fighting among your fellows where fighting is to be done, than dawdling here."

"Who are you, sir, and by what right do you prejudge us?" I answered warmly. "There is a limit to the endurance of horse and man, and we only take needed rest. I respect you, old gentleman, as devoted to the cause; but you are not more so than are we. I am called home to what may be the deathbed of my father, and have been two days in the saddle. My name is Anthony Gresham of Groton, and I may yet fight with you; but to go home is my first duty."

At this, he drove his panting horse to my side, and held out a hand as tough as leather, saying:

"Aye? Then there is no lack of mettle in ye; I was a trifle hasty; I insulted ye and ask your pardon. When ye see your way, come, as I know ye will; and now take with ye the best wishes of Israel Putnam, and so—God speed."

And with that he bowed to Harry, shook his horse into a run and went thundering over the road we had just traversed.

"I have heard that name," said I, as we turned our

horses into the ford. "It must be Putnam of Connecticut, who did good work in the French war. He's as blunt as the butt of a log, but made amends like a soldier."

Little I thought at the time that we had interrupted the progress of him whose wild riding would go down in history, and whose name would become a symbol of patriotism and disinterested devotion to his country.

Both horses and men being freshened by food and rest, we drove along with all speed, my soul bent on our reaching home some time during the coming night. As we drew near Groton my impatience increased. I hoped that when we reached there I would be able to pick up tidings of my father's condition; but on arriving at the village the hour was late, the road deserted, and every house as dead as though uninhabited.

By this time it seemed as though both horses would give out before the last five miles that lay between us and Hardscrabble could be covered.

My faithful companion, as rugged and strong as an ox, was well-nigh in a state of collapse; but it is to be remembered that he had held the saddle twice as long as I, and four days of hard and unusual riding had told heavily upon him.

For the last few miles I had been living on my nerves, and they still served me. With heel and whip I urged my exhausted steed to his remaining strength, and left Harry in the rear to follow.

The river road never struck me as so long or so rough, and when, after what seemed an interminable length of time, I came where a gap in the forest allowed a view of the house high on the hill, I strained my sight as though its very appearance would inform me in some manner as to the state of things under its roof.

It was as bare of light as any house in the village, and stood out silhouetted against the faint sky like a black block.

What to argue from its darkness, I knew not; but as my horse stumbled up the stony acclivity his pace dwindled to a staggering walk, and his nose reached the ground. He fell to his knees with a loud groan, and believing him dying I dropped from the saddle, and with my heart beating like a trip-hammer ran the rest of the way on foot.

Over the wooden steps that led across the garden wall I sprang, and cut through the young shrubbery, regardless of paths or flowers as straight as the flight of the bee, to the back door.

It was never locked, and in an instant I was in the dining room. A fire was burning in the great fireplace, and though fast falling away it gave light enough to distinguish objects. Before it, with a book upon her lap, over which her little hands were clasped, and her beautiful hair streaming around her pretty face, sat my sister Charlotte; her cheek drooping close to her shoulder, and her sweet lips half open, fast asleep.

She was dressed in her nightgown and well wrapped up in a bed quilt for warmth, and as the flickering firelight played upon her, bringing out the richness of her color, and tinting the soft white ruffle around her throat, I felt that a lovelier sight was never vouchsafed to man.

Upon a tea-stand by the side of her chair stood a burned, out candle and some knitting work in white wool. For the rest, all seemed as unchanged as when nearly two years before I had said good-by to home.

The tall clock ticked loudly in its old corner; the same red spread covered the dining table; the chairs were arranged just as of old; even the same potted plants graced the windows, and the dishes on the old dresser glinted back the flash of the lowering flame. The heavy sideboard still held the cut glass decanters and glasses freely disposed, and the oval mirror reflected no new features in the familiar room.

The intensity of the stillness gave an air of peace that

touched everything like a benediction, and as I stood
above my sleeping sister I knew all was well. The
book, the knitting, the nightdress, told the story in an
instant. My father was not yet dead, or these things
would not be.

That he was living I knew as I stood there as well as
though I had it from his own lips. I had been expected,
and that Charlotte was waiting up for me with book and
knitting to beguile the time, was plain to be seen; but for
her to have had recourse to these had death or extreme
danger been in the house, was impossible; and equally
impossible would have been the soft slumber and regular
rise and fall of her bosom.

How great was my sudden relief no words can describe.
My strained nerves gave out as I uttered aloud, "Thank
God! thank God!" My eyes filled, and as a heavy, choking sob shook me from head to foot, I dropped on my
knees before her, buried my face in her lap and burst into
a deluge of tears.

With a frightened scream she awoke and sprang to her
feet, flinging me from her; but the next instant a realizing sense of the situation dawned upon her, and she threw
herself into my arms with a cry.

For a few moments we stood wrapped in close embrace,
her tears mingling with mine; but finally, as the nervous
excitement quieted, we seated ourselves by the fire, for
though the hour was late, I knew that even exhausted as I
was, there would be no sleep for me until I had learned of
my father's present condition. It was as I had intuitively
foreseen. He was in no immediate danger, and considering the short time that had elapsed since the stroke, his
improvement had been marked.

"I marvel I did not waken Aunt Jane by crying out,"
said Charlotte. "In truth, I hope I did, if I have not disturbed father. Not a night's rest has she lost through all
the fearful time, for she claims to be useless in the sick-

3

room of one she loves. But come! It is time you were abed."

I wondered greatly that the scream had brought no one downstairs; but I was aware how heavily slumber comes after relaxed anxiety, and though I could have talked on till daylight, I now knew all that was of moment and so rose and bade Charlotte good-night.

Such was my homecoming from college, and from that day for many years I never experienced heartache caused by sickness in the family. My presence gave an additional fillip to my father's returning health, and (to slightly anticipate the time) by midsummer he seemed to have recovered every faculty, there remaining only a slight numbness of his lower limbs, which compelled him to forego all rapidity of movement and necessitated the use of a cane.

My father was a retired shipmaster, a whaler, and had left the sea upon his marriage with my mother, having in his calling amassed what was in those days something more than a merely comfortable competence. This was increased by the fortune brought to him by his wife, a Maryland lady of an old family, who had some pretensions to birth, breeding, and education.

My paternal grandfather had also been a follower of the sea, but a series of misfortunes on the ocean had overtaken him when past middle life, and he had retired from active service.

Having purchased the whole of the headland on which our house now stands, he erected a dwelling upon its most commanding point, that he might be near and have in continual view the broad water for which his passion never abated. By clearing away part of the adjacent forest and devoting the soil to tillage, and by utilizing the natural, rocky barrens for pasturage, he eked out a fair living; but such were the discouragements pretaining to the coldness and almost sterility of the soil, and the labor of getting anything like an adequate return for his investment, that he called the place "Hardscrabble," an apt term to describe the rocky nature of the estate and the difficulties of obtaining a living therefrom.

In the days of my greatest activity our house was considered somewhat pretentious, but at this writing (1830) it is looked upon as a fair type of the style known as Colonial, and has fallen from its former prestige.

Standing as it does on an eminence better suited as a site for a lighthouse than a dwelling, it commands a vast prospect of land and sea, from a point beyond the rush of the white water of the Race which marks the eastern limit of Long Island Sound, to where, far south, Long Island itself lies a blue sheen in the distance. At the foot and to the west of the promontory on the apex of which stands Hardscrabble, flows the Poquonnock River, a tidal stream of but few miles in length. Well-nigh on a line with its mouth lies Fisher's Island, its whole extent showing like a map from the headland, its half score of miles a green gem in summer and a stretch of purest white in winter.

Such was the prospect we loved and which, despite the isolation and inconvenience of location, bound us to the spot.

Being removed from the village, our neighbors were few and far between. Halfway to the Mystic Bridge at the head of the river was the farm of David Bailey, a stanch patriot. Near the bridge and facing the road which runs over it, was the house of Squire Beauchamp, and in later days this man bore heavily upon my life. These were our nearest neighbors, the Beauchamps being about three miles away.

The outside and domestic arrangements of Hardscrabble were in charge of an old negro couple named Freeman, brought from Baltimore by my mother on her marriage. They were known as "Uncle" and "Aunt" respectively,

and were supplemented by three children: a stalwart
young man called George, a daughter, Nance, and a boy
about my own age, born on the place, whose name had
originally been Roderick, but who was known as "Rod,"
and by general understanding was supposed to be my own
especial property.

CHAPTER IV.

THE "WILL O' THE WISP."

By the end of April I had exhausted the novelty of being at home, for I had not left since my arrival. The affairs of the farm progressed as though there was naught to fear from threatened liberty, and the household moved on in its quiet, peaceful routine, though war looked to be a settled matter, and, judging from reports that flew from all directions, the whole country was in arms.

I felt and hoped that my inaction at such a time as this would not be of long duration. At present I was not becoming impatient, as the relaxation from regular duty, the absence of anxiety, and the glorious spring weather kept my spirits in good order. My greatest trouble was what people might think of my inactivity. Most of the able-bodied had gone to help their fellows in the north, and I had no excuse for not joining them save the illness of a parent now rapidly recovering. Further delay might reflect on my patriotism or courage. When at last I suggested enlisting, my father, whose will to me was law, forbade it.

"I need you here," he said. "There are twenty thousand men now besieging Boston, and more are unnecessary at present. This is not a mere revolt—it is *war!* England will never consent to our demands, nor will the colonies cease to rebel. I fully believe you will have enough to do in assisting at the defense of New London. I cannot give my consent to your leaving home at present."

And with this I was forced to appear content.

A few days later he wished me to see to the launching

and furnishing of the sloop, the plans for which, though complete, had been interrupted by his illness and the excitement of the town. The existence of the boat, incomplete and unnamed, had not been spoken of, and I had given it no thought.

I will not go into the details of the weeks before it was finished, launched, and fitted. I had only to follow out the plans, which were completed without my knowledge.

She was a keel sloop, thirty-six feet long on deck, with a beam of eight feet. Her cabin, finished in mahogany, was furnished with four sleeping berths, two on either side. Directly under the skylight was a folding table, and in front of the berths on either hand were cushioned transoms or lockers, running the length of the cabin fore and aft.

The most peculiar features of the boat were her overhang at the stern, her straight stem and flush sides; the shrouds being stayed by chain plates. She was steered by a wheel of carved mahogany instead of the universal tiller.

But the perfection and elegance of her fittings excited the most comment and admiration. A small boat or dingey swung from davits on the larboard beam, and mahogany steps were made to be placed on the starboard quarter for convenience in boarding her from alongside. For the last she was painted white with a narrow stripe of crimson below the gunwale, and her name was *Will o' the Wisp.*

Considering the times, and the laws of Great Britain, which prohibited the manufacture of metal work in the American colonies, the completeness of the vessel's construction was remarkable. I believe she was the only strictly pleasure craft along the New England coast; certainly by far the finest of her inches of any character with which I was acquainted.

Now as I have said, by midsummer my father was in good health; the lack of events and need of re-enforcements had quieted my desire to join the army, and most of the entire season I passed upon the sloop, well content to be idling as of old. The broad Sound became at last so familiar that I knew each menacing rock and shoal along our coast for the space of ten leagues about New London, and in a broad way might chart it fairly, though roughly.

But this aimless life came to a stop with the waning of the year. Then it was that my father arranged with Dr. Ambrose, our family physician, to have me taken under his tuition to advance my medical education as far as possible, and it was finally decided that four days of each week I was to ride to New London and there pursue my studies.

The winter passed slowly, but life moved along, albeit quiet to a degree, and I had the satisfaction of knowing that my days were not being wasted. Finally Congress, recognizing the importance of New London Harbor as a naval center, decided to fortify the place and raise a home guard to defend it if necessary.

This organization both Harry and I joined. It is not to be supposed that we were formed into a uniformed regiment and regularly armed. Such, indeed, was far from being the case. The majority of the enlisted dwelt in New London or Groton, but many lived at a distance. It was but at intervals we met for drill, the understanding being that we were subject to call in times of danger; while as for arms, each did for himself the best he could.

CHAPTER V.

AN EXPOSURE.

It was about the middle of August, and the weather had been extremely hot and oppressive. The constant scorching of the sun together with the prevailing drought had seared the bosom of the highland until the grass about Hardscrabble had the appearance of hay.

It was on an unusually suffocating morning without the slightest breath of air even at our altitude, that I was at the barns with my father on some matter connected with the live stock. We had been in or about the buildings some two hours, and were then in the barn, when a deep rumble attracted my attention and I stepped to the great open door and looked out. Away to the southwest the sky was inky with a coming storm. Toward the zenith, great thunderheads in smoke-colored masses, their edges creamed by the sun, were rapidly climbing the face of the heavens. There was no stir to the air. Under the edge of the heavy banks of vapor the waters of the Sound looked flat and dark, but before me the heaving roll of the sea still sparkled in the intense light. A becalmed fishing schooner off the end of Fisher's Island was taking in her sails as I looked forth, and even at that distance I noted the apparent hurry on her deck. The strident note of the locust had ceased; all insect life seemed suddenly suspended, and even the noisy barnyard fowls were under a spell. The landscape still trembled with the sullen heat, but relief was near, and, as I marked a spiteful flash that laced the edge of the squall, I was joined by my father.

"Rain at last, Tony. Thank Heaven!" said he. "Give

me your arm and we will get to the house. Let us hope the barns be not struck; 'tis coming fast and sharp."

Making our way through the garden, we reached the dining room just as the first great rolls of vapor met the sun, and the house suddenly darkened with a ghastly gloom. As we entered, Nance came from the kitchen to close the windows and was about proceeding upstairs when my father said:

"Where is Charlotte?"

"Dunno, cap'n. Specs she's with missus; deys here minnit or two since."

"Very well, so she's in the house. Tony, my lad, pour me a dram of Medford and fetch some fresh water from the well; you will have full time before this breaks."

I went to the sideboard and brought him a decanter and glass, but the jug which was usually there was missing. Noting a tray with cup and saucer standing on the table, and not waiting to search for the jug in the increasing darkness, I picked up the cup and hurried out of doors.

I was about to dip it into the full bucket that balanced on the curb, when my eye fell on its contents. They were tea leaves. Hardly believing it possible, for tea had been a long tabooed commodity at Hardscrabble, as well as throughout the colonies, I smelled of the grounds. Undoubtedly it was tea, pure and simple, and I turned back just as a few heavy drops admonished me to hurry.

"Father, what can this be?" I said, as I held the cup to him.

He took it, examined and smelled it, and then said quickly:

"Tea! How came tea into this house? Where did you find it?"

"On the tray," I replied. "I picked it up to bring water in and discovered this as I was at the well."

"Have the servants here at once," he said; "then find

Charlotte and your aunt and bid them come to me. I shall get to the bottom of it."

I found the negroes, and sending Nance to search for the others, returned to the dining room.

My father sat in the same spot by the table with the witnessing cup in his hand, and opposite stood the black giantess—Aunt Freeman—denying all knowledge of the matter, while her husband and sons were near her, their dusky features barely visible through the rapidly increasing gloom.

"Don't know nuffin 'bout it, Massa Cap'n," she said firmly. "Haint smelled no tea better'n foxberry for mor'n two year, and nebber dreamed dere was no sech a t'ing in de house tell dis instinct."

Nance and the rest proved no wiser, and indeed it was extremely unlikely that the servants would attempt to keep and drink tea, or anything else, outside their own quarters. Beside, they were too true and well tried to be suspected for more than an instant.

This part of the investigation had hardly been completed when Charlotte appeared, and walking boldly up, said:

"I know all about the tea, papa! It was Aunt Jane! I came in here and smelled it and laid it to her, and I told her I would tell! She tried to make me believe it was only foxberry at first, and then promised me anything to keep quiet about it. She has been following me around ever since to get me to say nothing. That's how she forgot the cup and saucer, and she won't come down."

If there was a black storm brewing out of doors, there was a blacker one about to burst in the house, and my father's voice and face furnished the thunder and lightning.

Wheeling on Aunt Freeman, he shouted:

"Get that woman downstairs if you have to carry her. Nance, light the candles; I want to see what I'm doing.

I thought my will in this matter had been long understood; but there will be no doubt about it hereafter."

In the interval of Aunt Freeman's absence no one spoke. Nance hurried to light the candles, and they had become necessary, for an appalling darkness had spread over the land, although so far the storm had only vented itself in menacing growls of thunder and a few large drops of rain.

Charlotte, impressed by the tragic air that spread over everything indoors and out, sidled up to me and slipped her hand into mine. Presently the door from the hall opened and Aunt Jane, followed by the negress as if to block off retreat, entered. The countenance of the lady was white as marble, and, as her quick glance took in the group, the unusual candles and the face of my father, who still held the cup and had his eye firmly fixed upon her, I thought she would faint.

There was no preface to his remarks.

"So, madam," he said, "it seems that you have no respect for my express commands in my own house, and have therefore attempted to do in an underhand manner what you are afraid to do openly."

His voice was under control, a fact that gave her enough assurance to reply:

"Listen, Robert; I thought you would not care, and I was——"

"Not care!" he suddenly thundered; "and was it because you thought I would 'not care,' Jane, that you attempted to bribe Charlotte to silence? You commit yourself and seem as careless of truth as you do of consequences. You are probably aware that were this known, my house would be published and my family viewed with suspicion."

"Be not so hard on me, Robert; I had but very little— and the day was so hot—and I was feeling *so* poorly——"

"And you selfishly risked everything for a forbidden

luxury, regardless of principle and my commands," he interrupted. "Now, whence came this tea? Did you buy it? By Heaven, if so, I will ruin the one who sold it to you!"

There was no answer.

"Did *you* buy it?" repeated my father, raising his voice. Still no answer.

"If you hope to gain time or advantage by this stubbornness, Jane, you ill reckon my temper," he continued. "I shall know from whom you obtained it before you leave this room."

The culprit had been twisting her hands in her apron with drooping head and eyes downcast, but as my father ceased, after a moment's interval, she stammered:

"I—I did not—buy it. I—had it."

"Do you mean," he made answer, with flashing eyes, "that you have had tea in this house—perhaps for the last two or three years, and have not used it till now? You will pardon me, madam, but I believe you lie! You have but recently obtained it, and by the Eternal! I shall know how and from whom at once, or to-morrow you shall be shipped back to Southold."

With this, he brought the hand containing the cup down upon the table with a bang.

The frail china flew to splinters and the untasted liquor in the glass jumped in splashes over the cloth. At the action, a blinding glare of lightning illumined the room, and a crash of thunder followed on the instant, shaking the house to its foundations.

Charlotte shrieked and flung her arms around my neck; my father sprang to his feet, and my respected aunt fell to her knees, burying her face in her hands.

As the report faded away in a rattling peal among the hills, and the pent-up rain came down in a roaring deluge, my aunt stretched out her hands and cried between her sobbings:

"Oh, don't send me back! I will tell all about it—only forgive me, Robert, this once! I know you will, Robert; you love me too well to send me hence. I'll tell, I'll tell! It was the squire who gave it to me. 1 tried to shield him. Please, please forgive me—I will give it all to you, only please don't send me away."

Without unbending his features in the least, my father replied:

"Bring it to me. Bring it to the last grain."

She left the room, still sobbing hysterically, and was gone some time; but she finally returned with a packet containing about a quarter of a pound of tea. My father promptly handed it to me, bidding me burn it in the kitchen fire, which I did.

From that moment the subject was never referred to. If, however, this incident was not spoken of, it had the effect of giving me food for thought as it brought to my mind the words of Bailey concerning my aunt and Squire Beauchamp.

That he was no true patriot was evident enough from my aunt's confession, and that he and she met on common ground was equally apparent. What the sequel would show was to be left to time; but I determined to keep my eye on the lady.

CHAPTER VI.

A COUPLE OF TORIES.

I<small>T</small> was with a sense of real personal loss that I awoke one morning and found a cold northeaster was stripping the last of the brilliant foliage from the forest and soaking the earth with a chilly deluge.

It was my day for New London and the doctor, and I was soon splashing through the muddy road, with the roar of the surf at my back and the rain driving in slanting sheets across the landscape with such violence that both my horse and myself bent our heads to meet it.

The great trees writhed and fenced with each other like giants at war, and over all the storm sung its mighty diapason. The moor which borders the river near its northern end was beautiful in its desolation, and even the driving rain and howling wind could not bare it of its color or contrast, and it was no small relief to get upon the "open," and beyond the roar and danger of the forest.

I had traversed perhaps two-thirds of its extent when out from the curtain of rain I beheld a horseman coming toward me. There was naught familiar in his figure, his face and body being so effectually concealed by the hat drawn closely down and the large cloak that enveloped him, as to make it impossible for me to recognize him.

Seeing me approach he reined in his horse, and placing his back to the storm, awaited my coming. As I neared him he asked:

"Am I upon the road leading to the house of one Beauchamp?"

"If you are from New London," I answered, "you

passed the house a mile back; if from Mystic, you have taken an unnecessary turn; in either case it lies the way you came; I am happy to be your guide. You are a stranger in these parts, are you not?"

"If you will confine yourself to directing me you will compass all I desire," he answered gruffly.

"Very well," I returned, piqued at his shortness. "Turn and follow your nose to the main road and then ride to the west; it's the first house you come to beyond the bridge."

Without thanking me for my information, he asked:

"Is he living alone or has he a family?"

The strangeness of the question gave me some surprise, but I answered that his sister was living with him and closed by asking him how far he had ridden, for he was literally soaked through, the water running from his saturated cloak in streams, while his horse, heavily splashed with mud, seemed greatly exhausted.

"Curb your curiosity, young man, and ride your way. I will follow at my leisure."

The words had hardly left his mouth when a fierce blast tore over the moor, and catching his hat from his head, hurled it against my chest, from whence it fell to the ground and went bowling along until it rested in a clump of bushes a rod or so away. With an outspoken curse he brought his hand to his head too late to save his headgear, thereby releasing the cloak which he had been holding to his face, and as the folds fell away it disclosed the features of a very handsome man of about thirty years. His eyes were black as sloes; his complexion swarthy, and his face adorned by heavy mustaches turned up at the ends.

"Curse the wind! Why did you let it go?" he burst out. "Get it for me, will you?"

This decidedly high-handed demand thoroughly angered me, and I returned:

"Your civility hardly makes it worth while for me to inconvenience myself. You will be your own assistant."

And so saying, I started my horse and left him muttering something I could not understand.

How thoroughly are we at the mercy of circumstances; how powerless to make or mar our welfare by our own unaided actions, so slightly does the best reasoning mind penetrate the future, was never better illustrated than by the extreme importance of the trifling incident I have just recorded, and certainly nothing could have been further from my thoughts as I turned and rode toward Groton than that this slight encounter with a surly stranger would lead up to the most important period of my life and prove a factor in most of my subsequent adventures.

Two days passed, and Nature, relenting of her merciless behavior, spread a warm smile over the earth like a benediction. We were blessed with that perfection of sky and air known as "Indian summer," and the senses languished in the exquisite softness that is so brief and so portentous.

It was hunter's weather, and beset partly by a desire to be in the woods and partly in the hope of bagging a late wood duck, I plunged into the region of the Black Ponds (or North Woods as they were sometimes called), with the hope of finding my game on one of the deep sheets of water or quiet lagoons which connect them.

Despite my caution in the approach, at first my search was fruitless; but after penetrating the woods for more than a mile, I came to a small lake like a jewel in a setting, the basin of which was as round as a bowl, and on its center I descried two of the looked-for birds, but they were well out of gunshot. Carefully crawling to a spot on the bank where the lagoon carried off the surplus water, I bestowed myself behind some bushes, thinking it possible they might finally place themselves within reach of my piece; and fixing myself comfortably, prepared to draw on my patience.

The intense quiet was only occasionally broken by the

cry of a bird. There was nothing to occupy the sense save the zigzagging drop of a dead leaf or the clatter of a nut or twig as they fell without apparent agency.

The warmth, the drowsiness of the woods, the comfort of my position and the monotony of my fixed gaze, had their effects and I fell fairly asleep.

How long I remained unconscious I know not, but I awoke with the certainty of having been aroused. No doubt some little time had elapsed, for my game was swimming within easy gunshot and close enough to shore to be readily secured, but I hardly gathered my wits when the report of a gun within a rod of me gave me a terrible start and the ducks rose with a whirr and disappeared over the tops of the trees.

The confusion of woodland noises occasioned by the shot had not quieted when a man ejaculated:

"Missed them both, by Heaven! What kind of a piece have you given me? I could have done better with a pistol."

"It is of no importance," came a reply, the voice being that of Squire Beauchamp, whose tones I recognized immediately; "if you care to try further we will row to the next pond; they extend still deeper into the forest."

"Not with this outfit," was the answer; "it isn't worth the exertion. This attempt is on a par with my whole undertaking—a damnable failure. I have a mind to start back to Newport to-night."

Though the screen that separated me from the two was barren of foliage, the thickly interwoven twigs made an effectual barrier to sight at a short distance, but being myself close to the tangled mass, I could readily see through it and beheld, not above twenty feet from me, the squire sitting in the stern of a flat-bottomed skiff, while facing him upon the bow thwart with a gun between his knees, sat the stranger whom I had encountered two days before upon the moor.

4

Why I did not appear and make my presence known save that the finger of Fate was upon me and held me down, I know not; but in fact I lay quite still and only peered through the bushes. The idea of hearing anything of moment never occurred to me. That I was playing the part of an eavesdropper did not enter my head. I simply waited, thinking each instant they would move away; hoping so, in fact, as I disliked the stranger and was too suspicious of the older man to be cordial.

But no motion was made to resume the sculls that lay crossed athwart the gunwales; instead, the stranger drew out a pipe, deliberately filled it from a package which he emptied and threw down, and striking a light, puffed away as though, contented with the spirit of the spot, he was endeavoring to enjoy it. For a few moments the silence was complete, it being finally broken by the squire, who as though referring to some past conversation, said:

"I greatly regret that no action was taken in this matter until the works had grown so strong. Had my advice been acted upon, the king would have held possession of the harbor two months agone. It is certain, with its maritime interests, to become a swarming place for privateers, and I know that 'letters of marque' have been already issued. With New London you might have held the whole southern coast at your mercy."

"I agree with you there," answered his companion, "but Howe had his hands full at the time, and the force he might have spared then would be useless now. It is a cursed shame that he thought more of eating pudding than of fighting, or he would have bagged Washington and his whole brood after that day at Brooklyn. It might be of some service to obtain plans of the fort in case of future action; but it would be compromising to have such papers found on one in this rebel-rampant quarter. You told me there were but few Royalists hereabouts."

"A very few," returned the squire; "and those, like

myself, dare not be outspoken. Were it known that I harbored an officer of the king's navy, or even had written him, I would have no house to shelter me by sundown—if I escaped with my life. I think as it is I am viewed with suspicion by some of my neighbors."

"Discovery would place you in a pretty pickle, I must confess," answered the stranger; "and as nothing can be done by staying in this nest, where it would be death to answer questions, I think I will take myself off to-night."

"But the plans of the fort!" exclaimed the squire. "It would be well, my friend, not to depart with your errand entirely fruitless. Both Howe and Sir Peter Parker would like to know something of the plan of the works. You could sketch them in a day."

The stranger blew a cloud of smoke into the quiet air, and I could see the intensity of his glance as he bent his eyes with a quick turn upon his elderly companion.

"And penetrate their lines to do so?" he asked sarcastically. "Perhaps you are not aware of the consequences of a British officer not in uniform being captured under such circumstances; or is it possible you are unfamiliar with the history of Nathan Hale? He belonged hereabouts, did he not?"

"His is not a parallel case," said the squire, "and it is naturally to be supposed that a man of the stamp of Lieutenant Bromfield would be too wary to be suspected."

"They would make it the same," answered the officer, with a scowl. "It is settled so far as *I* am concerned; the game isn't worth the candle—or at least the risk. Why not do it yourself, you are a civilian?"

"Ah, ha! It would never do for me to attempt it." And the squire shook his head firmly.

"Then get one whom you can trust; a woman might do it—your sister, for instance."

"My sister! She would bear her errand on her face," was the answer, with a half sneer. "It is not feasible;

but,"—after a pause,—"but you give me an idea. A woman *could* compass it, I believe, and I have one in mind who might prove an agent."

"Here?" said the officer, looking up quickly.

"Hereabouts," responded the squire.

"Oh! I thought you might have had it in your head to send for and utilize your niece," was the answer. "I was about to advise you against it."

"Are you so interested in the welfare of my niece that you object to her running a risk in the king's good cause?"

"In a time like this, Squire Beauchamp," said the officer, knocking the ashes from his pipe and standing up in the boat to stretch himself, thereby displaying the fine proportions of his stalwart figure, "in a time like this, frankness is not one of my attributes; but I will be frank now and confess that I *am* interested in your niece. If I cared nothing for the risk to her, I would for our interests, for she is as fascinating a little devil of a Whig as ever wore brown eyes and drew on a petticoat."

"So?" said the squire. "I was aware of my brother's rebel tendency, but I thought that Dorothy's residence in New York with your family would have cured any disaffection she might have acquired at home in Norwalk. I have not seen my brother or niece for some years, though I am that young lady's godfather as well as her uncle. No, I did not refer to her, but to one of quite a different stamp," and the squire showed his strong white teeth in a smile. "I will endeavor to obtain the plans at my own risk, but it must take some time. When done, I will forward them, as soon as able, to Howe, or Parker, or Clinton; but communication is not so easy as at the time of my former correspondence. It is useless, I suppose, to think of sending them to *you* to forward; you will be afloat."

"I dare say I shall be ordered on some prize as soon as I have reported on New London and Newport," was the answer, with a yawn. "The regular ships of the line won't have colonial-born officers on board, worse luck! so I shall probably be relegated to some refitted capture and sent the devil only knows where. Failing this place, I think the next move will be on Newport; it is practically defenseless." Then with a sudden fierceness: "Why in hell they have picked me out for this infernal spying on shore I know not."

There was a momentary pause, and he resumed:

"My idea of a brief campaign, which would be both practicable and romantic, is to make a descent on Norwalk, and then, by the little god of love! squire, I would carry off your charming niece, and like a pirate claim her for my prize."

This so tickled his fancy that, throwing his head backward, he laughed so loudly that the woods echoed. The squire hardly smiled; but holding up his hand quickly, said:

"Hush, Bromfield, not so loud! Who knows who might be walking within earshot." Then after a pause, "Your imagination is lively, and you express yourself rather too freely for good taste. Come, we had better be moving."

Bromfield, as though conscious of having gone too far, made no answer, but seating himself on the center thwart, shipped the sculls, and turning the boat's head, they were soon covered by a bend in the canal.

What my sensations were during this conversation it would be impossible for me to describe. Not knowing the consequences were I discovered, I lay as quiet as the rock beside me. Of the squire I had no fear; but I had reason to believe that the other was a character more or less reckless or desperate, and I had no desire to risk an encounter when my gun might become necessary for my defense, and no earthly good could arise by discovering myself and denouncing them. They were both Tories, then; a name coupling contempt with enmity. One was evidently appointed to the British navy and was at present doing

duty as a spy along the coast, with a view of finding its
weak points. The other, exerting his influence to draw the
king's troops upon his native town. The last was monstrous. He would have blood spilled, and see the lives of
his own friends and neighbors extinguished while he, without the bravery to take a single risk, would work through
the hand of a woman and shield himself by duplicity.
The inhuman scoundrel! I felt oppressed by the importance of what I had overheard. But what was I to do?
The Great Power that had guided me to this spot and fixed
upon me as the agent of discovery, had not placed within
my scope the means of entirely frustrating their designs.
The fort was unfinished, and weaker in its present state
than either of the conspirators dreamed. All that seemed
left me was to impart my information to the proper
authorities; my father first of all. This I must do or
burst with the weight of my secret.

It was growing dark in the woods by the time I quitted
them and came out upon the main road, and darkness was
over the whole land when I reached home.

At that age I was unschooled in the art of dissimula-
tion, and my countenance was too ingenuous to hide my
emotions from those who knew me. Undoubtedly its
expression disclosed something unusual the moment I
entered the house. My father looked up inquiringly, and
Hal, whose presence was no surprise, greeted me with:

"Hello! What's wrong, Tony?"

The room being cleared, it did not take long for me to
repeat the whole of the conversation I had overheard, as
well as to retail the incident of my meeting the stranger on
the moor. My father's face was a study in its growing
gravity as I proceeded, while Hal, with his elbows on the
table and his chin clasped in both hands, flashed his eye
alternately from one to the other of us. However, there
was no perplexity on my father's brow as I finished.

"That man must be taken to-night!" he exclaimed.

"Tell Rod to saddle and go to Colonel Ledyard's at once, and ask him here."

He left the room, while I stepped into the kitchen and gave Rod his instructions. In something over an hour the clatter of hoofs outside announced the arrival of the colonel. I met him as he dismounted and he followed me to the sitting room, where, with closed doors, the story was told again and a plan laid for the capture of the officer, if by chance he had not carried into effect his intention of returning to Newport.

As regarded the squire, the usually ready colonel was at some loss how to act. It was not a question with him as to what he had a *right* to do; but what would be policy.

" Were the war at or near our own doors," he explained, "I should not hesitate a moment; but as an old man and an old neighbor I am loth to arrest him, while I believe I have the means of repressing his actions. The officer I hope to bag, but for the squire I will determine later. He is a cowardly old fox, but I think I can hold him fast without locking him up."

CHAPTER VII.

THE arrangements were simple. There being no time to waste in gathering a force of neighbors, it was determined to utilize George and Rod, who, with the colonel, Hal, and myself, were deemed sufficient. The negroes were armed, one with my fowling-piece, the other with my rifle, I retaining only a pistol. Harry was to get his rifle as we passed his house, and thus we made a band strong enough to battle with a squad, there being almost an element of absurdity in the force of the equipment as intended for the capture of a single man in a neighborhood lacking the slightest possibility of danger. As it was an easy matter to mount the party from our stable, we were soon in the saddle and on our way.

We crossed the moor and dismounted near the road, picketing our horses in the edge of the woods; and here we received our instructions. The negroes were now made fully acquainted with the object of our ride and placed under the charge of Harry. The three were to make a guard around the house, allowing no one to leave it, while the colonel and myself were to enter and demand the officer. The night was clear and starlit, but dark enough to make concealment easy, so we had no difficulty in making our way to the house and posting the outside guard in such a manner that they could see without being seen. The hour was late—verging onto ten—and a careful détour showed no light in any of the windows. To me, this did not argue a successful ending to our mission, as I feared

48

that our prey had escaped and left the household to their usual ways of early retirement.

Nothing being discernible from the outside, the colonel walked openly to the front door and knocked loudly with the hilt of his sword. There was small need of a second summons, for almost immediately a window opened and the voice of the squire was heard demanding who was there.

"It is Colonel Ledyard," was the response. "Come below and open the door."

"At once, my dear sir; at once," was the reply.

This ready action was somewhat different from the embarrassed parley and tardy movement I had expected; but the delay was really no longer than any man would take to partly dress himself and get downstairs. There was a rattle of chain and the upper half of the door swung back, revealing the squire in shirt and breeches, wigless and sleepy-eyed, with a candle in his hand.

"Why, colonel; you startle me! How is this?"

"Open, and allow us to enter," interrupted the colonel; "we will do our talking inside." As, with his own hand, he reached in and unfastened the lower door, and we passed into the house, the squire glancing from one to the other in well-feigned astonishment.

"Well, Colonel Ledyard! well, my young friend! Pardon me, I am but half awake. What can you wish at this hour? Has anything out of the common taken place? How can I assist you? If any——"

"Come! come! squire," said the colonel heartily, "we won't beat about the bush. I am here to demand the person of one Lieutenant Bromfield of the British navy, known to be a spy and under your protection. I warn you that it is useless to think of escape or resistance; the house is surrounded. Where can he be found, or will you compel me to make search?"

For the first time I noticed a look of fear or uncertainty

come into the squire's face; but on the instant he recovered himself and answered:

"There is a great mistake here, Colonel Ledyard. There is no such person in my house. Pardon my inhospitality in keeping you standing; come into the kitchen; it is warmer there."

"Pardon *me*, Squire Beauchamp," said the colonel. "I can start from here as well as from the kitchen, nor will I allow further temporizing. Where is Lieutenant Bromfield?"

"Your meaning is beyond me, Colonel Ledyard," answered the old man. "I know of no such person. I have had a gentleman from Boston, a lawyer, staying with me for a few days. He departed to-night. If you will not move to the kitchen, please to consider me; I am but half clothed and cold. I will finish my toilet and return in a moment."

"By all means, sir; and, not to lose sight of you, I will go with you," said the colonel. "Anthony, take a man and search the house."

Leaving the two, I went out and found Harry, and after having posted the negroes at opposite angles of the building, so that its four sides could be watched, we returned together.

"I'm afraid he has got away, Hal. The squire takes it too easily; but we'll know presently. Wait until I face him down; he can't crawl around the fact then."

Together we searched the house, and searched it thoroughly, beginning at the cellar and going through to the garret, the squire himself preceding us for the most part, even through his sister's room, and showing how entirely empty the house was of such a thing as a British officer.

Matthew, the squire's Irish farmhand, was finally summoned from his room in the stable, where he was found fast asleep, and taken in hand by the colonel. He corroborated the squire's statement that a gentleman—a Mr.

Hunter, he thought his name—had been in the house for three days and departed that evening, describing him exactly as I had done. Beyond that he knew nothing.

Had he seen the squire and the gentleman together in the boat that day?

"Divil a bit." The squire, he explained, had sent him to Groton at noon, and he had only returned in time to get supper, when he was ordered to saddle the gentleman's horse. He had seen him go toward Mystic, and then having done his chores, had gone to bed.

As no further information was to be gained from him, and as he evinced no tendency toward concealment during the questioning, he was allowed to depart. But the squire was left to be dealt with.

We were now in the kitchen and fresh fuel had been thrown on the dying fire. The room brightened in the blaze, and the warmth was welcome, as the night had become very chilly. The colonel seated himself comfortably, throwing one booted leg across the other as he turned toward his host.

"And so, squire, it seems that our bird has flown—fortunately for him; but you are left to bear the brunt. I consider it my duty to arrest you for plotting with an enemy. What have you to say?"

As from beginning to end I had watched the face of the squire, I watched it now. The easy expression it had worn since our fruitless search suddenly changed to deep anxiety.

It was fairly plain that he had considered his troubles at an end as soon as he saw we were satisfied that his guest had departed, but the colonel's change of base took him aback, and he clearly showed it. He hesitated a moment as he stood with his back to the fire, his coat tails in hand, and then replied:

"I say, sir, that I am the victim of a mistake or a persecution. I have already explained who was my visitor

and on what business he came. I can say no more, unless
to tell you that I am aware of a distrust of my loyalty to
the colonies, and see herein the finger of special spite. I
would ask in turn from whom you received this false
report, in order that I may know my secret ill-wisher."

"You have no secret ill-wisher, Squire Beauchamp," the
colonel replied, "but I assure you I have you on the hip.
Anthony, tell this tale once more, after which I expect the
squire to rely more on the truth than he has so far!"

Thus appealed to, I began again my thrice-told story,
and as I moved on from point to point, the old man gazed
at me with unflinching eyes, while I wondered at the nerve
that kept his face so steady. My hope of bringing him to
bay and forcing a confession was doomed to a humiliating
disappointment, for though his eyes flashed a defiant look
of hatred into mine as I spoke, when I finished he turned
with a sneer to the colonel, and said:

"And am I indebted to that boy for this outrage, sir?"

"You are indebted to this young man for the discovery
of these facts and these events," answered the colonel.

"Then let me at once deny the truth of his tale," he
returned. "I have held no such conversation, nor have I
been in my skiff to-day."

Had the colonel drawn his sword and cut his own throat,
I should not have been more dumfounded than at this cool
statement which made me out a liar. Even the colonel
swung around and widely opened his eyes, while Harry,
who had been a quiet spectator near the door, made a
sudden ejaculation.

For a space no one spoke. My indignation grew apace
with the passing seconds, and I suddenly burst out:

"Squire Beauchamp, a man who would smuggle tea and
use a woman as a tool, would lie out of reason. It is my
word against yours. Which is the weightier? If you——"

"Easy, boy," said the colonel; "no one doubts you."
Then turning to the squire, he said:

"Is it likely that this young man would come here to-night with a yarn made out of nothing, deliberately placing himself in a position to be shorn of all further trust, when an hour would expose the falsity of his statement? An idiot would hardly be so foolish. No, no! we must have something more than mere denial."

"Nay, colonel, I hardly expressed myself clearly," said the squire, ignoring me. "I do not doubt the honesty of our young friend, nor the loyalty of his purpose; he is simply the victim of an hallucination, or more correctly, *I* am the victim. By his own confession he was asleep. I aver the whole thing originated in his brain. In short, he dreamed it, and being an impressionable and patriotic young man, it has taken as firm a hold as reality. I forgive him freely; let us say no more about it."

Here was an ingenious and unexpected twist that at least showed the activity of the old man's brain, and for a moment it brought us to a halt; but the colonel soon broke the silence by saying sharply:

"How could he dream of a man he never saw?"

"Oh, I had seen him!" I burst out, like a fool; "and hated him on sight." I then related again our meeting on the moor, while the squire, with a foxy laugh and triumph in his eye, said:

"There you have the animus, colonel! Was I not right? A vivid dream would account for it all!"

"Anthony," said the colonel, with a slow smile; "you tripped yourself that time. Let me deal with the squire." Then addressing him:

"Have you not a niece? A niece was also in this wonderful dream."

"I have several," was the answer.

"In Norwalk?"

"I know not where they may be now. Some are in England."

"Have you a brother?"

"Yes, I have two."

"In America?"

"One is, I believe."

"Are you godfather to your niece?"

"No, but if such——"

"That's a d——d lie, too!" I burst out, as I was seized with an inspiration. "One moment, colonel—hear me. In twenty minutes I can prove by a single fact that the squire has hardly uttered the truth to-night. When Lieutenant Bromfield filled his pipe he threw aside the empty pack and I think it fell into the boat. With your permission I will fetch it; going back into the forest for it if need be, for it will still be afloat if it fell overboard. 'Twill be something more than wonderful if my dreams hang on to details like that, and they come up standing. If so, squire," said I, turning to him, "then my dreams are as good as facts and equally bad for you. Let me take Harry as a witness."

"A brave idea, Anthony. Go by all means. If the pack should be found, Squire Beauchamp, you will sleep in Fort Griswold to-night and thank yourself for your quarters."

Snatching the pierced tin lantern I saw hanging on a nail, I lighted it, and we started for the ponds. It was no more than half a mile to where the skiff was fastened to the banks, and knowing its locality, we sped through the damp gloom on a run and were soon at the spot.

There was small need of a long search. There, under the stern seat, wet with the water that had leaked in and settled aft when the bow was drawn ashore, was the tobacco pack; somewhat muddy, as though having been ground under foot, but of much more value than it had ever been before. We looked for footprints on the shore, but the close turf came down to the water's edge and there were none shown.

On our return to the kitchen we found an addition to the party in the person of the squire's sister, who had made her toilet and was seated on the high-backed settle before the fire, awaiting events.

She was an elderly and prim spinster, silent to taciturnity, and possessed of a hard and unyielding countenance, but withal not unpopular with her neighbors. It was evident the squire had been explaining the occurrences of the night, but she preserved an unchanged face and made no reply to his remarks, which were closing as we entered.

Without comment, I handed the empty tobacco pack to the colonel, who examined it, and handing it to the squire, who appeared mighty indifferent toward this piece of evidence, remarked:

"Here at last is a clinching argument in favor of the veracity of our young dreamer; I see, too, that it bears a Newport label. Squire, I am sorry, but you will go with me to the fort. Your concealment of facts has convinced me that what has been charged to you is true. You are too dangerous to be left at large."

The old man was stubborn to the last. With grave dignity he answered:

"Colonel Ledyard, I protest against this action. To be outraged thus on the word of an irresponsible boy excites my deepest indignation. However, I will go with you quietly, as you have the means of forcing me. I trust you will remember my years and not allow me to be the subject of further insult."

So saying, he left the room, and the colonel, telling us to return home with the negroes, as he alone would escort the squire to the fort, followed him.

The behavior of the lady was most remarkable. She had not uttered one word in answer to the colonel, nor shown the slightest emotion during the conversation. Her hands remained rigidly crossed upon her bodice, and the

only indication of her consciousness of the proceedings
was the quick movement and expression of her eyes.
Even after her brother and the officer had left the room
she remained immovable; and as Harry and I quitted the
house she was still sitting before the fire as motionless as
though carven from stone.

It was on the evening of the day following the arrest
and I was on my way home from New London, when I
was mightily astonished to see the squire standing upon
his own doorstep. I had thought of the old fox during
the day as safely shut up in the fort; but immediately
concluded that the lenient commander had but kept him
a prisoner over night and administered a warning before
granting him freedom.

This I afterward found was nearly the case. The
squire was made to take the oath of allegiance to the colonies, curse the king and his tyranny, and finally told he
could go at large on his sworn promise not to leave the
town of Groton without military permission. Being
caught again giving shelter to an enemy or holding correspondence with anyone in the king's interest would result
in his arrest and treatment as a spy.

These humiliating conditions he subscribed to under
protest, but with evident relief that matters were no
worse. How he kept them in letter and spirit remains to
be shown.

It greatly surprised me, as the days rolled into weeks,
that the crafty squire was left in peace by the townspeople, who in time knew of his attempt to betray them.
Had it happened a year before, he would have been waited
upon by a committee of his neighbors and treated to a
coat of paint or tar and feathers, or suffered further in
person and property. But as the Revolution progressed
the sprit of wantonness had declined. At all events the
squire pursued his way unmolested and nothing was heard
of him as the weeks slipped into months and the winter

into spring, which season advanced with its alternate changes of temper toward early summer.

Late in April the war seemed to be about to thunder at our own doors, for then General Tryon made his famous descent on Danbury, and having laid waste the town, beat so precipitate a retreat to the Sound, with the furious Wooster at his heels, that his withdrawal lacked but little of being a rout.

This near approach of the enemy gave plenty of excitement to the people of New London; for what with Pigot at Newport to the east (that city, true to the prediction of Bromfield, having fallen into British hands), and Tryon to the west, there was great anxiety in town for fear that they might concentrate on us, who were far removed from the main army, with an enemy between us and it.

The forts had been completed, and Fort Griswold garrisoned by a handful of regulars; though the entire region and the very forts themselves were dependent on the militia for adequate defense. The fright served to put more strength and method into the means of our resistance should resistance become necessary. An additional earthwork was built between Fort Griswold and the river, and in it was placed a light battery. A signal of *two* guns was to be a notification that danger was at hand, the word to be passed to those beyond the sound of the discharge; while *three* guns at half minute intervals denoted victory, or danger averted.

CHAPTER VIII.

THE SPRING OF '77.

SUCH were the conditions as we waited. It was the latter part of May, and I was longing for settled weather in order to take my first cruise of the season. I mind me that as the evening fell, I noted indications of a blow before morning, and consulting the glass in the cabin (for I was on board the *Will o' the Wisp*), found a decided fall in the mercury. Fearing the result of a gale (for the wind was already rising), I hauled up to the moorings and dropped an anchor for additional security; then taking the dingey, went ashore and returned to the house, cutting through the woods to the orchard, where the bloom hung heavy on the trees and gave its delicate odor to the quick, strengthening puffs of the north wind, until the air was filled with its perfume. Stepping into the dining room, I took the telescope from its slings over the fireplace, and going down to the wall that was the southern boundary of the home lot, and which lay like a barrier betwixt it and a precipitous pasture that sloped seaward, I scanned the expanse of water before me; a proceeding that had become regular during the past weeks; and as the position was a commanding one, I could locate a sail east or south for a distance of forty miles.

Many a one had I seen during that time. Sometimes a fishing schooner scudding for the harbor, sometimes a privateer, easily recognizable from her speed and a certain jauntiness difficult to describe, sailing away for prize-money and glory, and, sometimes, one of His Britannic Majesty's ships of war belonging to Sir Peter Parker's fleet at Newport, bound to or from that port, always under a press of canvas, as though greatly hurried.

The war had swept the waters of small traders in legitimate commerce, and the nefarious traffic known as "London Trading," whereby the enemy obtained supplies of fresh provisions in exchange for forbidden luxuries, was carried on by night, whaleboats being commonly used for that purpose. But it was not for these I looked. My object was to discern the approach of an hostile fleet which might hover in the offing during the evening and descend upon the town at night, gaining by surprise what it would require a greater strength to take in an open attack.

Thus I had made it my business each evening to scan the waters as late as the light would allow me to distinguish a ship at a distance; but to-night nothing filled the . field of the telescope save one topsail schooner under all sail, making south through Plum Gut. She was too far away to determine her character (and little I thought I would ever know it), but she was flying before the stiff north wind at a great rate. Elsewhere the glass brought out naught save the heave of the ocean swell miles away, seemingly at hand; but the town would be at peace for one night more at least, as no ship of any tonnage would care to attempt to beat into New London Harbor in the face of a flawing norther, which was each moment increasing in force.

I had closed the telescope and was sauntering to the house when Charlotte came running up to me. It was as though the blast had blown her to me and would blow her by; but she stopped as she reached me and said loudly, to be heard above the roar:

"Mr. Bailey has gone, brother Tony."

"Gone! Where to?" I asked; for I had counted on him for my coming cruise.

"Gone to Niantic on urgent matters for his father—and gone for a fortnight. He asked me to tell you how sorry he was to miss being with you, but he had no time to see you and explain."

"Not so pressed but that he could see you, though, and explain fully, no doubt," I remarked, as we walked to the house. "Still, I cannot quarrel with his taste in selecting his messenger. And where did you see him?"

"Oh! I chanced upon him in the orchard."

"Chanced? Ah! And in the orchard! A fair place for a tryst, truly, for what with the wind, the blossoms, and the maiden, I doubt not he has little mind for the business ahead. Seriously, Charlotte, does father know of the leaning of you two? You are very young," said I, speaking with the dignity of twenty-two years, "and while Hal is an unexceptionable fellow, it is hardly discreet."

"La! What nonsense, brother Tony! What utter nonsense!" she repeated, and though her face was aflame, she showed no anger save the pretty petulance that maidens use to mask their feelings. "There was no tryst. I was in the orchard as he cut through on his way to say good-by to us."

"Aye? And could get no farther, owing to the maiden, the blossoms, and the wind; albeit the latter was at his back," I said; at which she tried to look very fierce, and answered:

"A great pity it is, brother Tony, that no girl of all those around should fill your eye and blind some of your sharpness in looking at the motives of others. As for father—trust father; he is quite as wise as you." At which she danced into the house and left me alone.

However, it was none of my business what the two thought of each other. I certainly could take no exceptions to her evident partiality for my friend; a partiality that to me was marked and growing, as numerous incidents through the past winter had shown; and if marked to me, as well marked to my father, who never put a stumbling block in the way of their intercourse.

Her remark, as applied to me, was meant as a light fling at my indifference toward the young girls of the country about. Not once had I succumbed to the influence of the fairest of them; not that I held myself in any way superior, but I had never been impressed beyond feelings of friendship or calm admiration, though I sometimes longed for a closer companionship, and envied, perhaps, the happiness of others as they fell into the toils of love and marriage. As yet, however, I was fancy free and had not dreamed of asking a yeasay or naysay from any maiden of my acquaintance, though knowing that I was far from being ill-favored and might fairly hope for success in several quarters. The whole business had little weight with me, and was gone from my mind by the time I had replaced the telescope in its slings.

CHAPTER IX.

THE DISPATCH BEARER.

THAT night I went to bed betimes and lay listening to the humming of the wind, the creaking of the great maple branches, and the tearing scrape of the limbs as they swung against the house. I never shrink, as do some, at the hurly-burly of a storm, and the deep music of a gale brings to me a sense of security, home warmth, and comfort, when to others it spreads the eyes with terror and drives sleep far away.

I was well into slumber when awakened by a knock on my door, and my aunt called to me, saying that a stranger had arrived, and my father desired my presence downstairs.

I hurried into my clothes, greatly wondering who could have come at that time of night, and for what purpose I was needed. As I passed through the dining room, the clock in the corner was on the stroke of ten, and, hearing voices in the east room, I took my way thither.

Before a freshly lighted fire, beside a table drawn near it, sat my father and the visitor; the latter just raising to his lips a glass of spirits, but, catching my eye as I entered, he bowed to me as though drinking my health, before tossing off the dram.

Upon the table were placed two lighted candles, besides glasses and a decanter, pipes and tobacco; and in my father's hand, which rested thereon, was an open letter. As I closed the door and advanced, he said:

"Here, Mr. Moon, is my son Anthony, and the one on whom you will be obliged to depend." Then to me:

"Tony, I have just received this from the fort. It must be acted upon."

The stranger rose from his chair, with a hearty, "Happy to know you, leftenant," and made a bow with a grace unexpected in one of his build; for, though broad-shouldered and heavy, he was short in limb, and while sitting, seemed to warrant a greater stature than that which was revealed when he came to his feet.

I bowed in return, secretly flattered at the title by which I was so unaccustomed to hearing myself addressed, for I had been but recently appointed a lieutenant in the local militia.

Taking the paper which was held toward me, I glanced at the signature and saw it was from Colonel Ledyard. It ran thus:

ROBERT GRESHAM, ESQ.

My Dear Cap't: The bearer, Jacob Moon, is an emissary from General Washington, now at Morristown, N. J., and desires transportation to Sag Harbor in order to communicate with parties on Long Island. His business is urgent, and its nature secret—though for one thing, he bears dispatches from the commander-in-chief. I have reason to believe you will forward him on his way. I know of no craft but yours that can sail thither without creating suspicion, and intrust him to your hands with the belief that your patriotism and wisdom will devise the best method.

I will guarantee a leave of absence to your son, Lieutenant Gresham, as he will undoubtedly be helpful in furthering your plans.

It is hardly necessary for me to add that the bearer's identity and errand is to be held strictly "under the rose."

Sincerely, etc.,

WM. LEDYARD,

Col. Com'd'g.

FT. GRISWOLD, May 27, 1777.

I glanced keenly over the top of the paper as I finished reading it; for the stranger's face had struck me as being in some way familiar, albeit I felt I had never met him before. As I gazed at him, it came to me that the likeness between him and a woodcut print I had seen of Christopher Columbus was remarkable. There was the same broad face, the same thick, long gray hair cut square at the bottom and not gathered into a queue behind as was the fashion, but hanging heavily from the sides; the same strength of neck, the width of brow, and the same expression to the firmly closed mouth, even to the slight dip or point of the upper lip as it met the lower. A self-reliant, honest face, and then and there I would have staked my existence on his bravery and trustworthiness, so completely was I taken with his countenance.

"You are welcome to Hardscrabble, sir," I said, as I laid down the letter.

"To which?" he asked, with a puzzled expression.

"To Hardscrabble, sir."

"What's that?" he asked, his large, clean-shaven face breaking into a smile.

"Why, the name of this place," I explained.

"Well, well, my son! I see. A rocky name for a rocky headland. I thought for an instant ye might ha' meant the liquor," and he laughed outright, a jovial laugh, only such an one as an honest man may give.

"'Twas a queer conceit of my parents'," said my father, "and we have always held the name."

"Aye? One can't quarrel with it. But if he had been a sailor like yerself, as the colonel tells me, he might ha' struck a little more o' a marine flavor into the naming o' the place. What with the sweep o' the sea that caught me as I came in, the climb, an' the wind, I take it that the 'mizzen-truck,' or the 'cross trees,' or the 'cro' nest,' or others, belike, might ha' hit it off. I' faith, the road up would do very well for the 'ratlin's,' an' the steps over the wall, for 'futtuk shrouds' an' Heaven knows one catches a reefed fore-tops'l gale on getting here; so ye ha' no lack o' marine reasons for changing the name when it suits yer fancy."

"Does it blow so much harder here than below?" I asked.

"A sight, my lad, a sight. One doesn't catch the sweep from nor'ards until he gets here, for though there be a sting to the squalls down on the river bottom, there's the howl of a devil in pain in it at this elevation. Hark now!" and as we listened the whole house shook, and the corners took up a whistling shriek that seemed indeed like the voices of beings inhuman.

"Ha, now! List to that!" he said. "Fortunately for the blue-jackets abroad the wind isn't bitter, but cold enough to give relish to this," and he touched a decanter. Obeying the hint, we filled around and all lighted pipes, for smoking was one of my recent accomplishments.

"Perhaps we had better bestow you for the night," said my father, "you may be well tired, and nothing can be done before daylight—or in such a gale."

"Nay, nay! captain, not for me!" said the dispatch bearer, "at least not now—unless ye wish to quiet the house for yer own sake. I ha' seen so much o' buffeting o' late that the chance o' enjoying a storm while indoors is one I don't care to smother in sleep—being as how I'm always something o' an owl, besides. Let us finish a pipe an' talk over the matter."

"As you please," was the answer; "I am used to later hours myself. As to the business in hand, I see no barrier in the way. The sloop is ready for a cruise, and my son will put you ashore as soon as the gale breaks."

"The sooner the better," said the stranger, settling into his chair and crossing his booted legs to the blaze of the fire. "Glad I am there will be no 'to do' about getting off, for I expect nothing less than a set-back on the other side. Though Meigs did a good and gallant deed, 'twill be an unfortnit matter for me an' my errand."

"How? I hardly follow you—I have heard nothing," remarked my father.

"Nothing!" exclaimed the old man, straightening up and looking surprised, "an' ye know *nothing* o' Meigs o' Guilford an' his whaleboat expedition to Sag Harbor? Why, man! well, 'tis but three days since, an' news travels slow. They sneaked across the Sound one night last week, an' surprised the British post at Sag, capturing a gunship an' a nest o' transports, besides taking nigh onto a hundred redcoats. By the same token, the big storehouse went up in smoke, an' the place was made useless to the British, an' all without the loss of a man. Back to Guilford they went with the plunder all safe, but if this coast don't pay for it before the next frost, my name's not Moon."

"Indeed—indeed! This is news! It were well done. But if they avenge it, it bodes badly for my house. We are both exposed and isolated and have little means of defense."

"I grant it puts you in some danger," said the other, "but it is the chance o' war—an' war is yer word, captain."

"It is one thing to make war on an armed invader, and another to surprise a defenseless dwelling," was the answer. "I would ask no odds in a fair field, but such predatory warfare is as cowardly as it would be for me to raise a force this night, and tear down and burn the house of the Tory, Beauchamp, without giving him a chance to defend himself, or even escape."

"An' who might Beauchamp be?" inquired Moon.

At which my father gave a history of the proceedings of the fall before, and the conversation led into various channels, all of which were to me of intense interest.

During the season of talk between the two I remained but little more than a listener.

I can see them now, though years have passed over my

head; my honored parent in his snowy wig and courtly
dress, paying close attention to the other's words; his long
pipe in one hand, while with the other he twisted an
empty glass on the smooth mahogany, or pulled at his
white mustache, his blue eye always fixed on the speaker;
while the dispatch bearer, with an alternate puff of smoke
or a wave of the pipe stem, talked on, with his feet
stretched out toward the fire, the picture of a man enjoying
a respite from hardships while he recounted them.

The flash of the burning wood played through the strata
of tobacco smoke that hung midway in the still air of the
room, and cast huge shadows on the walls, the crackling
logs making a comfortable accompaniment to the whistling
of the wind without.   Each closely shuttered window
became a black mirror, that reflected the rising and falling
blaze, and the candles burned dimly through the blue
vapor.

As the two talked, I watched the face of the stranger
with increasing wonder.   The broad smile or clear laugh
showed a perfect set of teeth, which seemed to give a
touch of perfection to his countenance.   He was perhaps
fifty-five, in perfect health, if appearances held good, and
his manner and conversation made him the most extraordinary character I had ever beheld.   What his nationality
might be it was impossible to guess; for, while at one
moment his language was purely English, the next it took
on the rich burr of an Irishman.   His regular calling was
equally mysterious and not to be gathered from either his
manner or dress.   A familiarity with nautical terms made
one sure that he was a sailor until his conversation showed
him to be perfectly at home in military matters; while
again, to all appearances he was but a plain New England
farmer.   The dress, too, was baffling.   He might have
been a boatswain on shore liberty, a soldier on furlough,
or a well-to-do farmer enjoying a visit to a neighbor.
With all the puzzle, he fascinated me with his smile, which

showed the broad arch of his teeth, his ready wit and familiarity with the world, and a cheerfulness which seemed to spring from self-confidence and a clear conscience.

Hitherto, as I have said, I had taken little or no part in the talk, being engaged in listening to the others; but the man himself had made such an impression on me that I could not forbear getting some hint of his past experience, or at least some idea of his calling in life, so I said:

"I would ask you, sir, if you are a sailor? Your words compel me to think that at least you have been."

"Aye, my son," he replied, "a sailor an' a soldier as well. Look here," he added, laying the back of his fist on the table and unrolling a bunch of thick, bent fingers. "May not that be the trade mark o' the sea? At the same time, may it not be the proper hook to catch a sword handle or crook 'round the trigger o' a musket? It has done them all, by the bye, my lad; from fastening to a cable or a brace, to coiling about the handle o' an oar or wielding a hanger. My lingo vexes ye, too, I'll be bound, but I lay it down on no line an' use the tarms as they come uppermost. It is but fair to myself to tell ye, though, that I am not the underling I once was, since they think my sense is o' more account than my sinews, an' Washington has given me a chance o' using what little I ha' learned afield an' afloat."

"You know General Washington well, then?" I asked, with an increased respect for the man who was trusted by the commander-in-chief.

"I take it that '*well*' may not be used in speaking o' knowing his excellency, an' that he knows me much better than I do him, ye can be assured. Our first meeting was during the days o' Braddock an' the French war—long enough agone. Faith! it was after the defeat of Du Quesne, that I nigh missed track o' him before I fairly knew him, for it was there I lost my scalp, though the redskin who took it little guessed he was doing me a favor for time to come, an' I little thought it myself."

"But you have your scalp—you wear no wig! Were you indeed scalped by an Indian, and still grow a heavy crop of hair?"

"Aye, I was indeed scalped by an Injun, an' the ways o' Providence are past finding out," he answered soberly, as he stuffed the end of a thick finger into the bowl of his pipe. "However, I'm thinking, captain——"

"Listen!" interrupted my father. "Anthony, see who is in the hall."

I quickly stepped to the door and opened it. The light that came from the room was sufficient to reveal my aunt at the foot of the stairs, clad in a loose gown of some sort, but bearing no candle to light her way.

"May I come in, Anthony?" she asked, in her thin treble, "might not the gentleman wish some refreshment?"

Before I could reply my father came out and took from me the responsibility of answering.

"Jane, what are you doing here at this hour?" he demanded. "Return to your room! We have no need of your services; go, and remain there."

She made no answer, but turned upstairs, while we went back to our guest.

CHAPTER X.

This slight interruption, which bore no significance to our visitor, I could see had irritated my father, and I had no doubt that the same suspicion which had entered my mind was held by him; for his brows were knitted and his eyes had an angry flash. He resumed his seat, however, and pushing a decanter to Mr. Moon, helped himself to a glass of liquor, while that worthy, carefully tilting the bottle, said:

"As I was about to say, captain, I have it in my mind to do ye a kindness, for methinks it lies in my power to stave off British interference with ye, should they perchance drop their vengeance in this neighborhood—a thing not unlikely, for ye must make a fair mark from the sea, an' stand out like a defiance or an invitation."

"In truth, your remark *did* start an uneasiness, especially as I have no means of protecting myself against a piratical raid. Tryon's trip to Danbury shows how much or little they respect private property," was the answer. "If, as you hint, you can show me how I may protect myself from their usual outrage, to do it will be more than kindness. We have no near neighbors; I am well-nigh a cripple, and I have a daughter. Our only defense in case of sudden attack would be my son and the negroes; too small a force to oppose any organized company. The result would be worse than disastrous."

"Aye, sir. It would be worse than ruin," was the answer, impressively made. Then suddenly changing his grave aspect to one more lively, the speaker turned to me and said:

"Young man, I'll put ye a riddle, an' when ye fail on it, an' I give the answer, as I needs must to serve your father, I warn ye I am giving my best secret into your hands; but I'll risk it—I never mistake my man," he continued, after a pause. "Look, now! I am a spy, though I like not the word; it must go for lack of a better. Where, bethink ye, do I carry my papers?"

"Do you dare carry them into the enemy's lines?" I asked.

"Aye, verily I dare an' do, an' have now a well-worded missive about me, to be taken into their lines as soon as may be—may confusion go with it! Where, ag'in, doth it lie, think ye?"

"Sewn somewhere about your boots or clothing," I ventured; "unless, indeed, you tuck it into a hollow tooth."

"Nay, then; the last is not such a bad idea," he said; "but it would be a small chest for a long letter, an' impossible. As for the first, I'm no such zany; that has ceased to be a trick. Ye might cut me to shreds, boots, hat, an' all, an' turn me loose for a drunken farmer, stark naked, but I would still have my letters. Come, now! I must reveal, though mayhap I am foolish—but I know ye of old, an' can trust ye. Bring me a bowl o' hot water an' a clout, an' I will soon make it plain."

"That's an easy matter," said I, wondering how and what he knew of me. "I will soon have them both," and, leaving the room, I betook myself to the kitchen, where I trusted the kettle would be found still warm.

As I passed through the dining room, a sweep of chilly air met me, and looking for its cause, I observed that the garden door stood wide open. Thinking the blast had caught it while insecurely fastened, I shut it firmly, went my way, and was soon back in the east room with the warm water and a cloth.

"Mark this," said Moon, as he soaked the cloth in the water and placed it in the shape of a warm compress to the crown of his head, where he left it and resumed his pipe. "Mark this; an' it will show ye what a favor the redskin granted me, an' at the same time discover how a man may carry weighty matters *on* his brain as well as in it."

For the space of a minute he allowed the cloth to remain, and then removing it, grasped his scalp-lock, and with a gentle tug lifted it clean from his head.

I marked my father's eyes grow wide with blank astonishment as the long gray tuft of hair was laid on the table. Lifting again his hand to his head, the man took from the deep concavity which he had thus uncovered a small, flat package, and broke into a hearty laugh at the sight of our faces.

"I charge ye both," he said, "never to mention this abroad; names or no names. Who knows to whose ears it might get! Look here now, my lad," said he, bending down, "look here an' see what a tank the heathen made o' my head, an' tell me could a surgeon ha' done the job neater? I could swear it would ha' been with less dispatch."

I looked into the hole and examined it closely, for it interested me professionally as well as curiously. It was, perhaps, three inches in diameter and circled by a narrow strip of baldness. Originally the flesh had been stripped clean from the bone. The sides were well-nigh straight up and down and appeared fully a third of an inch deep, while the bottom was covered with the lines of a fine cicatrix as though it had been seared by hot iron. The bone was but thinly covered by a scarlet cuticle, and it seemed as though the blood must burst through at the slightest touch; but on feeling it with my finger I found it hard and unyielding as parchment.

"Ye never thought o' the like o' that, now, much less

saw it," he said. "Wouldn't it bother the Evil One to touch on such a hiding-place? I might be shorn like a sheep, or combed with a curry, an' my papers yet abide; an' not the least o' the miracle—for 'tis nothing less—lies in the workmanship o' this," he continued, taking up the tuft from the table.

"It took something more than a common wig-maker to turn that out."

And it was a clever piece of artifice that he handed to me, after passing it to my father. It was human hair, indeed, and not the substitute of jute, horsehair, or dyed flax, used by wigmakers of the time. It was strung onto a substance that might have been the finest parchment, so perfectly did it resemble the scalp itself, and when in place, the closest scrutiny might have easily passed it unmarked, so delicately was it made, and so exactly fitting the aperture in his crown.

After numberless comments of wonder at the ingenuity displayed in this mode of concealment, the dispatch bearer carefully undid the oilskin covering of the thin package, and selecting a closely folded paper from the three it seemed to contain, laid it aside; then replacing the covering to the others, he was about to lift his hand to return them to the strange hiding-place.

At that moment a crash broke the silence. The heavy shutter to the window directly behind me slammed to with the report of a gun, and the fragments of a pane shivered by the shock flew onto the carpet.

With a strange exclamation, the dispatch bearer instantly jumped to his feet and blew out the lights; but nothing followed the explosion save the howl of the wind, and after a moment's intense listening by us all, he plunged a candle into the fire and relighted it as well as its fellow.

"'Twas but the gale," he said, drawing a long breath. "You must excuse me, captain, but I carry heavy matters, an' I did ye the honor to throw myself off guard in this

6

house; but that blow had the keenness o' a firearm an' brought my instincts into play ere I thought."

" 'Tis strange, indeed," said my father, when we had recovered from the momentary excitement caused by the crash. "I closed the house to-night myself. It is odd for the wind to catch a tightly fitting blind; such a thing never before happened."

Moon by this time had replaced the package, and having taken the scalplock in his hand, was moistening the edges with a wet cloth, when I noticed the sudden intensity of my father's gaze, as his eyes fixed on something behind me. Before I had time to make a remark or turn, he exclaimed in a hoarse whisper:

"My God! quick, Anthony! there's a face at the window!"

With a muttered curse, the spy was on his feet again; but not waiting to mark his further action, I rushed from the room to the front door of the hall, as the shortest way out. This door was always locked, the key remaining in it. My efforts to unlock it proved ineffectual, but I finally found that the key was turned and the door unfastened. With the discovery, the solution of the whole affair flashed through my brain at once as I tore into the open air. There was plenty of light, though the moon was well past its full and was dimmed by the clouds that were flying like wads of smoke across the sky from the north. The front of the house was free of anything human, clear to the wall, as I could readily see.

As I ran around to the side toward the garden, I fancied I caught sight of a whisk of drapery disappearing behind the further corner. I had another way of solving the matter, that to my mind was better than chasing an uncertainty. Quickly entering the house, I ran rapidly up the back stairs and knocked at my aunt's door. There was no answer, and I expected none, so I opened and entered. It was as I supposed: she was out. A few embers glowed in the great fireplace, and on them was placed a copper kettle. A lighted candle stood upon a small table, revealing thereon the paraphernalia which goes toward concocting tea—cup, saucer, spoon, sugar-bowl, Delft pot and milk jug; and to cap the climax, a small tin canister of the stuff itself, which to swear by I put to my nose, and inhaled, not without pleasure, its grateful aroma.

The whole appearance of the chamber betokened extreme neatness on the part of its occupant. It was easy to see that my aunt had made her arrangements in a methodical manner, and was about to solace herself with the forbidden luxury before retiring, when her persistent curiosity, or a less innocent motive, got the better of her discretion.

However, here was a flagrant disregard of express commands, and I knew as I stood there that the lady had reached the end of her tether.

Stepping to the head of the stairs, I called for my father to come up, which he did hurriedly, though with some difficulty, after apologizing to Moon for his withdrawal. He was a little astonished at finding me alone, but when I explained that the room was deserted and drew his attention to the table, his wrath shook him, though he gave no word of it.

Dropping into a chair, he said:

"Leave me and return to the guest. I will wait here till your aunt comes back. She has exhausted my patience. Close the door and leave me."

I did as he bade me, and descended the stairs. Moon was sitting in his chair with his head in its usual order, a pipe in one hand and a glass of liquor in the other. I had expected to be obliged to combat some expression of doubt or suspicion on his part, but if such existed he failed to show it.

Whether his benign humor was due to the spirits, of which he had plentifully partaken, or whether it arose from his extreme confidence in the ability to take care of himself, I know not; but he looked up as I entered, with a cheery:

"Sit down, lad. Did you catch him?"

"It was no '*him*'," said I, "but a '*she*,' and she is caught. It proves to be nothing but the feminine curiosity of an aunt of mine. However, I think an apology is due you for such an untoward interruption, though I trust you will forget it."

"Well, lad," he answered, between his sips from the glass, "it was a trifle lucky for the lady that your father saw her face peering in at the casement instead o' myself. Belike I had forgotten where I was for the moment, an' let fly at her. For an unbidden eye to be spying into my secret might ha' made me lose mind o' all else but to blind it."

Here he rose from his chair, and pulling up his waistcoat (or a garment that stood him in that stead), displayed the butt of a single pistol stuffed into the band of his breeches. With this illustration of his meaning he sat down again and picked up his glass.

"I wish she had chanced to see the flourish of that!" I exclaimed. "It would have done more to curb her passion for minding other people's business than aught else I know. But I take it you are ready for bed; shall we turn in?"

"Well—as you say," he answered; "but look to this for a space. It was what I was at when your good kinswoman came on. By the bye, think ye she saw the hole in my head?"

"It is hard to say what she saw," I replied, "but I fancy not. She was placed too low. At all events, I have reason to believe she will never guess its import or speak of it."

"Well, then, see this," he returned. "How I got it would make your eyes bulge; but the story is too long to tell."

And he laid before me the paper he had selected from the packet. It was heavily written in a bold hand, and read thus:

This is a safe conduct and protection to y° Person and Property of y° bearer, a good and loyal subject of His Majesty.

Howe,
Genl. Com'd'g. H. M. Forces.

N. Y., Sept. 28, 1776.

"You don't mean to part with this?" I said, as I looked up.

"Ye give a fair guess," he answered; "but there is nothing to prevent a lad o' letters, like yourself, laying it against a pane an' making a bold tracing. 'Twill go a length toward hoodwinking any who are likely to land here an' molest ye; but as for parting with it—why, lad, were it laid with gems the price couldn't buy it just now. I will give it ye by daylight to try your hand on; but have no prying eye on ye in this, for were the forgery discovered, it were a hanging matter, my son, a hanging matter."

This last remark rather dampened the enthusiasm I felt for the scheme as he unfolded it; but thinking it were as well to be hanged on a venture as shot off-hand in defending the house (for defended it would certainly be), to say nothing of the suffering of my father, and the fate, worse than all, that would befall my sister, there was no hesitation in my mind as I thanked him, assuring him I would do my best to make a fair copy on the morrow.

After this we fell into silence; not through any feeling of a lack of congeniality between us, but the eyes of my companion half closed as he gazed into the falling fire, and, as he volunteered no further remark, I did not offer to interrupt his half dreams or meditations, whichever they might be.

As the night waned, the gale held its violence. The
chimney moaned; the trees clashed their limbs; the windows shook by fits, and it seemed as though the very sod
would be torn up as the wind hissed over the level top of
the headland.

I sat and listened to these grewsome sounds until I heard
the labored footsteps of my father. He entered with a
look of relief on his face which I had not expected, and
addressed Moon, who had roused himself as the door
opened.

"I have to beg your pardon for this lack of hospitality,
Mr. Moon, but I was above, sifting the matter to the
bottom. It turns out as my son doubtless explained to
you, and no harm is done."

This was a very neat way of talking around the subject
until he could find out what I had told, but Moon unknow-
ingly came to his rescue by saying:

"Aye? Woman's curiosity is generally fatal to some-
body—usually herself, and it came like to being in this
case, as I told your son."

"It is fatal to her present mode of living," was the sur-
prising answer. "To-morrow she leaves this house forever. Anthony, she will go with you and may be set
ashore at Southold before or after landing Mr. Moon, as
will suit him. There will be some delay, as I see not how
she can get her belongings into shape to sail before noon,
or even later."

"'Tis of little moment," said the spy. "It were as well
I landed by dark as by daylight, an' mayhap in the face o'
recent events over there, 'twere better late than early."

"Very good! All points settled, we will go to bed and
gain the rest of the night."

We here broke up the party, and showing our guest into
the spare room next to mine I left him for the night.

CHAPTER XI.

THE EXIT OF AUNT JANE.

THE next morning found the household stirring with unwonted preparations. At an early hour had Aunt Jane a long interview with my father, during which she prayed for forgiveness and another trial, but to no purpose. He was unyielding in his determination to punish and be rid of her.

Nor was this as inconsiderate as might at first appear. She was not turned adrift, homeless and unprovided with money. She was in receipt of a small income, and her house at Southold was still in keeping of the parties with whom she had lodged when she lived there. To her, I have no doubt, the worst features were the separation from the squire and the residence in a village well-nigh cut off from the rest of the world by the war.

Having obtained the pass from the dispatch bearer, I retired to my own room, and, locking the door, after a number of attempts succeeded in making a traced copy of the document; which, when heavily inked over, bore such a strong resemblance to the original that I was satisfied it would never be suspected as a forgery. Folding the copy again and again to give it a deep crease and an appearance of some age, I considered it finished. Taking my rifle and fowler from their places I joined my father and Moon where they were seated on the wall enjoying the flood of warm May sunlight, and smoking as they talked.

A steady breeze had taken the place of the gale of the night before and now blew fair from the west, with a breath of warmth that hinted at summer. Overhead, a few white rags of vapor floated in the clear azure of the sky, and the immense expanse of blue water sparkled in the crisp light.

The long stretch of Fisher's Island had turned from brown to a tender green, and the eye plainly marked the thin, white line of the surf that beat upon its southern shore. The peace of the morning was unbroken. Even the neighing of a horse from the barns beyond the garden, and the noisy cacklings of the numerous fowls, seemed in keeping with the tranquillity; nor did the distant voices that wafted from the house break the universal harmony.

I was in some doubt as to Moon's opinion regarding the effectiveness of my copy, and was vastly flattered when he remarked, while holding the two before him:

"Faith! I would as soon have the one as the other! Now keep that close," he continued, as he handed the copy to my father and placed the original in his pocket, "and pray ye will never have to use it. What are ye doing with the guns, my lad? ye have little time for hunting ere we make a start!"

"They are for the sloop. I am going down and mean only to leave them aboard."

"I thought as much—but ye had better take only the arms God gave ye. 'Tis an errand o' peace we must seem to be on, an' firearms might prove a matter o' trouble were we by chance overhauled an' examined. The lady is a fair pretext,—I'm glad she's going,—but your irons ye might better leave behind."

This struck me as possible wisdom, and I returned the guns to my room, though ere long I had reason to regret my ready acquiescence to his suggestion. Then giving a word of haste to the packers, I hurried down to the boat.

It was well onto three by the clock before the last of Aunt Jane's luggage was gotten aboard and stored in the cabin, thereby making it well-nigh uninhabitable by the lumber of the boxes and packs she had taken, albeit it was but a small affair she had used on her arrival. The lady came on board with a face like white stone, and cheeks and eyes swollen with weeping, though no word or sob broke from her. I had it in me to give her a word of kindness, but had no taste for the dumb look or curt answer I felt sure I would get in return, for since the night previous she had not deigned to give me the slightest notice. She let herself down the companion-way, seated herself upon the edge of a box, and for aught I could see, never stirred from it while the light lasted.

Ha! Will I ever forget the keen joy within me, as we bent our weight to the halyards, and saw the hoops mount the mast to the music of the rattling blocks and the fierce rustle of the canvas as the wind caught the loosened sail, and whipped the reefing-points into a lively tattoo!

It gives my old joints a twinge as I remember the alacrity with which I sprang forward to cast off the moorings and then jumped for the wheel, while Rod mastheaded the jib and we bent to larboard under the pressure of the air. With the dingey towing astern, we skimmed swiftly over the level of the river's mouth to the sound of the steady, ripping tear of the cutwater as it slid through the small ripples, while Moon was giving a finishing set to both throat and peak halyards.

It was no easy matter to clear the river in a west wind, for the stream turned sharply toward that point as it skirted the beach; but I squeezed through, closehauled, without a tack, and then with sheets started, we met the small swell of the Sound water and stood out.

"This, now, is a bit o' life," said Moon, coming aft, while Rod busied himself in coiling down the loose gear. "Ye can lay a fair course an' never shift a point until well through the 'Gut,' if this air holds. I fancy the wind may go down with the sun an' then come lighter out o' the south. 'Twill make good the saying a howl from the north brings a song from the west, an' a whisper from the

south; we had our howl last night an' the west is now piping her song. Ye show a tidy pair o' heels with the wind
abeam," said he, as he glanced astern and marked the
dingey bounding along in the smother of the hissing
wake.

And it *was* life, as we lay down to the strong breeze
until the deck was aslant, the white water boiling along
the "run," and the bow shearing through the seas that
began to jump as we drew away from the land. Hand
and eye were both busy, for the wheel needed a firm grip
to keep the boat's head off the wind, and I was watchful
of the new gear that creaked and strained as we lifted to
the diminished Atlantic swell that found its way in
through the Race. I missed Hal, and pitied him for the
loss of this free rush of wind and water; this high exuber-
ance of spirits which the confirmed landsman can never
know. But my disappointment in not having him was
mightily tempered by the satisfaction I felt at my own
situation.

Seated low, as I was, I could make nothing of the land
ahead save the dim blue of the "Gulls" to the south, and as
forward it seemed nothing less than a blank ocean, I laid
our course by the compass S. S. W., which, by putting this
slight southing to our way to make allowance for the flood
tide, would bring the wind but a trifle forward and lead
us fair into the "Gut."

This point was perhaps the best to bring out the speed
of the little vessel, and Rod having finished forward, I
called him aft, and turning the helm over to him, prepared
to enjoy myself with more freedom.

Moon, who had stretched his legs out on the leather
cushion of the larboard locker, and with back braced
against the cabin was smoking a pipe in placid enjoyment
of life, waved its stem toward the fast receding coast, and
said, with a chuckle:

"Faith! the Britisher that boards ye ashore will not bo

surprised to find ye a Royalist; for by all that's dead! if ye don't look like the Union Jack afloat on the hilltop!"

I caught his meaning at once. The bright red barns had the proper color as they stood out in the sunlight, while a lively fancy might see the cross of St. Andrew in the white house partly screened by the two immense maples that stood betwixt it and the sea. Knowing that my aunt's quick ear was within easy distance, I jerked my thumb at the cabin and shook my head. He followed me and immediately changed the subject.

"Did ye ever try the log on her?" he asked, referring to the speed of the boat.

"Never," said I.

"'Tis a pity. I think she would make ye proud; ye must be unwinding at least seven knots as she goes, an' that, with the tail o' the flood which ye'll catch after getting through the 'Gut,' will carry ye into Southold by eight, or a trifle later. Will it be too dark for the lady to land to-night?"

"She *will* land to-night," said I softly; "but the luggage will bother me to get ashore without wetting. I know of no proper landing."

"Faith! I'll put ye into a proper landing," he answered. "There's a feeler that goes out o' the bay in'ards, where the water will be as still as a tub—even in a gale."

"Then you know the coast well?"

"Like my two fists. An' then we'll cut across the bay straight, an' ye may drop me off a strip o' woods I'll show ye, where, if ye'll haul off an' wait a bit, ye may be o' much help to me. Mayhap I may beg ye to give me a passage back. 'Tis like this, ye see," he continued, settling himself and bending his mouth to my ear, "I fear 'tis but useless for me to go to Sag, as the man I want has left it, past doubt, since the rumpus last week. But I think, mind ye, I know where to finger him, an' 'tis not an hour's distance from the p'int where I go ashore. Canoe

Place is full o' redcoats, an' so, mayhap, is Sag Harbor again by this,—an' the country between,—so 'tis a trifle o' danger I may be in to reach him. In an hour I can finish my business, get my answer, an' start the ball a-rolling. I can be back in another hour, so if ye will lay to,—or off an' on,—till midnight, ye may pick me up; for I am fain to go back with ye. But mind ye, if I turn not up by eight bells, ye may know I must travel; so sheer off an' get through the 'Gut' by dawn, else ye may meet with bothersome delays. I little doubt that Parker holds something afloat in these small waters, an' if ye be sighted here, they will be mighty hasty to come by your business so far from home."

"But how are you to get back, unless I leave the dingey ashore,—a rather risky proceeding,—or what signal will you give that I may make sure of you and send the boat?"

"I'll not bother for boat nor signal—unless it be a plain call—if ye'll stand on an' off not too far from shore," he said. "Trust me for ways o' getting aboard. List, now! Is that the lady?"

As he spoke, an unmistakable sound of distress came from the cabin, and craning my neck, I looked down the companion, only to see that my aunt had suddenly succumbed to the sickness caused by the violent motion of the vessel, which was felt more distressingly in the close compartment than upon deck, where the eye to some extent may account for the movement.

She had thrown herself backward, and was half sitting, half reclining, on her luggage. Her face was of ashy paleness, and, with one hand to her heart and the other to her head, she was vainly striving to stifle the moans that broke from her. Knowing her agony, I descended and did my best to persuade her to lie in a bunk, but she warded me off with never a word and barely a look. Thinking it might be her spite against me, I sent Rod below to assist her, and closed the cabin doors that she might feel more privacy, while I took the wheel and marked the strengthening of the blue land ahead, for with our rate of progress we were rapidly approaching Long Island, and would soon be in the troubled waters of the "rips" of Plum Gut.

The breeze held strong, and the sky clear in the blue overhead, but dappled to the south with little pellets of cotton, and I fancied the wind had backed to that quarter a trifle, but no more. There was a slight touch of mellowness to the horizon in the west, that told of the waning afternoon, and by the time we struck the first heave of the caldron that boils between Plum Gut and the Point the light had turned golden, and the force of the wind suddenly abated. However, in the wild tumult of the channel, the face of the water looked as though torn by a hurricane; for between the rush of the deep current that tears through the narrow way, and the obstructions that lie beneath, it takes but a slight waft of wind to turn the place into a wilderness of jumping waves that have no direction, but seem to play up and down, a world of surging froth, all teeth and hollows.

The war of the white-capped waves was like the sound of a leaping cataract, though not so monotonous, and made words impossible. Without wind enough to steady us, we were thrown about, a mere plaything to the force of the waters, often shipping seas over starboard and larboard sides alike. Once a huge wave came aboard the quarter, and rolling into the cockpit, completely soaked me from the hips down. It was well the cabin doors were closed, else we should have had a fine mess below and damp quarters for the rest of the trip; but it drained off through the pipes.

Like grief, the "Gut" had its end, and in less than an hour we were in the tranquil waters of Gardiner's Bay in a calm that was almost dead; though with good way on toward our destination, the tide still running flood.

As the dusk deepened, a light air came out of the south,

and for the first time we shifted the boom to starboard and slid through the water that was growing clearer and greener with every mile.

Quietly we stole past the town of Greenport with its few twinkling lights, hugging the shore of the island called Shelter—a very garden for beauty. It was fully dark when we had left its great cliffs of white sand and floated quietly through the stretch of the Peconic that lies between it and Southold, and were barely moving when Moon indicated the proper spot to anchor.

Not a light broke the somber aspect of the shore, but owing to the thick growth the place is not well seen from the water. A graveyard it seemed at that hour. The small piping of night sounds that came off the land in no way relieved the deathlike silence, and we naturally spoke in whispers.

The rattle of the falling jib as we came to, with the thundering splash of the anchor as it dove to the bottom, seemed like a roar that must bespeak our coming for miles around; but no hail greeted us, nor by the closest scrutiny could we discover so much as a small boat afloat.

When nearly abreast of Greenport my aunt had opened the cabin doors and come on deck. She asked no questions, but, taking a seat on a locker, fixed her eyes on the passing lights of the village. Her seasickness was gone, but since noon we had eaten nothing, and I asked her if Rod should prepare supper, meaning only to show her an attention. She shook her head and gave a sigh as though to witness how heartbroken she was, after which I let her alone.

As we swung to our cable, I had Rod bring round the dingey and we proceeded to load the boat as low as was safe; then with the negro at the oars and Moon in the stern to direct the course to the inlet, they hauled off and soon disappeared in the blackness of the reflected land.

As the boat passed from sight my aunt opened her lips for the first time, and betrayed her ruling passion.

"Anthony," said she, "who may that man be?"

I was surprised at hearing her voice at all, and more at the question, for I thought her curiosity had been taught to stay within bounds, but I answered:

"A friend of father's."

"And what does he here and yonder?" meaning our house.

"A sail, for one thing; if more—'tis his business and not yours or mine," I answered shortly, for I was vexed.

"It's a lie, Anthony! You're all plotting against the king. You are an ungodly family. 'Tis as wicked to lie as to pilfer, and to make war against the king is worse. Now I'm free and I'll make you rue it."

She had risen to her feet and stood shaking her finger at me, while she continued:

"I warn you you shall suffer for this outrage put upon me. To-morrow I shall tell the troops that something is afoot, and your designs will fail; *will fail*, I tell you. Do you mark me? I have good ears!"

She had wrought herself into sudden, hot anger. Her small eyes flashed, her voice growing high and sharp in excitement, while her fist, with its one outstretched finger, put a point on every word, with a spiteful shake.

By this time I was nigh as angry as she. Had she been a man I would have pitched her overboard. She had heard—but how much had been heard, or how much was simply to work on my fears, I knew not. I held my temper down and replied saucily:

"My dear aunt, it is strange for *you* to take lying for a text to preach on; as for the rest, care will be taken of it. For your own sake let me inform you that Southold is not a Royalist town, so if you give vent to your temper and sentiments in this fashion, you may be brought up as shortly as was your friend Squire Beauchamp. You are a woman, my dear aunt, but I have heard of women being ducked even at this late day."

She stood looking at me, not knowing what to reply to this; then sat herself down suddenly all of a tremble, saying:

"Anthony, I shall not leave this boat till I know who that man is and what his mission may be."

"Well," said I, "if your ears be as good as you intimate, you must know without my telling; as for leaving this, you surely will when the dingey returns—unless you prefer swimming to going ashore by boat. Out of here you'll go—and that as soon as possible."

This was all extremely brutal of me, I know, and with little excuse; but I was a very young man and am telling what I did, not what I should have done. My last remark was too much for the poor lady, for she began to sob and rock herself, partly in sorrow, but more, I think, in anger at being thwarted at all points. She now well knew I would set her ashore without giving her any satisfaction. Her curiosity and prying spirit appeared to be a disease, and I dare say she suffered from it as much or more than her victims.

When the last of her goods had been landed and the house notified of her arrival, it was late; but she made no more ado and was quickly escorted home.

If she ever took steps to be revenged for what she considered our cruel treatment of her, we never knew it. The poor lady died before the close of the war; not greatly loved by anyone, I imagine, her peculiar disposition forbidding it, but I saw her no more after that night, and indeed, scarcely heard of her again.

CHAPTER XII.

THE LIFTING OF THE FOG.

WITH the final landing of my aunt the first part of my mission was completed, and the cabin rendered habitable. My feeling was one of decided relief, for though I had fully determined that, come what might, she should not abide on board through the night and witness the landing of Moon, I had been possessed of a fear that she would prove obstinate in her determination not to go ashore until dawn, which would have incurred the disagreable necessity of placing her in the dingey by force; an act that might have proved dangerous to her own safety in case of a struggle, and a proceeding of little dignity.

However, here I was at last free of her with the loss of nothing but a few ill-tempered words, and with hearts easy and unaware of troubles to come, we took in anchor and moved across the quiet waters of the bay.

It was well onto eleven o'clock when we had finished a hasty supper and drew near the land to the south. I stood in as far as I durst, for the black line of the land met its equally black image in the water, and made it impossible to fairly calculate its distance. The jib was softly dropped and we stood well-nigh motionless with the bow in the wind's eye, while Moon and Rod again entered the dingey and rowed ashore.

"Ye may lie as near this spot as possible," said Moon, as he stepped over the side. "Take your bearings on a tree, or anchor if ye like; I feel it safe if ye stay hove short. If ye hear a shot off shore, ye may run, or if I am not back by moonset. I will be with ye shortly, I take it;

I may hail ye, or may not if hurried. God bless thee, lad!" and he wrung my hand in his huge fist until I could have cried out.

Left alone, I filled my pipe, took a nip of rum, and seated myself in the cockpit to await Rod's return.

It was a perfect night for an enterprise. The waned moon gave light enough to assist one in traveling, but it was too uncertain to clearly place an object at even a short distance. It put a polish on the dew that lay heavy on the deck and along the rail, and dispersed the intense darkness that gives one such a "shut in" and defenseless feeling, as the being ignorant of the possible approach of any enemy always will.

The stillness was only broken by the delicate splash of some leaping fish or the ripple of the reefing-points as they pattered against the sail when the light air softly swung it. There was a low heave to the bay in the shallow water near shore, and one could mark the crisp ruffle of a cat's-paw as the breeze struck the surface.

By the time the boat returned I was getting chilly, for the air grew damp and cold as it got later, so I stirred around and helped Rod make things ready for flight, if need be. We softly slid the kedge anchor over until it lay on the bottom with the line up and down, and found not more than a fathom under our keel. As that would hold us in the light air and was easily gotten in, I had the gaff-topsail set and the dingey hooked to the falls of the davits—but not hoisted, though ready on the instant. All being shipshape for a sudden move, I set Rod to watch for the dispatch bearer until the moon set, and went below for a nap.

My sleep was sound and restful, but none too long, I thought, when I was wakened by the negro, who called me from the companion:

"Mas' Tony, de breeze am stronger an' I t'ink we's draggin'!"

I reached the deck and found it even so. The wind was still south, but its force had increased slightly, and catching our top-hamper, had caused us to lose our slight hold, and we were slowly pulling into the bay.

The moon had fallen low, and now lay tipped on the edge of the distant trees. A half hour more would end our stay, and I was just ordering Rod to pay out more line to the anchor, when I saw a dark object move out from the gloom of the land and make toward the sloop. A glass brought to bear on it showed a man swimming slowly, and pushing something before him. I hailed as he came within easy earshot, and was answered by the cheery voice of the spy:

"Ahoy there! All right! Make off, make off! I will be with ye by then."

Without ado, I shipped the side steps, and together with Rod I hoisted home the dingey; we then laid onto the kedge line and soon had the little anchor aboard, and by the time the negro had hold of the jib halyard, Moon was at the side clinging to a log which he had used to support him on the trip from land, on the top of which was lashed his coat, covering his pistol and powder.

"Hoist away, lad, hoist away and be off," he said, as he threw his bundle aboard and crawled dripping over the side. "We must be out o' this ere daylight. There's a king's cruiser to sail from Sag this morning, an' a detachment o' redcoats will pass on its way to meet her—but they will never get to Sag Harbor, though I can say no more on that head now. Ye will be seen from shore, an' ye are too trim a craft to be a nonentity; so let's make way an' get into broader waters."

While saying this, he was stripping himself of his boots and clothing; pouring quarts of water from the first, and wringing out the latter, until finally he stood naked; after which he went into the cabin, and taking a bottle of rum from the locker, took a long pull from it. Then, with two blankets wrapped around him, he came up and seated himself in the cockpit, as cheerful and unconcerned as was possible for a mortal to be.

"Ye'll pardon my freedom," said he, his face lighted by his handsome smile, "but I never give the rheumatiz a chance, for it soon makes a man a sheer hulk, be he young or old, an' with it, life for me would be spent."

"You are wise, and are welcome to all that's aboard; but what of your errand?"

"'Twas a failure in most ways. My man is a prisoner at Canoe Place, an' I hear 'tis like to go hard with him— he being mixed in the muss along o' Meigs. *That* part o' my business is smoke; but I fancy I ha' started other smoke more to the purpose. Look to this end o' the land some day when there's a gale from the east, an' if ye don't see a merry smudge that will tell o' the burning o' the redcoats out o' this nest, it will be no fault o' mine or the lads I have but left."

"Do you mean they will fire the forest and burn out the king's troops?"

"Just that same," he answered, "and with little risk to anything but fences. Every farm is cleared, an' the troops lie in the heart o' the wood. Pray God they be caught and scorched, for we have no other force to drive them."

And this, indeed, happened, as I afterward found out, though I did not see it nor have ever known it laid down in history. The forest was fired during an eastern gale, and the Royalists driven down the one road that leads along the backbone of the island. After retreating before the flames for some five miles, they made a stand at a certain stone in the road, which stone lies there to this day, and is the only one larger than a pumpkin (and that, not much) on the eastern end of Long Island.* Here they tried to fight the fire, but to no purpose, and were fairly driven off the field. They continued their retreat to

* The stone still lay in the same spot in 1891.

Brooklyn, and bothered the colonists of the East no more.

While thus conversing, we had paid off before the wind, directing our course the way we came, deeming this safer than would be the shorter cut to the south and toward Sag Harbor. With the boom far out, the wind astern, and the additional pull of the topsail, we moved rapidly though quietly through the dark bay, the jib hanging loose and useless, though at times giving a sharp flap as it filled and spilled itself.

The moon by this was settled low behind the forest, and it was nearly the darkest hour of the twenty-four. With the tide now at ebb, we fled past Greenport and into Gardiner's Bay, keeping a wide eye for the shoals that there abound; for to stick on a sand spit with a falling tide might mean more to us than mere delay.

By the time we had made this stretch of water the east was glimmering with the coming of the dawn, and a fine smoke began to rise from the surface of the sea and drift across us; for we were hauled east and on the starboard tack. I noted, too, the lightness of the air, which instead of increasing with the break of day, seemed to go out and leave a flat sea. By the time we should have put the helm up and stood into the "rips," we were hardly moving; while the fog seemed to gather strength and pour in upon us from every point.

It was soon seen to be impossible to breast the strong ebb that was running against us through Plum Gut, as well as impossible to direct our course in any direction, for as the air fell, we were more and more at the mercy of the strong swirl of water that boiled about us with flat eddies, and we were, ere long, drifting helplessly to the southeast at a rate that would soon take us out into the broad Atlantic. The muck had grown so thick as to shut out the land, bidding fair to limit our vision to a few fathoms, this lack of sight of shore making our rate of

speed uncertain; but I well knew of the terrible rush of
the current, and marked how slightly faster than ourselves
sped on the funnels of the little whirlpools.

We drifted without regard to stern or bow, sometimes
sidewise and often spinning about—as I saw by the compass.   It was now broad day, and the fog was like a silver
net with the brightness of the sun, which, despite the
blur in the air, was dazzling.   By this I knew it was fine
overhead and would clear away as the heat strengthened,
but in the meanwhile we were getting miles away from home
and out of all bearings—though that troubled me but little.

Aunt Jane was housed and the spy had done his errand.
Thus my mission was over, and I might make a day of
pleasuring; for my father need only look abroad and see the
fog to know what detained me, and have no cause for worry.

Therefore we breakfasted royally and without fear.   I
knew we were clear of all obstructions, and if not, the
very force of the stream would tend to keep us shy of
rocks; but Rod was kept on the watch for the lifting of
the fog or any untoward thing, while Moon and I enjoyed
ourselves.   Then the negro was sent to eat and "turn in,"
for he had been up all night; and the spy, stretching himself along the cabin cushions, was soon fast asleep, while
I sat myself by the wheel, whistling softly for a breeze and
a sight around me.

Ere long I noticed that the swirl of the water was less,
and that we had taken up the motion of a long, low swell;
by which I guessed we were well free of the rush of the
stream and out at sea.   The deck was swimming in the
moisture of the white cloud around us, and the water
hung in great beads along the bottom of the boom.   Every
line was taut and black with the wet, and so thick it was
that the end of the bowsprit softened off into a ghostly
point.   The reefing lines beat a soft tattoo against the
sail, and the spars creaked as we swung to the gentle swell;
but all else was quiet.

By the time I had finished my pipe and whistled my fill, I felt the heat of the sun and knew that ere long the fog would be gone. It went suddenly when it once started; blowing nowhere—for there was no breath of air that I could feel, though I whipped my finger in and out of my mouth and held it up a dozen times. The vapor simply vanished in the growing heat, and in a quarter of an hour I could see the horizon.

Away to the northwest Plum Island looked faint in the distance, and to the south of it hung a long, blue sheen I took to be Gardiner's Island. But the point of interest lay not in that, for betwixt us and the land was a topsail schooner with all sail set, as thoroughly becalmed as ourselves.

As I reached into the cabin doorway for the spy-glass that was bracketed to the side of the companion, Moon turned over and awoke.

"Are we still beset, captain?" he asked good-naturedly, and with a yawn.

"No longer by the fog," I answered; "but there's a schooner yonder I wish to make out. Mayhap she is from Sag Harbor and is the Britisher you spoke about early this morning. I fancy I saw her through the telescope last night."

I got a bearing on her and soon made out she was no trader, for she was armed, as I could see from the polish of a brass piece forward of her foremast; though whether she was an enemy or a Yankee privateer I could not tell. I saw two men on her quarter-deck, but failed to discover if they were in uniform or not. There was no flag at her peak, and the one thing in our favor was her small size and decidedly American rig and rake. As we then lay, she was off our starboard quarter some two miles.

I had handed the glass to Moon, who had come up, when a small cloud of smoke broke from her larboard bow, and presently a dull report floated to us.

The shot was blank—for I marked not the skip of the ball, but at the same time a flag went up to the head.

"That's the colonies," said Moon, with the glass to his eye; "but means nothing. Hoist your own in answer."

I jumped below to the flag locker without disturbing Rod, for I knew the lad needed sleep. While bending the bunting to the signal halyard I heard Moon mutter to himself:

"The bloody villain! The cursed pirate! The last craft I ever hoped to see! If ye be not the *Dragon*, may I never eat more."

"What's the *Dragon?*" I asked, as I run the flag to the peak, where it hung like a wet rag.

"She's the devil, an' well named—a British patrol for the Sound, an' given to picking up small fry like ourselves. I never thought she would venture so far east. That schooner was a peaceful trader plying on the Hudson until we lost New York; then she was stolen by the redcoats, who need small craft rather than great ones for these waters, an' armed an' called the *Dragon*. I know her well, an' God help us if she boards us an' I am found!"

"And why so bad?" I asked.

Without directly answering me, he continued:

"It means the prison ship *Jersey* for you, my lad—an' death for me. I' faith! I prefer my lot to yours, for a taste I've had o' the *Jersey*, an' a taste is but a draught o' hell! God forgive me, lad, for leading ye into this coil! What will your poor father do? But who would ha' dreamed o' the only vessel I feared turning up as though dropped from the clouds!"

"What is all this, Jacob?" said I fiercely, giving him his first name. "Do you fear I am a coward that you take a turn at testing me?" For the horrors of the *Jersey* had spread through the land, though then the half was unknown excepting to those who had suffered imprisonment on board. IIis reference to my father had also given me a twinge I cared not to express.

"Nay, nay! lad; I ha' no reason to doubt your stoutness of heart," he returned as kindly as a woman. "I know ye of old, though it's doubtless a surprise to ye to hear it; but let us below an' I will give ye a tale. I had better not be marked from yon deck. I take it they will have hard work to make out our colors, as there is no wind to spread them."

IIe went down the companion, I following, and we both stood looking out of the oval windows of the cabin as he talked. IIe began at once, never shifting his eye from the schooner:

"I know ye of old, I tell ye, though your memory might well ha' played tricks, for our first acquaintance was short. 'Twas at the White IIorse in Cambridge, on the eve o' 'Lexington,' that I marked your mettle. And now, mayhap, ye will discover the man who fell atop o' the redcoat, an' bid ye fly. Aye! I it was!" he interrupted, as I began to speak, "an' knowing ye is the reason I trusted ye with my secret last night—but enough o' that."

"What became of the sergeant?" I asked, for a moment forgetting our situation.

"I know not. I quieted him with a trifle o' choking when he turned ugly, an' dragged him into what I thought a closet—but fear 'twas the cellar stairs, for he went out o' sight suddenly when I let go my hold. IIe's still alive, for I ha' seen him since; there's no blood o' his on my hands. But let me get on. I served around Boston, an' after the loss o' New York I was taken at Fort Washington with Magraw an' the rest when the place fell. What became of the mass that remained alive is beyond me; but some fifty of us were thrust into the *Jersey* after a spell o' being shut up in different places. I learned enough in my short stay there to prefer quarters in hell to another turn o' it, though then it was a new thing; but I was taken out an' put on board the *Dragon*, this very vessel yonder, when it was found that I could pilot Hell Gate an' the Sound.

"'Twas pleasant enough, barring the fact that a marine was always by me with a loaded piece, an' orders to shoot or run me through if I as much as touched ground, whether by chance or ill will. This worked very well for them, for I was careful to make no miss, but I began to get mightily sick of seeing the small stuff fall into their hands through my own skill. My very blood used to boil at their treatment o' the poor devils who were caught, though they had no more hand in the war than unborn babes.

"I have seen them seized-up an' lashed till nigh dead, because their small tubs were worthless, or they had no fish or loot aboard an' would give no information. They acted like devils straight from home, an' presently the *Dragon* became a terror from the 'Gate' to New Haven; but further east they durst not venture for fear o' the Yankee privateers o' New London—an' I wish by all that's dead that a wind would heave one in sight at this moment!

"I stood this for three or four weeks, with a letter from Magraw to Washington snug under my hair the while, for I was caught in the fort, an' was not a regular soldier. 'Twas on board, too, I stole the 'protection' ye copied at home, an' that lay with the other. By then, they were beginning to get used to me, when one night we were becalmed like this off the Sawpits, only on the Long Island side, an' there I saw my chance.

"My guard was like a wart on my elbow, forever at my side, an' though he never prevented my going whither I would, he followed always, a pace or so in the rear.

"The officer o' the deck was half asleep, an' forward all was quiet. The night was a black one, an' it came to me in a minute to be off. I stepped to the bulwark to knock the ashes from my pipe, an' the red-laced devil followed me close. As I reached the rail at the waist (for I was amidships), I suddenly turned an' hit the fellow a blow with my fist. It was badly aimed, for its being so dark, but it knocked the musket off his shoulder, an' he jumped an' grappled with me. There I had him foul, for I'm no weakling, an' knew my life hung on it, so one hand having a grip on his windpipe, an' the other on the slack o' his breeches, I pitched him clean over the rail into the sea. The fall o' the gun an' the scuffle an' the splash, brought the officer on the quarter-deck to his senses, an' he gave the alarm. Someone came out o' the darkness aft, I know not who, but by that time I had the gun in my hands an' gave him the full foot o' the steel bagnet in the bowels, an' then I ran across the deck an' threw myself into the water on the shore side. There was a hue an' cry, ye may well think, an' many a shot; but all went wide o' me, for I finally got ashore, well blown, I tell ye, an' hid in the woods for the night. They made no search, knowing it was useless, an' at early dawn I saw the *Dragon* stand away, nor ever did I lay eyes on her again till now, an' I know her as well as I know my own face.

"So ye see, my son, the fact o' my being here aboard will damn ye as a rebel, an' finish me at the same time."

"And when did this happen?" I asked.

"'Tis not more than six weeks agone, an 'there be plenty yet there to know the pilot, for they've doubtless made little change in either officers or crew."

"What's to be done, then?" I inquired, beginning to quake a little. "We have no wind to take our chances in running, and no arms to fight, desperate as we are."

"Aye! that last is my fault again—who could tell?" said he dejectedly, "but," with sudden wrath, "by Heaven! they'll not have the pleasure o' seeing Jacob Moon dance at the yard-arm; an' mark me, if I fail to see sunset this night, there'll be others struck with the same blindness— at least one more."

As he said this he pulled out the pistol from the band
of his breeches, and taking a powder flask from his
pocket, carefully reprimed the weapon and laid it handy
on the cushion.

"Might you not hide and let me take my chances?" I
asked.

"Where, lad?" turning full toward me for the first
time.

"In the lazarette. I can clear out enough to make
room."

"Aye! I had thought o' that, but the dunnage about
would look bad; besides, ye are bound to be searched there,
as the only place where a cat might hide. Were it dark, I
might get aloft an' wrap me in the bunt o' the tops'l, but
that's out o' the question. There, now! There goes their
true colors; get up an' see if it be not so."

I went on deck and with a spy-glass could plainly see
they had lowered the Colonist flag and put the Union Jack
in its place. At the same time I marked a number of men
at their davits and saw a boat lower away. I looked around
for a sign of a breeze to aid our last desperate chance
of running, but nowhere was there a ripple, although
a bank of slate-colored clouds to the north showed from
which way the wind would finally come. The ocean was a
vast stretch of swells, low and long; their parallel lines
reaching for miles, their tops like burnished steel in the
sunlight as they rolled inward, lifting us easily and passing on to break in a thundering surf somewhere on the
coast to the north.

The sky was becoming hazy, another sign of wind, but
was in no way overcast. Again I directed the glass to the
schooner and saw the boat—only one, putting away from
her. How many she contained I could scarce make out,
they were so huddled by distance; but I easily caught the
glint of bayonets and knew they came fully armed.

CHAPTER XIII.

Two miles. Less than half an hour would certainly bring them to us, and then tragedy, captivity, suffering, and Heaven only knew what more.

I marveled at my own calmness, but have since come to know that the inevitable will often quiet a coward. It is uncertainty that flutters the heart, causes the brain to whirl, and the breath to thicken.

The situation had a hopeless cast. I had been well frightened, I am free to confess, but fright no longer mastered me.

Without any special reason I mechanically hauled down the ensign, and, going to the locker again, tied on the Union Jack and ran it up.

As I belayed the end of the line, I noticed for the first time that since the lifting of the fog we had not altered our position in relation to the schooner, the swell keeping us both in the trough of the sea and parallel each to the other. As I marked it, an idea sprang into my head, and I stepped slowly to the cabin that the haste in my heart might not show in my actions, albeit it was plain enough in my excited speech.

"Jacob," I exclaimed, "they are well on their way, but there is one chance yet. We have been stern on for an hour and are likely to stay so, as it is time for slack water at the ebb. Go you through the galley and out at the hatch, keeping under the comb of the cabin, then swing yourself into the water under the larboard bow, and hold your head out by a grip on the bobstay. By Heaven! they will never think of looking overboard save they have some suspicion, and I will try to lull that. I'll engage to tie them up on the starboard quarter and keep the boat there. Quick, now! Leave nothing behind to tell of your going. They've not seen you yet. If they've marked two, Rod will account for the second."

"Ha! 'Tis a chance! How long have we, think ye?"

"Twenty minutes, perhaps; not more."

"Then I've time. Give me some water in haste."

I crawled into the galley and kicked Rod awake, bidding him go on deck through the cabin, and, pumping a jug of water, handed it back to Moon, who, scooping several handfuls, applied it to his crown, thereby loosening the false scalp.

"Methinks your head will win yet," he added, as he lifted the hair and took the packet from its hiding-place. "Here is Howe's 'safety' ye copied from. I put it back last night, little thinking I would need it to save my neck so soon. Use it on the gulls when they come aboard. Faith! it's a quick brain ye have. I'll do your bidding— an' in truth 'tis all that's left; but woe to the man that catches sight o' me—for alive I'm detarmined not to be taken. If I go down, my lad, remember that Jacob Moon would ha' loved ye as a son, an' if by chance ye slip away, mayhap ye can get word to Gen'ral Washington that Moon has gone, an' his last dispatches safely with him."

"Never fear! The plan will work if they be not too curious; but budge not till you hear me call. Get gone! I must give Rod his lesson while they are yet at a distance."

"Here goes, then!" said he, giving my hand a squeeze; and, taking his pistol, he crowded his bulky form through the narrow passage to the galley.

The hatch above was open, and he crawled out. I put my head up after him and saw him snake himself forward to the heel of the bowsprit and drop gently into the water.

"Are you all right?" I sung out, in a low voice, for I could not see him.

"All right, but a bit damp, an' I'll not bile here, either. Make a short shift o' it, if ye can."

His good spirits braced me, and the sudden reaction that came with the chance of possible escape made my own rise suddenly, albeit it set my heart beating rapidly. Taking up a cabin cushion, I made a small slit in the bottom of the lining and thrust in the paper he had given me, to make a show of secrecy, and then I went on deck.

"Rod," said I to the negro, who was all eyes as he looked at the approaching boat, "do you know what that is yonder?"

"No, Mars Tony."

"Well, it's a Britisher. They are coming aboard to search for Mr. Moon, and if he is caught we will all hang together. Now mind what I tell you. Mr. Moon is overboard at the bow. Our business is to keep their boat aft, if possible; so when they come alongside take their painter if they offer it, and make a land-lubber's knot when you belay it. Remember we are Tories, and this boat hails from Newport. My name will be, for the time being, Forbes" (as a common one came to mind), "and we have been to Canoe Place and among the red-coats there, but you are not to know wherefore. Tell them naught if you are not questioned, but talk to them here when I go into the cabin. First and foremost, keep your eyes from the bow and don't look frightened. Do you understand all this?"

"Yes, sah. We wants to fool dem an' make dem t'ink we's Britishers. Golly! Yes, *sah*, Mars Tony. I un'stan' —we's Fo'bes."

"Very good! Get forward and make as though busy, but come when I call you."

I then again descended into the cabin, and going to the locker, took from it a bottle of rum and one of brandy, with glasses, and set them on the table. Then going into the cockpit again, I seated myself quite carelessly, though inwardly trembling, and proceeded to fill a pipe.

Gradually the boat drew nearer, lifting over the glassy hills until at last I could mark the flash of the oar blades and count the inmates. As it came on, I saw four men at the oars, and astern sat two marines with muskets, and an officer in uniform. When they came close, the order was given to cease rowing and back water, which was executed with tolerable precision, and finally they lay not five fathoms astern.

"What boat's that?" shouted the officer, standing up with the yoke lines in his hands.

"The *Will o' the Wisp!*" I sung back, with my heart thumping like a drum. "What schooner's that?"

"The *Dragon*, of H. M. Navy, out of New York. What are you doing here?"

"Waiting for a breeze," I answered, with an attempt to appear easy.

"D——n your impudence! Where do you belong!"

"Newport. Won't you come aboard?" for I saw the boat slowly forging ahead, and was afraid of her getting on our beam.

Without further parley he gave an order, and the boat shot alongside.

Calling Rod aft, I directed him to ship the steps, and then said to the bow-man, who stood ready with boathook in hand:

"Pass your painter, friend, and I'll make fast. Look out for my sides!"

He threw the line aboard without remark, Rod passing it through a scupper hole, and I saw him fussing over it as I turned to the officer and offered my hand. He disregarded it, however, and leaped aboard, but without being followed by his men.

All this suited my purpose to a hair, but I had scarce time to think before he spoke.

"Why did you hoist that rag first there?" said he, scowling, as he pointed at the peak. "What are you? A d——d rebel, I believe! Where are your papers, and what are you doing in these waters?"

This was delivered with a pomposity that would have caused me to laugh had we not been in such a dilemma, and as he asked his questions, he threw out his chest and looked about as though remarking the completeness of our fittings.

I saw with half an eye the character with which I had to deal. He was a young man, whose rank (that of a lieutenant, as his uniform showed), sat heavily upon him, and I figured him a light weight mentally and physically. There is no conciliating such. They need a rough hand; but I was hardly in a position to give him a lesson, though I knew any meekness on my part would make him top-heavy with arrogance.

"As to the bunting," I answered boldly, "you can hardly criticize it, as you set the example yonder. How did I know you were not a Yankee?—you look it by your rig at this distance. There are my colors!" and I pointed to the limp, red flag aloft.

"You are a blatant Yankee yourself," he blurted out. "Do you think to trick *me?* Who have you on board?"

"Only the negro."

"Well, you and the nigger will step into the boat and go aboard the schooner."

"I think not," I replied very coolly, for I had gotten the mastery of my nerves again, though I was far from feeling the confidence I expressed. "I have been on an errand in the king's name, from Pigot to the encampment at Canoe Place, and am returning to report; nor do I propose to be stopped by anything but an enemy or a lack of wind."

"Where are your papers, then?" he demanded.

"They are delivered; nor would I show them to you if
8

they were not, for the service was secret. If you will but step into the cabin, I can satisfy you in all respects. There is no soul else on board, and you are safe, for we are not even armed by as much as a cutlass."

I forced a laugh as I made the last remark, and dove down the companion steps, while he turned to the crew of the boat before following, and said :

"Lay where you are and stand handy for a call."

Seating myself at the table, I motioned him to do the same ; but before complying, he drew his sword and gave a quick glance into the bunks and about the cabin.

"You'll moisten your lips, sir," I began, pushing the bottle toward him, "and in two words I can make this plain. You lay at Sag Harbor last night, did you not ? "

" We did. What then ? "

" I knew it. Did you not hear of the coming of a detachment from Canoe Place this morning ? "

" We did," he answered, softening a little in his interest, " but got word about dawn that they would not be there to meet us."

" Then *that's* a Yankee trick, for my business was to carry instructions to them from General Pigot, to proceed at once to Newport and make requisition on the first vessel that touched at ' Sag,'—though neither the general nor Admiral Parker then knew of the havoc that the rebels had made. The detachment has been cozened in some way. It is a dangerous spot, and I was told to sail out by night. Were you bound for Newport ? "

" We were, but only to trans-ship an officer—but I'm not discreet," he added suddenly, "I'm saying too much. You are evidently possessed of some important facts, but I cannot let you go on the strength of these and your unverified word. Who are you personally ? "

" I am the son of a citizen of Newport ; by name, Forbes. I have chosen to do the king a service, and not

the first, without the protection of his uniform. You
yourself see how easily I might pass as a rebel, for I have
not half convinced you of my loyalty."

"You have not, indeed. I am by no means satisfied, and
though I may be making a mistake, I must insist on your
going aboard with me. We will move at once, so make
ready. I will leave men in charge of the sloop."

Here then, was I driven to my last throw, and if that
failed, there was nothing for it but to give up or fight,
though how we could do the latter with such odds against
us, I failed to see.

"Perhaps this will satisfy you," I replied, rising and
turning over the cushion, when thrusting my fingers into
the slit, I drew forth the paper and laid it open before him,
then threw myself carelessly on the locker.

He picked it up and read it two or three times, turning
it over and over in his hands, as I knew he was doing in
his mind. As I looked anxiously at him, I then and there,
quick as a flash, made up my mind to fight if he caviled at
it, and was ready to spring at his throat and throttle him
the moment he showed signs of disapproval.

I knew that even if destruction followed the act it would
make little difference, for destruction was certainly in
store if the sloop became the prize of the schooner. I
could easily master this stripling, and kill him with his own
sword and without noise; then by obtaining the pistol,
which past doubt he carried, and getting the spy on board,
we might make a fair show of resistance until help came
for the enemy.

This sped through my brain as I waited. Outside, I
could hear Rod talking to the boat's crew, who were evidently amused by the negro, for anon, I caught the sound
of a muffled laugh in answer to his chattering. Finally the
officer laid down the paper, and the pucker on his forehead
relaxed as he said :

"This puts a new face on the matter, and I must believe

it genuine, for I have seen his Excellency's writing. And why did you not show this to me at once?"

"Because, beyond your uniform, I was by no means sure of your identity. Suppose now that you were a Yankee privateer in disguise ; what would be my position with this paper in my possession?"

"True ! Well, you may go your way," he returned, evidently disappointed. "But lastly, I desire to search you if only as a matter of form, that I may give a complete report. The darky, I think, we will have to press in the king's name, as we are short-handed."

"Nay, sir. The darky is my property, and this paper covers him as well as myself and the craft." For it never entered my head to give up Rod as a sacrifice to save myself.

"The devil take your paper !" he said pettishly. "Can't you lend us your man?"

"His Excellency should hear your respect for his authority. As for the boy, I need him myself. Do you think I could handle this boat alone if it should come on to blow— as I think it will?"

"Send a man aboard !" he shouted, without answering me ; and presently a marine came stumbling down the step.

"Search the lazarette and all on board," ordered the officer.

This command was a relief, for I thought he meant the call to refer to Rod, and I knew not how to act.

The sea-soldier pulled away the steps and opened the doors ; but the little hold was packed tight with ropes, spare canvas, and a large anchor. He pulled out a mass of stuff, poking his head and shoulders into the space, only to draw back and report nothing but gear within. He then opened all the lockers, though they would not have hidden a good-sized dog, and passed through to the galley, which he took in at a glance, then climbed through the hatch overhead.

Now I listened with bated breath for the shot that would come if he sighted the spy. He had left his musket lying along the transom cushions, a godsend to me in case of need, and I coiled myself for a spring on the instant, until my muscles were as tight as fiddle-strings. The officer, too, was thoroughly off his guard, for, taking the search as only a form, he was helping himself to a glass of brandy, little knowing how near he was to sudden death.

I scarce breathed as I heard the marine's footsteps, but in a few seconds, though they seemed like hours, his form blocked the light from the companion door and he called down :

"All clear and in shape, sir!"

I unsprung myself with a long breath of relief, and turned to the table, pouring out a stiff glass of brandy, which I downed to brace me against the shake which I feared would come as a result of reaction. Then, passing up the musket to the waiting marine, I called Rod and ordered him to re-stow the lazarette. In the meantime the officer was in deep thought, but finally his face cleared a bit as he said :

"Though you insist on not parting with your man, who, by the by, I am half inclined to take, you can hardly refuse to do a favor and help us right the muddle at Sag Harbor."

"Anything in my power for the king's cause. You can command me, but I don't care to be crippled for lack of my only hand."

"Well, sir," said he, courteously enough, "we have an officer aboard who must get to Newport at once. He is also on secret service for the king. If you will take him with you and land him there, we may return to Sag Harbor, look after the detachment for Pigot, and punish the freebooters who have dared to meddle with this movement. I cannot now say that this will meet the approval of the captain until I have reported ; but you will not sail

if the wind should rise. Work toward us. If we decide
not to use you, a gun will be fired and you may proceed on
your course ; if we need your services we will send the
officer aboard as soon as possible. I believe," he concluded,
rising and looking out of the window, " we will have wind
enough ere long, so I will get away at once."

"The king's health, sir, and yours," said I, pouring out
two glasses of liquor. "Send your man aboard by all
means, and I promise to have him ashore to-night."

We picked up the glasses, bowed, and drank. He then
turned up to the deck and jumped into the boat.

After much fumbling and swearing the painter was cast
off, and it was with thankfulness that I heard the order to
" Give way ! " and saw the boat started back to the schooner.

So far, so good, thought I. If they send this fellow
aboard, there will be only one to three. I will see to it
that it is mighty little use his arms will be to him. Put
him ashore ! Aye—by the mark ! but 'twill be strange if
Newport be the point. A fine thing will it be—to not
only bedevil the schooner and get away free, but to capture a British officer as well. 'Tis a smooth ending,
indeed ; but let me not whistle too fast, for the end is not
yet; only, so far, so good.

I watched the boat as it receded until they had gotten
at such a distance that I knew they would not return on
an afterthought.

There was less brightness to the sea than when they
came, and the clouds in the north were breaking from a
solid mass into lumps that told of wind, as plain as reading.

But now I wanted no wind, for I cared not to work
toward them, and for a wonder it held off in spite of the
appearance of the sky, though I knew that when it did
come it would make more than a " lady's day " of the ocean.

The boat was no more than a few good strokes from the
schooner before I dared move to call Moon, but at last I
got my head through the galley hatch.

"Jacob!" I shouted.

"Ahoy, there!" came back cheerily.

"Get aboard now; they are far enough."

"'Tis easier said than done. I must have a hand; your sides are too high."

At this, I ran back through the cabin and hauled on the larboard jib-sheet until the sail came around and formed a screen; then going to the halyard, I let it down halfway, where it hung as if jammed, and, while pretending to fuss over it, for I knew not what glass might be on us, I gave Moon a hand, and, with much tugging, landed him on deck—pistol and all.

Under the sail he crawled and dropped into the galley while the canvas was lowered and showed a clear deck to any who might be looking.

I joined him by way of the cabin, and found him sitting in a puddle made by the water that drained from his clothes.

"Well, my son," he said, looking hard at me, "ye are one to be proud of. I would hug ye were I less of a mop."

"Are you the worse for your bath?" I inquired, handing him the bottle of rum; for he had been in the water nearly an hour.

"Not now," he replied, stripping himself; "but when ye went below I thought ye were both taking a nap over the matter, for then I could hear nothing; an' what betwixt the cold o' the water on my body an' the heat o' the sun on my brain, I was nigh having a fit an' letting go my hold. But ye laid it down to him finely at the outset. I hardly thought ye would have the daring, though I might ha' known ye would not be backward. An' what was the upshot?"

I repeated at length what had transpired in the cabin, even to my thoughts; and then we laid our plan for the capture of the officer should he be sent to us.

" 'Tis easy," said Jacob, as I showed him how simply and quickly it could be done, " an' high time I were doing more than hanging like a pickle in brine. Have the darky handy, and the line stout."

Calling Rod, I let him into the plan and detailed his part to him, he nodding sagaciously as I went along.

"And you had best arm yourself with a belaying pin in case a rap is needed to quiet him," I concluded.

" Hi, Mars Tony ! I got sumfin better'n b'layin' pin ; I prick 'im wif dishere."

Here he reached into a space between the top of the upper lockers and the deck carlines, and drew out a short spear which he handed to me for inspection. It was a crude affair, made of a piece of straight, peeled hickory, about four feet long. In the thick end, which had been split to receive it, was a murderous-looking knife blade, fashioned out of a broken scythe, ground to a double edge, and brought to a needle-like point.

" I aint much use wif a gun, Mars Tony, but I kin plunk an aig twenty foot off wif dishere, mos' ebbery time. I kin frow dis an' kill a chicken in de haid," said he, with evident pride.

And indeed he could, for I afterward saw him do it ; but then, though I had often noticed him playing javelin, I had no idea he was making a practical effort, and of the existence of the weapon I had no knowledge.

This is but a slight incident to remark ; but Rod and his spear have gone down in history long since, and are therefore not unworthy of notice here.

Telling him the spear would do as well as the belaying pin, I ordered him on deck to look out ; but he had hardly gotten his woolly head through the hatch, when he sung back :

" Dar's big breeze, Mars Tony."

I ran up and saw the northern rim of the ocean turned dark blue with the coming wind. The streak stretched broadly from east to west and would soon be on us.

"Douse the tops'l, Rod!" I shouted, as I sprang and cast loose the main sheet; for we stood broadside to the coming blast, and I had no notion of finishing with a capsize. "Clew up; then take the bonnet off the jib. Work quick at it, and bear a hand to reef."

But hurry as we might, the wind was upon us before the great sail was half reduced. It came with a rush that heeled us to starboard as it struck us, and created a rumpus with the loose canvas and slackened ropes; but it brought us into the eye of the gale, and as there was no sea on, we lay steadily, though all seemed confusion overhead. There was less weight to it than I expected, after the first gust had passed, but 'twas a merry double reefer and would soon get up a lively sea, I had no doubt.

As the last point was knotted and the sail run up, I betook myself to the spy-glass and the schooner, and noted that a boat had put off from her and was a third of the distance on its way to us. Evidently they had acted quickly on the suggestion of the young officer, and had no further suspicion as to our character.

The vessel had taken in her square sail, fore sail and flying jib, and was standing off for headway to tack, so I concluded it were better for me to move toward the visitor and not create remark.

CHAPTER XIV.

THE STRUGGLE IN THE CABIN.

The straining oarsmen were doubtless glad to see us bearing down on them, for the boat was making but little progress against the wind; at times seeming barely to hold its own. My attention was taken from them as we swept past and rounded up, for I was busy getting the jib to windward in order to lay to, that they might come alongside, and the officer was aboard ere I finished belaying the sheet. He tossed a black portmanteau to the deck, and followed it immediately with a jump, the boat sheering off and making for the schooner still to leeward, before I caught sight of his face.

When I finally did I was staggered.

There before me and within arm's-reach stood Lieutenant Bromfield; his dark countenance as supercilious and impatient as when I first met him months before on the moor. He was dressed in plain black as of yore. The same cloak, or one like it, hung from his shoulders, and in his hand was a sword around which was wrapped its belt. His keen, black eyes snapped a look at me, but showed no recognition—which was not remarkable, as he had never had a fair look at my face before. He quickly turned his attention to the cabin and the fittings about the deck, bending to peer into the former and letting his gaze play rapidly over the latter, before he deigned to speak. Then with a suddenness that went well with his temper, he said:

" You have a tidy enough craft; I hope you will give me a quick passage. Will you have your man take my traps below? "

Now in courtesy I thought something due me in the shape of introduction before he ventured to make half demands ; and as my first fear of his possibly remembering me had given place to a feeling of security, I was somewhat nettled at his tone, which was none of the smoothest.

Rod, without waiting to be told, disappeared with the bag ; and I, with all the ease I could muster, let go the sheet to windward, hauled aft to leeward, and seated myself at the wheel before I answered :

"The sloop is well enough ! As for the passage, you can direct your prayers to the wind. Pray, sir ! whom have I the honor of addressing ? My own name is Forbes."

This while I was trimming the main sheet for a run on the larboard tack.

We careened to the gale as we gathered headway, and were tearing along at a rate which ought soon to raise Block Island dead ahead, before he gathered sufficient politeness to reply.

"My name is Beverly—of His Majesty's service," he said. "Have I not seen you before ? " and now he looked fixedly at me.

Perhaps something in my voice and semi-defiant manner may have awakened a passing memory in him, which I evidently dispelled when I returned :

"Not to my knowledge surely, though it is possible I have met and forgotten you. I have met many in my day."

"Very like ; but the first is not a broad compliment to me, if so," he replied indifferently, throwing off his cloak and standing on the sloping deck with graceful ease. "Have you any eatables below ? I am well-nigh famished, and 'tis high noon or more."

"Certainly," I replied; "I am sharp-set myself. If you will tighten your belt a bit we will go below together," and calling Rod, I ordered him to place on the table whatever the larder afforded.

His suggestion necessitated his going to the cabin, thus carrying out the first part of my plan, for in it must come the final action, and the prize would be greater than I had anticipated.

Though no wise doubtful of the result, I was nervous about the onset, as I knew enough of the man to believe he would not tamely submit to becoming a prisoner, no matter what odds were arrayed against him. Force must be used, and it would take tact to make the opportunity when it could be used to the best advantage. The first was provided for; the latter he was himself leading up to.

Bromfield presented a picture of illy-controlled impatience; his standing was but an expression of it. He would have walked like a caged animal had there been sufficient space. His white teeth gnawed his mustaches, as with knitted brows he looked ahead for land, and astern at the schooner already nearly hull down on the horizon; his fine figure swaying with the vessel as the seas, which were now growing tumultuous, swung under us. I looked at his powerful physique with a feeling of something more than mere respect, as I saw at what a disadvantage I would be in his hands; for he was undoubtedly my superior in both size and strength. He had no inkling of the trap yawning to receive him. Suddenly he turned and said:

"What time, think you, will we reach Newport?"

"I hope to have you ashore shortly after dark," I truthfully returned; "but we are a small vessel and are well at sea."

He mused a moment and then asked:

"What force has Sir Peter now in the bay, and what progress has Pigot made?"

Here was a poser. I could but hazard an answer, and if by chance I made a blunder, matters might take a sudden turn for the worse. What to say puzzled me. My brain worked quickly. I saw the necessity of getting matters to a head as soon as possible, and of placing myself near

Moon, who I knew was on end for action. To gain time, I called Rod to hasten, and then said :

"Sir Peter's force is shifting so frequently 'tis not easy to say just what ships are there. Of course I know naught of his plans."

"Is the *Cerberus* there ? "

Here again was a poser, and one that demanded a direct answer. At a venture I said "No," trusting he was asking for information and not giving me test questions out of suspicion. He evidently wished to know, for his manner remained unchanged and he made no further queries. To take no chances, however, I called Rod to the wheel, giving him a sharp look (which he understood), as I directed him to hold the course, and then motioned Bromfield to go below. This he did quickly, as though glad of a change, but to my great relief leaving his sword in the cockpit.

I placed him on the starboard side of the table and seated myself by the galley entrance. The officer was evidently hungry, for he fell to with the gusto of a hungry man, while I dabbled with the food before me, getting more and more nervous with suppressed excitement until a mouthful would have choked me. For a space, no word was spoken by either. The timbers creaked as we lifted to the seas ; the lockers rattled their contents and the galley curtains blew in and out with a flap as the strong air drew down the hatch.

Knowing that the time was at hand, and he would be at a greater disadvantage while seated on the depressed side of the cabin, I stepped on deck as though to look about ; then, albeit in plain sight of the officer, I told Rod in a low voice to bring the helm up and careen us to starboard as far as he durst, when he heard me shout the word "*king;*" then, going down, resumed my place.

"I regret," said I to Bromfield, "that I can offer you neither tea nor coffee. 'Twould have been dangerous for me had I been overhauled by a Yankee and either found aboard ; they have a prejudice against these small matters, but I can recommend this *Medford*," raising my voice on the word 'Medford,' as the agreed upon signal to Moon that I was coming to the point.

"Rum is a fair substitute," he replied.

"Very good ! Fill, and I will give you a toast you rarely hear," and I handed him the bottle. He was no novice at it, for he filled his glass almost to a level and passed me the liquor ; then setting the tumbler betwixt his fingers to steady it, waited for me.

"Now," I began, rising, and with all the smile I could force (which must have been made ghastly by my inward tumult), "here's long life to General Washington,—God bless him !—and confusion to the *king !*"

For the space of a moment he stared at me with amazement, his black eyes flashing like fire ; then catching the situation, he uttered a terrible oath and hurled the glass at my head, at the same time springing to his feet.

The frail glass took me in the forehead, and though lacerating the skin to the bone, was too light to stun me. At the same instant the head of the vessel paid off until we were nigh broadside to the gale and lay almost on our beam ends. The sudden tip threw me across the table and drove Bromfield into the bunk at his back with the mess of the meal on top of him.

As we both struggled to gain a controlling position, I heard a loud "Ha-a·a!" behind me, and grasping the bulkhead of the bunk, I pulled myself upright.

There, halfway though the galley door and as naked as on the day he was born, knelt Moon ; his right hand, in which he held a cocked pistol, resting on the table in such a way as to have the weapon leveled full at the prostrate Royalist. His face was terrible in the intensity of its expression. Every element of kindliness was gone. His lips were drawn back against his teeth till they showed like an angry dog's. With eyes literally blazing and breath that came and went with a snarl, he glared at his victim. Every fiber in the man was trembling like a leaf in a breeze, and I expected nothing less than to hear the report of his pistol and see Bromfield die; but as the seconds sped, the shot came not, nor did either move.

"Let her come up!" I shouted to Rod, for nothing could be done with the vessel at such a terrible incline, and we gradually swung into the wind until the floor became a heaving level. Even then the situation remained unchanged. The two looked to be in a trance as they glared at each other without moving, Bromfield seeming fascinated by his opponent's face. It was a dramatic tableau; but no time was to be lost, for the blood that was pouring from my forehead was blinding me, and like one in a frenzy, I threw myself upon the British officer and drove him onto his back. Even with this disadvantage, he would have made short work of me alone, I fear, for his grip was like iron; but Moon came to the rescue, catching him by the legs and hauling us both to the cabin floor, where there was room to work.

Will I ever forget the maddening dance of the cabin lights as we swung around, each striving for mastery! The struggle for a foot-hold, the crashing fall and twist for recovery; the clutch at the throat, and the devil that shone in the eyes of the Tory.

It was a fierce encounter—a confusion of oaths and blows; at the end of which I was thrown against the wood-work half stunned. I was so dazed by my exertion and the loss of blood, I have small memory of the detail of the fight. But we won it. 'Twas but a few seconds ere the proud Royalist was tied hand and foot, wound round and round with a coil of signal halyard, and laid upon his back on the floor; for the tossing of the vessel would have thrown him from a bunk.

I could barely tell what happened, so great was the confusion of my brain, and it was not till after Moon had

bathed and bound up my head and backed his treatment
with stimulants, that I realized all we had planned had
been carried out. The details of our scheme had somewhat miscarried by reason of the gale, which had not been
taken into account, but the end had been attained. I was
too dizzy and sick to fully realize the import of our success,
and the nausea that assailed me was in no wise lessened by
the pitching of the little craft. Continued nervous strain,
lack of food, and hard blows had worsted me, for a time
rendering me helpless; so, feeling I had earned a needed
respite, I crawled into a bunk and turned my attention to
the captive.

Though he was incapable of movement and a great gash
on his head showed where he had been struck in the *mêlée*,
I bade Rod get his spear and mount guard by his side;
while Moon, still naked, took the wheel until I could pull
myself together.

The most virulent hatred was expressed in the officer's
eyes when I spoke to him, and though it be not manly to
exult over a fallen enemy, there was something mightily
like exultation in my voice as I said to him:

"Lieutenant Bromfield—alias Beverly, I shall land you
as I promised, but hardly at Newport. To Fort Griswold
you will go, and you can then see the works, as you once
had a desire to do; but it will hardly be to your advantage,
nor that of Howe, Clinton, Parker, and the rest."

"Who, and what are you?" he demanded with an
oath.

"Your inquiry would be needless had you stayed at
Squire Beauchamp's a few hours longer on the occasion of
your spying last fall," I answered; and I then detailed the
manner in which I had acquired my knowelge of him, ending by stating how I had hoodwinked the officer who came
aboard, and where Moon had been concealed.

He twisted in his coil of line as he listened, and when he
heard that Moon had been over the bow, vented his rage

by heaping maledictions upon the head of the young officer for being so readily deceived.

He made no inquiries as to our intentions in regard to himself, but I voluntarily told him that he would be taken to Colonel Ledyard, before whom he would be questioned and searched. If compromising papers were found on him he would probably be hanged as a spy ; in any other event he would be held as a prisoner of war until exchanged.

"But even as a spy, I am not taken within your lines," he snapped out.

"You make a fine point ; but for the matter of that, Nathan Hale was not taken within *your* lines, yet he suffered. You have set us the precedent."

"I am no spy, nor have I doubtful papers ; I was merely being trans-shipped."

"The better for you," I answered, "unless your previous errand to Beauchamp counts against you. We will wait and see what Colonel Ledyard finds on you."

I had decided not to risk loosening his bonds, as would be necessary in order to give his person a thorough overhauling. He had been gone over for arms, but beyond his sword, he carried nothing but a pistol of small and unusual pattern, and that not loaded.

He gritted his teeth at my answer and became silent ; while I slept or dozed, until, awakening with a start, I realized that Moon was still at the wheel, clad like Adam before the Fall. Leaving the prisoner to Rod, I went on deck to relieve the old man. That worthy was in an angelic frame of mind, albeit he presented anything but an angelic appearance.

From beginning to end, no word had passed betwixt him and Bromfield, but when I first saw them face to face, I felt they knew and hated each other.

"By the powers ! my son," said he, with his old smile as he relinquished the wheel, "ye have the devil's pet cub below there."

9

"Was he aboard the *Dragon* with you?"

"Much o' the time, an' he was the most cruel o' the bloody gang when they took a prize. I know little o' him except that he was forever on the p'int o' j'ining a Line ship, an' always failing, which seemed to sour his addled temper; for I never heard him speak without an oath slipping off his tongue. He's a Jersey Tory, an' bitter as sin itself. But faith! 'twill be a tall feather in your cap for this day's work."

"There would have been few feathers for me, save wing feathers as an angel, had it not been for you. I am not his equal in strength, and you deserve the credit for his capture."

"Nay, nay, man! I was but a pistol backed by so many stone weight o' bone an' muscle; 'twas your head that plotted the whole from start to finish, an' ye fought like a shrew. To say nothing o' bagging this brute, I owe ye my neck an' I can't tell ye what I feel for ye." And his eyes glistened as he put his arm around me and inquired about the wound on my head.

"I'll soon be right," I replied, honestly flattered by his words and touched by his affection; "but we had better get about and lay our course for New London. If you will give your duds a swing in this air you will soon have a dry rig. You've been damp since last night."

The wind was neither stronger nor weaker as we came about on the starboard tack, but the seas had gotten to be monstrous for a craft of our size, and I determined to make for the lee of the Connecticut shore by the straightest line I could sail. The great somber combers had an ugly look as they broke about us with a hiss, and if they continued to grow we would be in a danger but little less, though of a different sort, than that through which we had just passed. I laid our course due northwest, or as I judged, for the eastern end of Fisher's Island, and with the fervid hope that we would face no further interruption, settled down to master the surrounding element.

It was fortunate that we lay on the wind closehauled. To have laid a course with the wind abeam in such a sea would have been impossible.

As it was, sailing was difficult enough. Our progress was almost stopped at times by the crash of some huge billow striking our bows, while ever and anon the jib boom would bury itself in the depths of a charging torrent and threaten to snap off as we lifted. The jib was soaked wellnigh to the head, and the deck forward so deluged that the galley hatch was shipped to keep the flood from getting below.

As time progressed, the weather turned dirty. The sky flattened into a dull slate color and a few drops of rain splashed on my face with a sting that showed the force of the wind as we beat against it. With the wearing hours, my sufferings increased. My head throbbed as though the brain was loose, and a nausea, for which there came no relief, made me blind and dizzy.

My impatience to get home became, in my fevered state, more like a thing than a condition, and though barely twenty-four hours had elapsed since our departure, I felt as though we had been away a week; and the events of yesterday seemed long since passed, so thickly had the time been strewn with incidents.

Our progress appeared rapid as we jumped into the seething green hills, but I knew it could be measured by feet rather than fathoms, and that our seeming speed was due to the rush of water and not to ourselves.

The land was yet a blue cloud, northward, differing but a shade or two from the bleak sky above it. Its distance was indescribably depressing.

Meantime, while I sat in abject misery at the helm, Rod kept ward over the prisoner with an attention as fixed as though the rope-swathed victim was liable to burst his bonds at any instant. With spear in hand, and an unswerving devotion to his duty, he never marked my condition ; but Moon, who was at last getting into his clothing, observed me sway from weakness, and promptly came on deck to order me below ; an order I was fain to obey.

Once more crawling into a bunk, I soon yielded to my exhausted condition and slept, and was only awakened, hours after, by the rush of the anchor chain, to find we were lying near the old rope ferry in New London Harbor, and that the voyage was over.

It was dark. Consulting the cabin clock, I found it was past ten. I felt refreshed and relieved, albeit somewhat light-headed from an empty stomach, and, while Moon and the negro snugged matters for the night, I rummaged about for something to eat.

Bromfield lay with his eyes closed as though asleep, but on my asking if he were hungry he gave a negative reply and demanded water, to which I helped him. He was decidedly weakened by the pressure of the cord and his enforced rigidity, but was still unsubdued in temper or spirit.

Owing to the lateness of the hour, it was suggested that the captive be kept aboard till morning, but on his own earnest appeal to be sent to the fort, where his bonds at least would be taken from him and the pain of the stricture released, I dispatched Rod with a note to Colonel Ledyard, and in the course of half an hour I had the satisfaction of seeing Lieutenant Bromfield escorted to the works under a strong guard.

He could scarcely walk, his limbs had become so stiffened, and despite the little love I bore him, I was struck with pity for his suffering—a waste of feeling, doubtless ; but with his departure from the *Will o' the Wisp* my responsibility for his safety ended.

CHAPTER XV.

BEING far from pessimistic, and no misanthrope at that time, nor since, for that matter, it can readily be imagined with what zest I took in the compliments that were poured upon me. Moon had told the story his own way, which despite my earnest protest made me the hero of the cruise, albeit my companions were not without their meed of praise.

It turned out that aside from the risks we had so successfully encountered, we had done nothing of great moment in the capture of the British lieutenant. The closest search had failed to uncover papers of any consequence, and though it was to me a source of satisfaction to have thus proved by my recognition my previous knowledge of him, I much regretted that no collusion betwixt him and Beauchamp could be shown.

Bromfield was tried before a military court and finally held as a prisoner of war. Though confronted with the squire, he would only admit an acquaintance, and that his previous visit was purely on matters of private business. His confinement to the fort did not last long. Within three months from the date of his capture he was exchanged.

'Twas but little I saw of him at this time, but I saw and heard enough to know that his temper was morose and well-nigh ungovernable, and his malice and threats of future vengeance were directed less toward those who had taken him than toward Colonel Ledyard, against whom he seemed to feel the wild hatred of a madman.

If I ever thought of him after, it was only casually. I was far from dreaming that this devil incarnate would crop up in my life again. But as some men are followed by adverse fortune, which seems to hang like a demon over their lives, as though waiting for an opportunity to work them evil, so this dark-browed Tory became my *béte noire*, as the French say, and a thorn in my side.

So far, we were opponents only by the chance of war ; but the future held for us an enmity occasioned by circumstances that fostered an antagonism to which war was a mere pastime. Fate was to determine whether the victory belonged to the dashing man of the world or to the country stripling.

I will not load these pages with the minor doings of my every-day life, nor devote my space to the military movements of the time, however interesting might be the latter theme. Every reader of history can supply the events of the years 1777 and 1778 ; events in which I played no part.

The war had extended to such a length that to us it had become almost a matter of course, and, aside from the temporary public stir on the receipt of news which came only at long intervals, there was no excitement.

Only once was the town in danger. On the last day of August, 1778, Clinton, with a fleet of one hundred sail, threatened us ; and but for the providential interference of an adverse gale, which prevented his working into the harbor, history would have had another bloody page to unroll. But he sailed back to New York and left us to pursue our course as onlookers over a theater that was extending more and more, until finally the war drifted to the south, and we heard of defeat after defeat, as one listens to disasters occurring afar, without a full or even fair realization of their import.

My excursions by water had become restricted, owing to the prevalence of the enemy's vessels, and I always kept within easy running distance of New London. The saying to the effect that whomsoever one meets in the desert is sure to prove an enemy, had its counterpart on Long Island Sound in those days. I fled from a sail with all dispatch, having no stomach to again try a policy of deception or to possibly run into the arms of the *Dragon* herself.

The face of the great sea wrinkled or smoothed itself as it frowned or smiled, and the twinkling edge of the surf lazily lapped the beach or bit into the sands with its varying moods. The forests turned brown and green and brown and green again before my time was ripe to bear new fruits of action. All nature alternately dressed herself as a bride and fell into the barrenness of age, and this great world swung twice through its course before my story again takes up its thread and spins a line which still glitters through all the years that have since gone.

But erstwhile, under the blossoms of the orchard in spring, beneath the shelter of the summer forests, and beside the fostering warmth of the great fires in winter, had grown a quiet romance; for Charlotte and Hal had put aside all concealment and stood before us betrothed. At present marriage was not spoken of, for times were hard and the future too uncertain to make such a step advisable. The grasp of poverty hung over all, and even we, who had never known its hand before, now felt its grip and were forced to forego luxuries that had hitherto been considered necessities.

This was far from being remarkable, for the money of the Confederacy, which had been freely taken when first issued, had now fallen so as to be worth but four cents on the dollar.

Little, however, did poverty trouble the two, for at their ages love was enough. The curse of heartache, through waiting, was not near them, and my sweet sister grew sweeter and more beautiful as she stepped onto the throne of first love, the throne a woman occupies and feels the dizzy glory of but once.

Moon had long gone, and we had seen him but for a brief space since our adventure; but he had promised a speedy return, a promise he had so far not fulfilled. For myself, the days had found me no laggard in the main, and the people had grown to know me as a young practitioner, while the old doctor, on whom each passing month now told heavily, depended on me more and more.

I cannot say that I had an abiding love for my profession. A life of greater activity than could be found in the shady streets of the quiet old town would have suited me better ; but I knew no other road into which to turn, and those two years which saw me emerge from the unformed student into something less negative were tinged with but little color, and held no great hopes for the future.

I confess to the keener pleasures of my home, over the moderate activity of time spent in following the path of my manifest duty in town. I confess to the greater satisfaction of an hour's day-dream while reclining on the top of a certain high, chestnut-shaded bowlder that pushed from the side of the hill overlooking the sea ; a great halfrounded rock, standing ten feet above its fellows, with a depression on its top like a cradle, in which I was wont to lie and pretend to study, while my eye and brain drifted away from the *materia medica* and went fog-hunting or wool-gathering, as you please.

To this same bowlder a strange thing happened the following winter, during the "great freeze" of January, 1780. On a quiet night in the middle of the month, when the still air seemed to crackle with the intensity of the cold, and all nature shriveled up in the terrible temperature, the rock split from top to bottom with a wonderful report that equaled the discharge of a heavy cannon, and was heard for miles around. I mind me that it was in the dead of night, and the ground feet deep with snow, when the noise

that shook the house broke upon us. At first we thought
it the bursting of the ice on the river or along the Sound
shore, due to the swing of the tide, and not until a day or
two later did I make the discovery that my cradle had been
split through its center and gaped widely. It had been an
immense toy to me in childhood, and I can remember dig-
ging away the earth at its front and putting my little
shoulder to it in the vain hope of seeing it topple from its
place and roll down the steep declivity into the sea. And
there the old rock still lies; a wonder to the country
around, at the mighty power in the freezing of a few drops
of water in its heart. In its nest Charlotte and I had
played, summers in and out, while over it further and
further the chestnut spread its arms. On it I had dreamed
as a youth, dreamed and hoped as a young man, and was
so dreaming and hoping on the afternoon of Sunday,
July 4, 1779, when my half-dozing senses were aroused by
a sound more portentous than that of a splitting rock : the
distant boom of a single cannon that vibrated through the
quiet air.

I had hardly realized the nature of the report when it
was followed by another, and then all was silent but for
the swish of the leaves above me and the chirping of the
crickets.

Suddenly I felt its significance in full force. Inaction
had fostered a feeling of security, and the import of the
dull, rumbling shots had come slowly, but I was fully alive
to them now.

Throwing myself from my perch, I tore up the hill and
into the house shouting :

"The alarm from the fort! Where's Harry ?" for I
knew he would be somewhere on the place, as I had seen
him and Charlotte together but a while since.

My father, who was writing, looked up anxiously, then
rose and walked slowly to the open door. The outside
world was exquisite in its aspect of peace and beauty,

and it seemed impossible that war should mar its perfection.

"Are you sure you heard aright?" he asked, as he looked out onto the barren stretch of blue water, for no sail specked it south or east, and the west was hidden from where we stood.

"Hark! there again!" I exclaimed, as the sound of two more reports came from the distance. "'Tis a call from the fort. What force could have approached us unknown— yet what else would demand an alarm?"

"God grant it be not what I have long feared! There is but one thing to do. Haste to the fort, Tony; I will send Rod to follow and bring back tidings."

I rushed to my room for sword and rifle, and, starting for the barns to saddle up, I met Harry hurrying through the garden with Charlotte, whose face was white and scared.

"I heard it," he said briefly, as he turned and went with me, while Charlotte, without a word, followed. None of the help was about, but it was short work for us to saddle a couple of animals. It was not so short a business, however, to get clear of Charlotte, who clung to her lover as though it were to be an eternal separation and the cannons were his funeral salute. She held him as only a woman holds the man to whom she surrenders, giving vent but little to words or tears, but with a desperation that was pitiful from its very earnestness.

"Heaven help me! What am I to do, Tony?" he cried, as he strove in vain to unclasp her arms from about his neck. "It's as cruel as death to leave her in this state, yet I must get hence. Sweetheart, for the love of mercy, let me go!" he urged, his face growing set as he looked at her. "You should be the first to send me off and not the one to make me prove a coward. Unclasp me, love; I will be back soon—the alarm may mean nothing."

As if to give the lie to his words, two more sullen booms broke on our ears and worked him to a pitch of frenzy, though he plead and struggled to no purpose. But this combat of love and duty ended suddenly, for my sister became limp in his arms, and fainted.

Leaping on to my horse, I rode through the garden to my father, who still stood where I had left him, and bidding him farewell, told him to send Aunt Freeman to Charlotte, and made my way to the gate. Here Hal soon joined me and we sped away. At his house a brief halt was made that he might gather his arms, and we then hastened onward.

Never but once, and that later, have I urged a horse to greater speed. As we turned into the Mystic road, clouds of dust before and behind marked the quick gathering of the militia. We passed them going on foot, on horseback, and in carts—men, women, and children on the way to fight or look on, all unsmiling and all filled with suppressed excitement. We saw them cutting across fields and climbing fences singly and in pairs, and my heart gave a bound of delight at seeing how promptly the people sprang to arms in defense of their homes, albeit they were far less prompt in joining the regular troops.

I scarce knew what I expected to see as we approached the fort, but in fact there was nothing unusual to behold beyond the numbers that poured in and out of the gate. A company was already formed in the field, which marched down the road to the ferry as we came up, and I learned it was dispatched to the feeble works of Fort Trumbull across the river.

There was no sign of an enemy in sight, and it was with some little difficulty that I gathered the cause of the alarm, but the cause was sufficient.

Five British ships lay in the offing, either preparing to work into the harbor later, or to land troops under cover of darkness to do their work by night. It seemed strange to us that they should have thus given a chance for the countryside to rise before making an attack. Presently word came from the lighthouse that there were no troopships or transports among them, and that the fleet meant only to block the port.

This proved to be the fact, though until we knew the reason, it kept us on the alert. Though most of the militia returned to their homes that night, a large number remained to garrison the fort.

A week passed with the silent enemy before our eyes, and the rattle of our own drums and notes of preparation in our ears, when, on Sunday afternoon, as I was placing a patrol on the beach back of Pine Island, I received an order to report to Colonel Ledyard, and immediately repaired to headquarters.

In the meantime enough had come to our knowledge to stir the blood and make inactivity well-nigh unbearable. Tryon had suddenly fallen on New Haven, burning it and the surrounding villages. Outrages unspeakable had been perpetrated on the defenseless inhabitants by the foreign troops. The movement had none of the dignity of military strategy, and had been foreshadowed in the action of the British Parliament, which had determined that predatory incursions on defenseless points had become necessary to break the spirit of rebellion. Tryon had given the key of his intentions in a proclamation to the people, issued from the fleet then before the town, which ended by saying :

"*The existence of a single habitation on your defenseless coast ought to be a subject of constant reproof to your ingratitude.*"

The war vessels before us were thus accounted for. The eastern end of the Sound and the port of New London were blocked from interference by water, and the move was too sudden for resistance by land. Having no knowledge of the whereabouts of the main fleet, or intimation of where the next blow might be struck, we were in a lamentable state of fear and uncertainty on the day I was sent for by Colonel Ledyard.

I marked an air of expectation as I entered the fort and saw a line drawn up on the parade as if for inspection, but not stopping to inquire the cause, I proceeded to the colonel's quarters and entered.

In the room were a dozen officers and men of importance in the town, all gathered about a table at which sat the colonel in earnest conversation with a noble-looking old gentleman in a white wig, who was a stranger to me. That he was a person of importance, I knew at once by the deference paid him. I mingled with the group for some time without attracting attention, until the colonel at last, looking up, caught my eye.

"Here, Anthony," he said, rising and beckoning to me, "let me present you to Governor Trumbull. Governor, this is Doctor, or rather Lieutenant Gresham, the young gentleman of whom I spoke. Shall I give him his orders?"

Governor Trumbull of Connecticut! So this was the man, who, next to General Washington, commanded my greatest reverence. The friend and adviser of the commander-in-chief, and the one on whom he most relied. The spirit and backbone of Connecticut, who never for a moment wavered in his faith in our ultimate triumph. The man who proved himself the "Solon of the East," and whose resources seemed never at an end.

He rose from his chair and shook me warmly by the hand, saying :

"The State is already indebted to you, lieutenant, but with your permission I will increase the debt."

I felt both honored and confused at this notice given so freely and in such company, and bowed with my best grace, while I murmured something to the effect that I was at his service.

"As it is not in the line of your regular duty," he continued, reseating himself and apparently studying my face, "you are not *ordered*, as the colonel intimates, but asked to volunteer on a service not necessarily attended with great danger."

He paused as though waiting a reply, and I managed to get my tongue and say that I considered Colonel Ledyard's wishes as orders.

"Excellent!" he answered. "You of course are aware of the disaster which has overtaken the Commonwealth. The enemy have withdrawn to Huntington Harbor on the Long Island coast and are refitting. This much we know and this is all. Messengers by land are plentiful, and we now need one by water. You will take your vessel, which I hear has already done good service and seems fitted for the duty, and sail around these gentry outside by night, bearing west till you meet this fleet which is at the back of Tryon. If you can determine their movements in any direction, return with the information. Place on shore the messenger I shall send with you, and make your return as safe as possible. If hard pressed and in danger of capture, run your vessel ashore, and the State will indemnify you for all loss. You may ask for volunteers to the number you think you may require, and they too may be set ashore at different points at your discretion, to make their way back with such information as you acquire. The whole will be under your command. Do you understand this plainly?"

"Perfectly," I replied, losing all diffidence in listening to his concise orders, and feeling the prospect of immediate adventure. "I will ask for three men and start by dark to-night."

"If your action is as prompt as your answer, there is little to fear, and all will go well," he returned. "Commend me to your father, whom I know and admire. I wish you a fortunate trip."

"I trust your Excellency will hear a good account of me. I will prepare at once. Is your express ready to go with me?"

"Not here, lieutenant, not here yet; but he will be instructed to meet you a little after sunset. Good-by to you!"

Considering this as a dismissal, I withdrew with a bow to him and another to the assemblage and, flushed with pride and gratification, set about finding Harry, who would of course form part of the expedition.

After much trouble and inquiry I came upon him seated on top of Avery's Knoll (an elevation just outside the fort), where he was sucking a pipe and gazing pensively out at sea. He became all animation when I stated the nature of my business, and readily agreed with me as to the advantage of taking the Rose boys, upon whom I had settled in my mind as being suited to make up the needed number.

These were two brothers who lived near the ferry and were competent watermen; a qualification I deemed necessary. Both had been with the army around Boston, and we had known them since boyhood. Their names were Ben and Amasa respectively. Jolly, devil-may-care fishermen in times of peace, and equally brave and devil-may-care in these days of war. They joined us eagerly, and such was the looseness of the military organization that the matter of asking for leave of absence was not considered. They simply stated their intention of leaving—and left.

Not knowing the state of the family larder, and doubting its ability to provision us on so short a notice, we drew what rations we could from the commissariat, and with light hearts set out for Hardscrabble, more like boys bound on an errand of pleasure than like men going on an expedition that might prove disastrous—even fatal.

CHAPTER XVI.

FOUND ON THE SAND.

BESIDES laying in every available weapon, with a supply of ammunition, and taking on board such provisions as could be spared from the house, there had been little to do. Otherwise the *Will o' the Wisp*, like a blooded hound, was always kept trim for a run, and was tugging at the leash of her moorings against the young ebb. We were only waiting the coming of the Governor's messenger and the darkness, to be off.

As a fighting force on the start, we would have, with Rod, six men ; and I had small fear of our ability to take care of anything of our draught. Our numbers precluded the possibility of fatigue from being short-handed, yet left ample room to work ship, fight, or live comfortably, as the future decreed.

Good-bys and God-speeds had been given, though in Harry's case it seemed a protracted function. We were all aboard save Rod, who with the dingey was ashore waiting the completion of our complement of men. Slowly the light sank and the shore lost its details. The water rippled under our bow, the tree-toads and frogs started up their night concert, and still no messenger appeared. What would be my duty in case of his non-arrival bothered me greatly, and I was about calling a general council when the stroke of oars reached my ears, and a boat appeared from up the river and swung alongside. Before I discovered it was not Rod in the dingey, the figure of a man stepped from it to the deck. His first words introduced him.

"I'm late, lads, but through no fault. Where's your captain?"

There was no mistaking the voice and gesture. It was Jacob Moon.

In a trice the old man was wringing my hand, while the others stood wondering. The greeting was warm and short enough, for there was no time to be lost.

"Let's be off," he said, as he released me, "the wind's fair an' we should make New Haven early; there'll be plenty o' time to palaver."

At once all hands were busy. Rod was recalled and the sloop got under way; and ere the low west was fairly freed of the glimmer of the sun's last light, we were standing out into the Sound and bearing south to make a long loop around the blockade.

The night was hot and bid fair to be dark enough to suit our purpose, for the thin haze that oft accompanies a south wind veiled the light of the stars, and there was no moon.

"Keep a sharp watch ahead till we round them," said Jacob, as we drove out into the blackness of the Sound. "The ships may be moving abroad; 'tis just the night they would be on the lookout, but ye can give them the slip though they sight us, for they fear shallow water as the devil fears a cross."

We made our way to the south, however, without seeing any sign of the enemy, and then stood west until we had put the harbor well on our starboard quarter. It was nine o'clock when we started, and by half-past eleven I considered it safe to run in and get the land within easy distance, for there was no knowing what cruiser we might chance upon in the depth of the Sound. We made the land near Millstone Point and then bore away west again, just near enough to the coast to make its black outlines barely visible against the sky, yet far enough to clear the outlying reefs.

To have Jacob aboard was the one thing that completed

10

my appetite for the expedition, and as we had much to talk over, we took the first watch together while the rest turned in below.

"How happens it, old fellow," said I, "that you drop on us in this fashion like a meteor, when I have figured you as being leagues hence ? "

"Faith ! 'tis a long story," he replied. "Since I had the last o' ye I ha' covered a power o' ground. From ye to Sullivan at Providence, then on to Boston, then to Falmouth, and from there back to headquarters, with many a side road and many a delay. I fetched Germantown in time to winter at Valley Forge. I tell ye, lad, I ha' been better clad, better fed, an' better housed before an' since that time, an' many was there penned in who were about ready to give up an' return to the king, only no one had the backbone to propose it for fear o' his fellows. Good Lord ! those were black days, my son ! I thought the cause the same as lost during the early winter. But the chief—God bless him !—is made o' iron, methinks, for he was always the same, blew the wind east or west; an' now, albeit I see not how, we look to be climbing the hill. 'Tis the French that ha' put the heart in us again and given the king a fit, mayhap; for do ye mind, I think this matter o' burning houses an' shooting unarmed men, an' robbing an' outraging, is a token o' weakness among the red-coats, an' that matters be on the mend.

"I'll not be telling ye what ye know, but how I happened here. Washington got wind o' this movement o' the Bloody Wolf,* an' sent me to you fine old gentleman, your Governor, an' he sent me to Glover's Brigade at Providence ; but it is far too late, if I may venture an opinion, an' now I am ordered back to Washington by this route,— which delighted my heart when I heard o' it,—an' will take him what scraps o' matter we pick up, if so be we pick up any."

* The name given to General Tryon by the Americans.

"Are you to leave us, then, before we return ?" I asked, mightily disappointed at so soon losing him.

"Aye, lad ! When ye start back I quit ye—an' sorry I am ; but we'll meet again, past doubt ; my loss is the greater for the quitting. An' now that you have a coarse cutting o' my doings up to this night, ye'll tell me o' yourself."

I gave him my history for the past two years, but being devoid of incident, it took little time. When at last I told him that our prisoner had been exchanged, he snapped his fingers suddenly, and said :

"I know it, an' by the powers ! but I came near forgetting the news I had o' him. He's out o' the navy. He throwed up his commission on blue water an' wants a berth in the army, which he hasn't got yet, if I hear aright. I had the story down in Princeton, where he hails from, an' there is little love borne him even among his friends. I heard no good o' him. In or out o' the service he is one to keep clear of, for he can't arguefy save with a sword, an' is fond o' a pistol an' ten paces an' doesn't always wait for the fair word. Why ! 'tis but a short time agone, and since we caught him, that he as good as murdered a boy— Bowden was his name, a young ensign with Parker at Newport. The lad was drunk at mess, an' in his high flight (an' high they all get), he insulted our friend some way—though how he could do it beats me ; anyhow, Bromfield called him out then and there, an' they fought with swords, though the boy—for he was naught else, being but eighteen—knew nothing of the art, so I am told, an' was too far gone in liquor to manage if he had been a master. 'Twas cold murder as ever murder was, for Bromfield run him through before they had more than crossed swords, an' a devil o' a time there was made o' it, for the lad was o' high society. The upshot o' it was that our friend had to give up the navy, an' that is how he lacks a job at present. The affair was winked at some way, an'

now he's after the land branch o' the service. His family's
a good one an' well to do. He's the black sheep on't."

I was surprised to hear this, but not surprised at such an
exposition of his character, for it seemed in keeping ; the
topic was one of but momentary interest and was soon put
aside.

In such manner of conversation the time slipped by, the
wind holding steady and driving us at a good speed, for
the sea was not boisterous.

At one o'clock I called the relief, and Moon and I took
their places below and soon slumbered. When I awoke it
was broad day and we were still making progress. We
breakfasted at once, the wheel was relieved, and Hal and
Amasa, who had held the last watch, turned in for a nap.
By eight o'clock we were off Guilford, and by nine thread-
ing our way through the " Thimbles."

The day bid fair to be intensely hot. The sun was
bright and the sky without a cloud, but the steadiness and
weight of the wind made the heat bearable, and I hoped
that, for comfort alone, we should not be overtaken by a
flat calm. The telescope had been in use since daylight,
the horizon being constantly swept in search of tokens of
the fleet, but nothing marred the dazzle of blue, neither
did any craft put out to meet us as I had hoped, and we
sailed along in total ignorance as to what might be going
on ashore.

We had lapsed into the silence that always comes to a
boat's company after the novelty of the situation wears off
and the immediate future holds out nothing of interest;
and the "Thimbles" dropped astern. Before noon we
were off New Haven harbor, but not caring to lose time by
tacking out, as we would have to do if we went in, I
decided not to enter, but stood for a point known as Savin
Rock, a few miles west. Here we dropped anchor and
sent a boat to the beach, trusting to pick up news from the
farmers in the vicinity. To give them a taste of what

they might be required to do later, I dispatched the Rose boys with it, and after an absence of nearly two hours, during which time we suffered greatly from the heat, they returned with the information that the disaster to New Haven had drawn thither most of the yeomen of the surrounding country, and the only positive fact that could be gathered was that the fleet had left Huntington Harbor, its destination being unknown to the inhabitants of the coast hereabouts.

Not considering this of sufficient importance to warrant sending back a messenger, we hauled up anchor and continued on our course.

The afternoon passed without incident and with hardly a word among us, so depressing, despite the breeze, was the closeness of the atmosphere. The cabin was intolerable, while on deck the direct sun was terrific, the planks radiating heat like molten iron. I overcame the latter by having the decks soused with water, and, by dodging into the shade of the main-sail, all but the one at the wheel managed to exist without suffering.

So wore the hours until we were abreast of Black Rock and running close to shore, when we marked a small boat with but one man in it, put out from the land and pull as though to intercept us. Having no fear of him, we luffed up and let him come alongside.

By his dress and speech he appeared half fisherman, half farmer, and his first words awoke us all.

"Go no further!" he exclaimed excitedly, as he came up, "unless you want to fall into the hands of the Hessians. Tryon is out again and at Norwalk since last night, and the town is burned. I had the news scarce two hours since. The whole fleet lies off the creek and you will be taken if they catch sight of you."

"Was there no resistance?" I asked, as he sat in his boat holding onto our side.

"None that I wot of; there are no troops thereabouts,

and the militia is weak. My own house at Fairfield was burned on Thursday, and I escaped here. I saw you coming and felt it my duty to warn you."

Further questioning brought forth the fact that the people along shore were terrorized and ready to move at the first sight of the hostile fleet, but there was no knowing whether it would work destruction along the coast east or west.

My mind was at once made up to dispatch one of the Rose boys back with this news, and telling Ben that he would have no difficulty in getting the means of transportation to forward him, I sent him ashore with our informant. He was loth to go from us, but I put it in the form of a command, and with short leave-taking he stepped into the boat while we filled away.

With the whereabouts of the danger located, we centered our attention ahead, and as we opened and drew around each point of land, it was with relief that we discovered it sheltered no sail, and held on, not knowing what the next point might reveal.

I figured that the position of the fleet lay ten or twelve miles west of Black Rock, and though they might have been seen from the middle of the Sound, our policy of hugging the shore cut off a view far ahead and made it possible for us to come upon some detached vessel of the enemy's before we were aware of its proximity.

But we slipped by the wooded points and black reefs, and nothing met our gaze that changed my determination to proceed. The wind, which had been without a flaw since sunrise, now shifted to the west and began to head us off and blow fitfully. My expectation of a squall, which the heat of the day had led me to look for, seemed about to be realized, for as we made a tack toward open water, I marked a heavy cloud hanging over the horizon, and called Moon's attention to it. He looked at it a moment and then went below to consult the barometer. As he came up he said :

" We will have thunder, past doubt, for the glass is falling, but I take it 'twill not be from yon cloud.   'Tis not far out to say that yonder smut marks Norwalk, an' 'tis the smoke o' the burning town ye see.   The wind has drawn west an' 'tis bringing it down on us, but there's a black squall behind.   Ha !   The Bloody Wolf leaves a broad banner to mark his work, an' hangs it high," he continued, as the cloud rose rapidly ; " an' yet the tears he causes were almost enough to swamp the fires he kindles.   I would to God I could settle the matter with him single-handed ; I'd willingly lay my life for the chance," and the old man's face took on something of the expression I had seen in the cabin when he captured Bromfield.

On we went, with alternate short tacks, the sun dipping lower and lower as we covered the distances; but our progress was slow, owing to the nature of our course, which zig-zagged in and out, until finally the wind dropped flat as we were close ashore, and we lay rocking to a slight swell.

Our position was then off a point that I judged was not more than four or five miles from the burning town, but beyond, no sight could be had, as the Norwalk Islands, which lay thick off the mouth of the harbor, blocked the way.   The smoke that rose spread like a pall over us and dimmed the sun that was near its setting, though the water lay clear and golden in the mellow of the evening.

We were doubtless in for a blow, as all signs showed, from the drop of the wind to the bank of clouds that was now but partly hidden by the thick haze of smudge.   Here I took in the light sails, for we had been carrying both gaff and jib topsails all day, and lowered the jib itself until the squall should break.

After a general consultation, it was determined to set Amasa ashore to make his way to Norwalk by night, and from thence home, bearing such news as he could gather. It was a difficult undertaking, but not dangerous, as I had reason to argue that the town was deserted by the enemy, and the man was full of resources. With the parting injunction to report to the commander of any patriot force, if such were near, and offer himself as an express to the east, I sent him ashore with Rod in the dingey, and saw him land and disappear in the thick wood that covered the point and came down to the water's edge.

Everything was now snugged for a sudden change, and we sat watching the climbing of the clouds and the faint flashes of lightning that lit them with an angry glare. Blacker and blacker grew the sky as the sun went down. At last our expectation was broken by the first heavy drops that splashed on deck like bullets, quickly followed by the roar of the rain that tore the face of the water into spray, and sounded like a cavalry charge in its advance. The line that marked its edge was on us in an instant, and in a twinkling we were soaked ; but we sat some minutes in the down-pour before the wind struck us. The sloop was saved from the greatest fury of the squall as it broke by the point in the lee of which we were lying, and she met it in the best possible position, bow on.

When the first blast had roared itself out, the wind steadied into a pouring of cool, fresh air, and the sky behind the black front of the storm lightened a bit, though the thunder and lightning increased in force and frequency. Wishing to make the most of the faint remains of the day, we got up the jib and stood out for the Norwalk Islands, among which I knew we must pass the night (and it bid fair to be a stormy one), for there I could find a harbor in any wind—though it blew a hurricane. But the night fell rapidly and I was glad of the gleams that shot from the clouds so often, for without the lightning I know not how we could have progressed through the narrow passages, so intensely dark had it become. It was dangerous work at best, and I felt my way slowly until I came to an opening made by the triangle of three small islands. As here there was room enough to swing, everything was let go and the anchor dropped in four fathoms of water.

The fitful flashes that opened and shut the prospect showed the island to the west to be slightly wooded, while the other two and those beyond were low and barren of trees, though covered with bushes and thick short grass, with here and there a rock to break the surface. So far into this little archipelago had we penetrated that the water was without a swell, and when we had nosed up to the wind, we lay as steady as a house ashore. It was no easy matter to furl the great, wet sail in a down-pour of rain, but we got it in " stops," and once snugged, I felt safer than at any time during the day, albeit we now lay close to the British.

Nothing could find us in this labyrinth, and our presence was unsuspected. It was near ten o'clock by the time the last gasket was tied, and determining to get some comfort after our experience, I ordered Rod to block the cabin sky-light and windows, and with the companion closed, we lighted the lamps and had supper like Christians.

However, our comfort was short-lived. The closeness of the quarters, owing to the heat from the galley and the lamps, together with tobacco smoke and steam from the wet clothing which we had stripped from us, made the place unendurable ; so, with extinguished lights, we opened everything to the sluice of cool air outside, and, wrapping ourselves in blankets, prepared for the night. By eleven the rain ceased and a few stars broke out overhead ; so I went on deck for the first watch. Hal was to relieve me at one o'clock and be relieved by Rod at three, and with this understanding all turned in, leaving me to my vigils.

For two hours I smoked, slapped the mosquitoes that came in clouds, and harkened to the slatting of the halyards against the mast, with no other sound for company save the chirrup of one lone cricket on the island hard by,

or a mysterious splash that once in a while broke from the
waters about.   After the heat of the day and the cabin,
the wet night air was like wine, and I drank it in with
long breaths, but was drowsy enough by the time I called
Hal and turned in.

It was gray dawn when I awoke, and I lay looking at
the square of pale sky framed by the open companion,
when I saw Rod put his head through the opening and
look around.   Seeing that I was not sleeping, he stepped
softly down and whispered :

"I reckon dar's a dead woman on de island yonder, Mars
Tony, but dey aint mos' light nuff to see fo' sho."

I jumped from my bunk and went up to the cockpit,
from whence he pointed out a black object lying along the
sand close above high-water mark, but whether a woman
or a log I could not determine.   Reaching for the glass, I
brought it to bear on the object, and with a start, plainly
made out a female ; but whether dead or not it was impossible to tell, there being no movement.   Turning to
the cabin, I roused the others, and we got into our damp
clothes, while Rod brought the boat alongside.

Leaving him in the sloop, we rowed quickly to the spot,
and were soon by what appeared to be the corpse of a
young woman.   I say young, for, though the face was
drawn and white and her dark hair threaded with gray,
there was nothing but youth in the small, girlish form
that plainly showed through the clinging water-soaked
garments ; and the face itself, though pinched by suffering, had an oval that only goes with youth or early
maturity.

She rested on her side, with her small hands thrown out
loosely, and her face, attractive even in its plight, turned
half upward.   By the fact that the body lay some way
above high-water mark, I knew it was not a case of drowning and being washed ashore.

The first sign that made me think life remained in the

body was the swarm of mosquitoes that had settled on her,
but not the faintest breath could I discover coming through
her pale, half open lips. We turned her over gently, while
I stripped the dress from her bosom, that I might get my
ear close to her heart, and as the white flesh was uncovered I saw with surprise a gunshot wound in the shoulder.
Further examination showed that the ball had passed clear
through and out at the back, without touching the bone,
but the rain had washed away all traces of blood; so I
could make nothing of the extent of the hemorrhage,
though I doubted that being the cause of death.

I held my ear to her heart for fully half a minute, listening with the greatest intentness the while, before at
last I heard a faint click, and then another, proving the
poor creature was still of this world, though about crossing the threshold of the next.

"There's life there yet!" I cried, as I jumped to my
feet and met the inquiring eyes of my companions. "The
woman has been shot, and has, past doubt, lain here all
night in this state, and the Lord knows how much longer.
Shock, exposure, and loss of blood have brought her to the
last extremity, but perhaps something may yet be done.
Jump aboard, Hal, and get some brandy and water and a
blanket; also fetch the telescope!" for I determined to
take a look toward the enemy from a tree while we were
still on the island.

It would have been natural, mayhap, to have taken her
aboard the sloop at once, but I hesitated to move one
so low in vitality until I could see the effect of stimulants, and the air here was better than that of the cabin.
While I set to work chafing the hands, Moon walked down
the little beach, but soon came back and reported an empty
rowboat ashore just around a small point. Both oars were
gone and the boat deep with water, but it accounted for
the woman's presence on the island.

"Some poor thing from the town," he said, bending to

assist me. "If she pulls out o' this, she can thank her stars that her luck landed her at the door of a doctor, though I'm not hopeful; it looks to go hard with her. 'Tis fit to make one's eyes run blood to see war in this shape. Are the scarlet-backed devils afeard to meet men, that they come in force to murder helpless women? Aye, aye!" he continued, shaking his head vigorously, "God's will be done! But what a footstool He's made o' this world, that a man can't breathe free air without fighting for the right, an' dragging babes like this into the muss!"

But while venting his indignation in this manner he was working away with the tenderness of a woman. When Hal returned I took the poor head on my knee and poured a few drops of brandy and water between the lips; then, laying her down, we covered her loosely with the blanket, and, with all possible delicacy, removed her wet clothing.

I knew little of woman's rig in those days, and greatly felt the need of one of her own sex; but there was no time for false modesty, as I saw the only chance of bringing back the spirit was to get warmth into the cold form.

In constant chafing of the limbs and small doses of brandy we passed an hour working like beavers, by which time the sun was lifting over the land and the day well begun. The heart was slowly increasing in action, but no outward sign of life was yet visible. During the whole time the mosquitoes were a perfect pest, swarming by the hundreds, greatly interfering with our efforts at resuscitation, and I verily believe they alone would have killed her had she been left much longer on the sand.

The first token that I had of her returning vitality was a slight flow of blood from the wound in her shoulder, and soon after the small mouth trembled an instant, and the lungs took up their work, for she began to breathe, though very weakly. With what means I could gather I bound up the shoulder, that she might lose no more blood, and, wrapping the blanket closely about her, Jacob took her in his arms like a child and carried her to the dingey, Hal rowing him to the sloop, while I, picking up the telescope, made my way to the other side of the island for a look about.

The little island was some two acres in extent, and it took me but a few minutes to cross it. As I waded through the thick, wet grass the mosquitoes rose in clouds and made this small jewel of the Sound nothing short of purgatory. I fought them off as best I could, and found on arriving at the opposite shore that there was small need of a tree to assist me in viewing the British fleet, for from where I stood they were in plain sight, and lying about five miles off the mouth of Norwalk creek.

I counted a dozen ships of all sorts, and as I stood watching, there were signs of activity among them, the nature of which I could not make sure. Hurrying back, I called the boat and sent Moon to take an observation, bidding him stay until he could determine their intention, if the insects let him live to do it, while I tended to the patient.

She had been laid on a transom cushion, and was still unconscious, though breathing with more freedom, some warmth having come into her extremities. For a long time I sat watching her while awaiting the return of Moon, with no change to be noted save that the breathing became deeper, and the face lost something of its pinched appearance.

While thus waiting, I had a chance to study her. The gray in her hair, the drawn look of the features, and the blotches caused by the mosquitoes, made it difficult to tell her age, yet I thought her to be not more than nineteen or twenty years old. Her feet and hands were small and finely molded, the latter soft and white, showing her a stranger to coarse, manual labor. The homespun garments we had removed were no indication of her position, for in those times of war with the mother country, the highest ladies in New England covered themselves with material

woven by their own hands. Who she was I could give no
guess, nor was there anything about her to help me form
an opinion ; yet I would have sworn she was of gentle
birth, for the stamp was set in the close, well-shaped ear,
and small, straight nose with its delicate nostrils. By
and by the little hands began to work ; a weak and pitiful moan broke from her lips, and presently she opened her
eyes, but there was no intelligence in the look she gave,
though they played over my features in a puzzled way.
Soft, brown, frightened eyes they were, but I had little
chance to study them, for they closed at once, and with a
half turn of her head she sank into her former state.
Soon after this, Moon hailed us and was brought aboard.

"The whole grand legion o' Beelzebub is off," he said,
"an' gone west. I waited till I saw the last o' them string
away, an' I must be moving to follow along shore. I take
it ye'll go no further, seeing your orders are to return as
soon as ye get their bearings, an' faith ! 'twould not be
safe. Just give me a bite and let me out."

As this was plain duty I made no demur, though it gave
me a feeling akin to homesickness to have him go. During
breakfast I conceived it would be a good idea to have
Harry accompany him to the ruined town and return to
me with news of the extent of the disaster ; at the same
time inquiring into the identity of the unfortunate girl we
had found. This was acted upon, and with a short shift
of leave-taking, the two were set ashore on the mainland
some mile or so away, with the understanding that the
boat would meet Hal at sundown.

The day was a long and wearying one. The patient had
opened her eyes several times, but made no answer to
the questions I put, and beyond taking the only nourish-
ment I could give her—an egg beaten up in weak spirits—
required little attention save to see that she was not pes-
tered by the swarming insects.

The sun finally set in a great glory of color and fire, like a ball of burnished gold, and the dingey was dispatched for Hal, who came with a heart-rending tale of all he had seen and heard. General Parsons had arrived with a force of militia, but too late to save the town, and death, destruction, and suffering were rampant in all directions. It was common report that the rapacious Tryon had sat in a chair upon a hill-top, and laughed to see the Hessians chasing and bayoneting the fleeing inhabitants of the town, and this I have seen verified in history.

Of the identity of the lady, for such she undoubtedly was, there was not the faintest clew. Too many were missing to mark a particular one, and those who remained had sorrows of their own to occupy mind and heart. The fleet had gone west, probably to New York, and Moon had left him at midday to join Washington, whom he had heard was at West Point.

Such was the breadth of his tale, and it seemed there was nothing left for us to do but make sail for New London, carrying the unfortunate girl with us. It would be a relief to do the first, if only to be rid of the flying pests that abounded, and the second went not against my desires, as the brown eyes had awakened an interest in me, and I would have been loth, at this juncture, to have lost the little woman whom I had brought back to life at least, if not to reason.

CHAPTER XVII.

DOROTHY BEAUCHAMP.

THE return trip was uneventful. I noted with great anxiety the symptoms of the sick girl, the bounding pulse, the low muttering of delirium, and the uneasy rolling of the head, which, together with a high fever, betokened trouble with the brain. We were miserably equipped for such an emergency, and I could offer no relief to her suffering.

Fortunately the wind blew strong and fair, mile after mile slipping beneath our keel. At Niantic I ran in to wait for night, to round again the blockading ships off New London. It was a useless precaution, as I afterward found they had gone, we probably having passed them in the darkness of the night before. At midnight we were once more at our old moorings.

It was a short matter to arouse the household, but an infinite difficulty to get the patient ashore, carried up the steep hill, and placed in a bed in my aunt's old room. What with the greetings, questions, story-telling, and wonderment, and the care of the sick girl, there was no sleep for us that night. And many a night thereafter was the house a scene of unrest, for the patient had plunged into the depths of brain fever.

She would call out for her father, or start up in bed with shrieks and wild words about fire, and a broad stretch of water that would never let her rest for its heaving. Horrors came in the shape of darkness and blood, and strange, uncanny things she thought she saw, but no word or name did she drop to give a hint of who she was. All the time

Charlotte nursed her like an angel, and Nance helped her, a figure of mercy in ebony.

The old doctor did his best, but with many shakes of his white head, and I followed his lead, using my few wits, working night and day over her, seeing her grow to a poor shadow, so thin she became, until at last she fell into that state of lengthened stupor, the change from which meant to slip into life anew, or glide into the great, blank beyond.

As the days had passed my interest in the unknown patient had grown, knowing it would be a fine thing for my reputation if I could carry her safely through so violent an illness; therefore I was only away from the bedside when my duty called me elsewhere. But either skill, or youth, or both, with good nursing, conquered. One night, while we were hanging over her, anxiously watching for the change that I knew was due, she opened her eyes at last, and with no horror in them—only a vague, wondering look at the faces about her; then closing them, slept, and I knew she would live.

A poor, broken, snowflake of a thing she looked against the pillows, with her hollow eyes and cropped hair; and many a day went by before she really began to mend, or I would allow the slightest question put to her or an answer given, save that she was getting well and was among friends.

There was a world of pathetic sweetness in the glance that showed plain thanks for the drink given her, or the pat to the pillow and the countless little attentions bestowed; and surely no mother ever nursed her child with more devotion than did my sister nurse this stranger.

Her look would follow my every motion as I prepared the medicine, or her lips would form some question which I was forced to stop with uplifted finger and a shake of my head. Little by little she gained, until she would greet me with a wan smile that strengthened the sweet, patient expression of her face; but she never spoke of the past, till one day,

11

when I deemed it safe, I made up my mind to determine
her identity, and putting my questions gently, to my astonishment I found the life behind her was a blank and
that she had not retained even the recollection of her own
name.   The detailed story of how and when she was found
made no impression ; nor did the name of "Norwalk," and
the recital of the attack on the town, give her any help.
She would only clasp her poor head, looking wildly at me,
and then I desisted, fearing to force her into a fever; telling her it would all come back when she grew stronger.
And I had no doubt it would, for these lapses of memory
are common after brain fever, when caused by shock and
suffering.

The curtain lifted slowly; and once I found her in a half
wild state, for she could tell of being in an open boat that
was gradually filling from a leak, and had a recollection of
the fierce thunderstorm, and finally of drifting against the
land, when she got out in fear that the boat would sink if
it floated again into deep water.   Why she was in the boat
and whence she came, worked her half distraught in striving to think ; so I gave her a quieting draught and left
her, telling her to be comforted, as it was plain to be seen
that her memory was slowly returning.

Thus the summer days drew on with no change in her,
save gaining strength, until at last on my home-coming one
afternoon, I was met by my father, who halted me as I was
going to my patient, and led me outside and down to the
stone wall.   There we sat in the last of the day's sunlight,
while he told me a strange tale, which I give as he gave
it me.

"The brain of our charge has come to life at last, Anthony," said he, "and at present she is divided betwixt
joy upon the recovery of her memory, and grief for all it
has revealed.   Her home was in Norwalk, and she lived on
the bank of the creek with her father, who was a stanch
patriot, though an Englishman by birth.   When the British

first entered the town they committed no worse outrages than the ruin of public property, and had they been unmolested, 'tis possible 'twould have ended there ; but it was more than flesh and blood could abide, and they were fired upon by a few brave townspeople who got together in haste ; among them her father.

"Tryon but needed that as an excuse for his usual course, and the little band was defeated and fled to their homes. With the firing of the first dwelling, all the misery began. The Hessians caught the spirit, and to the general burning was added a general slaughter.

"She gives me no details beyond her own experience, and that was too harrowing for her to go into deeply. Defending his own home, her father was shot and bayoneted before her eyes, and the house fired. She was driven from his body by the wretches who had killed him—a squad of half a dozen, and only saved herself from foul outrage by hiding in a closet, from whence she heard them making search for her. But ere long, the house being well ablaze, they were forced to quit, and doubtless thought she had escaped.

"In fear of the flames and trusting they had gone, she climbed from a rear window and fled to the boat that was moored at the foot of the garden. She had scarce made her way into the stream when they discovered her, and one of the ruffians ran to the bank and, deliberately kneeling to aim, shot her in the shoulder, as we know.

"All this she remembers clearly, but then comes a blank, and she must have fainted from fright and loss of blood, for the next she minds is lying in the boat with the water almost covering her. When she raised herself she found the oars gone, a storm coming on and it was getting dark.

"She recollects striving to paddle with her hands to some land hard by, but the exertion made her weak and the motion of the boat sickened her, so it seems she must have been out of the river and drifting east with the ebb tide.

Then she sat and waited while the storm broke, and the water kept deepening in the boat. It grew very dark and she had no idea of her whereabouts. She was probably in a dazed state when at last the boat grounded, and she got ashore and then fell, after which of course she remembers nothing. In landing, she probably pushed the boat away, and it floated off to where it grounded again and was found.

"The horror of it all overcame her as she told me the story; mainly the knowing that her father is dead and his body burned with the house.

"She has no relations in Norwalk, and of course knows naught of the friends she left. The poor waif would be welcome to stay here, for Charlotte has grown very fond of her—as indeed have I, for her disposition is winning; but she has more legitimate shelter hard by."

"Indeed! Where?" I asked, with a mind divided betwixt pity for her and wonder at the last remark. His reply amazed me.

"Her name is Dorothy Beauchamp, and she is the niece and goddaughter of our neighbor, the squire. You may call to mind the conversation you overheard betwixt the squire and Bromfield. He spoke of his brother in Norwalk and his niece Dorothy. The brother is her father, and she—the niece—is the young lady in whom Bromfield showed so much interest. The squire must be notified. He is her natural guardian and nearest relative, and will doubtless be glad to have her with him."

"But she should not go yet," I replied warmly; "nor for some time to come. The change from here to yon gloomy old house, with a human gravestone as her only companion, would work her an injury," for I thought of the squire's prim and silent sister, and the cold, colorless life of the two.

"Well! as her physician you will of course be consulted in the matter; she is welcome here as long as she chooses to stay."

And so it had turned out that this was the "fascinating little devil of a Whig," for whom Bromfield had as much as confessed his love. She certainly belied the description in her present state, but I nothing doubted that time would improve both looks and spirits. She was still a subject for nursing, though she sat up every day in a big chair, looking out at the Sound water, with the flickering lights and shadows made by the maples shifting over her, and the summer wind that whipped the muslin window curtains into a dance, bringing her new life and health—though alas! happiness seemed far off, if judged by the expression in her eyes.

The squire was told of the presence of his niece, and came often, having many interviews with her, the nature of which none of us might guess. Then with the permission of the authorities, he went to Norwalk and was gone a week, but told us nothing on his return, save what we had feared—that the house was a ruin. Her father's bones had been found and decently buried. He did not press for her immediate removal, a point on which I was prepared to fight, but left her to the tender care of Charlotte ; and between them there grew a love that never failed.

By the time the golden-rod nodded its plumed head in the fields, and its purple companion put on the ancient mourning color for the summer that had passed, and sprinkled its signals of the waning year along the roadside and in the fence corners, Dorothy was strong enough to get out into the open air and walk to the stone wall with Charlotte's assistance or the aid of my arm ; and sitting there, talk quietly of the grand prospect before us. Sometimes she would visit the barns and pat the smooth noses of the horses, talk to the cattle and coax the poultry, or do what most people would call "senseless things." Or in the jungle of the garden she would bury her little nose in the depths of the late flowers and gather huge bunches of them for the table.

She was a child in the ease of her entertainment, yet there was no lack of good, hard sense in our long conversations. Many a day I cut short my stay in the village to get home for a talk with my patient, as I still called her, and later, as she grew stronger, for longer walks under the trees of the forest or on the crescent beach that lay below Hardscrabble like a white sickle ; and all the time I saw her figure gradually fill to its perfect proportions, the cheek and chin grow round and touched with color, the smile that showed her pretty teeth come more freely and more often, and the step take on something of the bound that a healthy girl's should have. The cropped hair had begun to grow, but with more shining lines than when I found her, and she had curled it up to get rid of the "awkward shortness" of it, as she said, in a way that became her mightily in my eyes. It was strange indeed to see so young and fresh a face crowned with hair so thickly threaded with silver, but it only increased its interest and gave no suggestion of age.

Together we would saunter along the edge of the surf, or sit in the hot sand and build houses like children as we chatted, or pick up shells to cast away again. I beguiled the time by telling her of my adventures and the capture of Lieutenant Bromfield, and she in turn, told of his family as they were when she visited them in New York early in the war ; of his mother and sister, and a thousand other things ; but of Bromfield himself she had little to say.

Charlotte would never follow us in our longer wanderings (which I thought was strange), but somehow I never pressed her ; she always seemed to have some work to do, or was about to meet her lover, which was enough to account for it. She would dance off with a wave of her hand and a smile, and leave us to ourselves.

It was a glorious autumn somehow. I never knew the sky to be so soft or the foliage so brilliant. I never knew the surf to crawl up the sand with so musical a hiss, or the brooks to tinkle so clearly. I never knew the sun to move so fast or the chill air and dusk of evening strike so suddenly, nor did I, poor idiot, know the cause of it all or of my vague unrest, until the sun had drawn well to the south and the flaming forests dropped their dead fires in ashes of brown leaves ; not until I noticed the birds had fled and the golden-rod was blackening in the frost ; not until the meadows had lost their depth of green and the garden was a tangled mass of withered shrubbery ; not until the broad fires were lighted on the dining room hearth, and in its cozy glow we heard the patter of the autumn rains through the evenings, all too short. Not until then, when the squire came at last and took his niece home with him, did I awake and know that I loved Dorothy Beauchamp.

CHAPTER XVIII.

THE "GREAT FREEZE."

I KNEW it by the blankness of home, that never before in my life had I noticed. Somehow the place became suddenly barren, and small things, that erstwhile held an interest, flattened into tameness, while others, equally trivial, grew into importance because of their associations with her.

If there were anything needed to re-enforce the consciousness of my love for this girl it was shown in my moody walks over the haunts we were wont to frequent together, and the spirit of retrospection which possessed me during these wanderings.

I knew perfectly well what ailed me now, as I fancy did my father and sister, but no word of it did either say. Charlotte was fond of talking of Dorothy, and found in me a willing listener, though I affected all but a professional indifference on the subject. No doubt her womanly instincts fathomed my trouble, for she was unusually attentive to the wants of her "big brother." I was not living in a "fool's paradise,"—my state had not lifted me so far,— but in a lover's purgatory ; and even then I honestly believe I hugged my melancholy, and would not have changed to the matter-of-fact days when I was "heart whole and fancy free."

Yes, I was in love—deeply ; and I was a miserable man, though the object of my affections was but three miles away, and there was no obstacle to prevent my seeing her.

I am afraid what strength of character I possessed was on the wane in those days. Neglecting my practice, I took to haunting the neighborhood of the squire's, calling

on Dorothy, of course, and basking in the light of her
brown eyes, after which I cudgeled my brains for an
excuse to go again without a reasonable wait. But my
wits failing me, my bashfulness and fear of discovering
my passion to her (who had never given me a word or look
that I could translate into encouragement) kept me often
away.

I tried to content myself by going past and around the
house (which all at once had an individuality), and sitting
at the edge of the woods where I could command the
home-lot, hoping to catch a glimpse of her and vainly trying to deceive myself into the belief that I was not needed
elsewhere, and that I was playing the part of a man; which
latter, by the way, was exactly what I *was* doing, as nine
men out of ten will testify, if they be honest.

When, at times, the period of waiting gone, I would
summon up courage to approach the door and enter, a boy
of sixteen could hardly have been more diffident. Somehow I felt we were losing the old, free, companion feeling
which used to exist between us, for then she would never
color under my gaze, while now, when I took her hand
in greeting, she seemed to shrink within herself, and the
pink would flash through the rounded cheek as though her
face had caught the rose of the setting sun.

There were, however, no wanderings for us, not even to
the edge of the woods or to the brook that bounded the
the farm, for the late season was boisterous and gave
early indications of the severity of the terrible winter of
1779-80.

History tells of the rigors of that winter. It tells of the
sufferings of both armies, not only from cold, but from the
absence of necessary supplies. It tells of the isolation of
communities, of slow starvation and rampant disease, and
nature gave early warning of what was in store for the
land.

I had marked it in the death-like stillness of the nights;

in the extra brilliancy of the autumn colorings and the sudden and complete fall of the leaf. It showed in the dead brown of the fields that lay full to the southern sun, albeit hitherto they had always retained a suggestion of green until the snow fell. It was plain, too, in the way the frost struck its spurs into the ground and never loosened its hold.

The weather seers of the community predicted a hard winter, but they never imagined the like that came upon us and pinched us till life was almost gone before it eased its grasp. There had been but little rain that fall, and the brooks had run low, their faint murmurings sounding like the distress of weakness. By the end of October the land was a desolate waste, lying like one crouched to receive a blow. The sun rarely shone clear, but gave its light from behind an impalpable haze that threw a melancholy cast over everything, making land, sea, and sky one vast monotone of gray.

November entered with an increase of the steady cold ; a deadly, windless cold that silenced the small streams and all but locked the river. Then the haze thickened over the sun deeper and deeper each day, until at last noon was like twilight. The snow was gathering aloft and finally it fell; gradually at first, as it does in long storms ; then thicker and thicker it piled on the solid bed the frost had prepared.

There was no wind, so that it fell evenly and steadily, until the night succeeded the day, and another dawned and died without a cessation of the feathery downpour. When at last the sickly sun looked out, it seemed to be only as a warning of further tempests, and shone down on a scene unequaled for its purity, but attended by most serious conditions.

No prisoner behind bars was ever more shut from the world than were we by the miles of snow that lay between us and the town. Deep, driftless snow ; snow that came to the saddle girths and made even a passage to the barns a matter of infinite labor. The walls were gone. The woods were dwarfed to half their height. Every branch was clearly outlined by its white covering, and stood out in sharp contrast. The headland was a smooth, spotless bosom that descended to the gray waters of the Sound, with only a soft mound here and there to mark a hidden bowlder. The quintessence of purity was almost painful, and the silence hardly to be borne. Our isolation was complete. To break a path to the main road through the yielding mass would be impossible ; there was nothing to do but wait, but the wait was not long.

A comparatively warm rain at once followed the snow-storm and drove the white covering to half its depth. Here and there the top of a wall appeared, and the largest of the rocks cropped out above the surface of the snow. The forests were washed clean and black, and the edges of the river became sodden. But this was only the beginning. A hard frost turned the mass to marble. Then came a succession of storms of snow and sleet followed by thaws and rains ; then more snow, that drove in drifts and penetrated the crevices of the house like dust, until on the first of the year, the land lay under successive slabs of half snow half ice, and all artificial boundaries were obliterated.

The climax came in the " great freeze " of January, 1780. Such a protracted spell of cold had been unheard of in this region, and the very marrow of one's bones seemed to contract in the terrible temperature. The river froze solid from shore to shore, salt though it was. The Sound threw a snow-covered boundary further and further from the land, which sometimes broke with the lifting and falling of the tide.

It was during this period, when the cold was most intense and every atom of moisture was extracted from the air, so pure and dry it was, that the great rock of which I have spoken was rent asunder during the night.

I discovered it in one of my walks, for now travel was

as easy as though granite was under foot, and on foot I
always went, as it was worse than cruel to sit a horse and
face the terrible north wind. One would have frozen stiff
in scarce a mile, and many a one did freeze to death that
season, the cold numbing the faculties without warning
its victims.

I had, myself, felt the creeping of delicious drowsiness
on one occasion when coming home at night, and pulled
myself together with a sense of horror that set the blood
bounding, while I started and ran as though fleeing from
a demon. Thereafter, I never ventured far from shelter
without being in violent motion ; going to and from the
town on skates, using the level of the river as a highway to
the bridge, then skirting the edge of the road on the
adamantine crust of the snow.

Now the days were dazzling in their brilliancy, but the
sun gave no heat to soften the armor of ice. The north
wind held during the light, but the nights were still and
terrible, the sun and wind going down together ; the
former in a steely glory of violets and cold blues which
barely faded before the splendor of the Northern Lights
would flash toward the zenith, for at this time they were of
constant occurrence.

During these still nights a crash would come, and by
the character of the sound that died in many echoes, one
could tell whether the ice had cracked or a tree in the forest
had been riven by the frost ; for the former gave way with
a ripping noise as the opening progressed, ending in a roar,
while a tree or limb would split with the quick report of
heavy artillery.

Fires were piled high throughout the house, but, even
with these, water froze indoors during the dark hours.
The windows were thickly mailed with frost while the fires
were at their fiercest, and to the north and west the light
was completely shut out by the immense drifts which had
banked against the building. Our supply of water was

gotten from melting blocks of snow hewn out with an ax, as the well, which had never been known to freeze, was apparently solid. No icicles hung from the eaves to mark a temporary relenting, but all was firm, clear-cut, and remorseless. The Arctic Circle had extended south, and winter seemed to hold the universe with a hand as stiff as Death's.

This period of intense cold lasted more than a fortnight. None but the hardy ventured abroad without the force of necessity. No news from the outside world broke the monotony of existence.

The dazzling brilliancy of the days became a source of irritability, and the severe beauty of the nights and unearthly clearness of the sky and crispness of the few stars which withstood the light of the aurora, commanded a feeling more of awe than of admiration. Nature lost her half-tints between sunset and sunrise ; her tones were positive. The shadows cast by the moon that sailed high above the horizon were black and sharply cut, and the whole picture a drawing in the most intense black and white.

Necessity detained me at home during the mornings, for the negroes became semi-torpid, like chilled snakes, and it was but by using measures akin to force that they could be gotten to move from the great settle before the kitchen fire. Snow was to be melted for the live stock, fodder provided, and fuel brought into the house, and most of my time was occupied in seeing that they performed these simple duties, for they were prolific in excuses to return to the house, and was my attention relaxed for half an hour I would find the fire dying under the caldron in the barnyard, the ax neglected and the gang huddled together in the kitchen.

Visitors we had none, saving Harry, if he could be called one, for the day never passed during which he did not appear at some hour, his road lying along the ridge above the river, down which he came before the wind on skates, for the crust was hard and strong as an ice block, and no fence or waterway broke the course.

I envied him his warm welcome, his contentment, and the air of happiness that he brought with him, and which clung to him like the stream of cold air that followed and gradually diffused itself through the room, freshening it.

CHAPTER XIX.

BROMFIELD DECLARES WAR.

THERE was no cessation in the regularity of my visits to the squire's. It would have been a wild storm, indeed, that would have kept me from fulfilling my intention made days ahead, and many a time did I go determined to loosen my tongue and end the harrowing uncertainty which clung to me like a weight, but there never came an opportunity.

Were Dorothy the veritable Angel of Light and I the Prince of Darkness, she could not have been more jealously guarded ; for, while during the early winter we often had moments—few, indeed—alone, now not for an instant were we rid of surveillance, for either the squire was there, or his sphinx of a sister with her knitting, or both of them. The lady would move her lips on my entry, but never vouchsafe a word during my stay. I had grown to think of her as a nightmare with a mission to watch, and was torn by impatience, indignation, and pity, to think that my darling was having her young life flattened and her vivacity ground out between the squire and his gloomy sister, while I was powerless to interpose.

I hoped and prayed for an opportunity to unburden myself, and this possibility had lately kept my spirits from waning.

The month of January was nearing its end, albeit the winter held its severity, when one evening I strapped on my skates preparatory to making a visit at the squire's house. A week had passed since my last call, and I expected nothing more nor less than the old conditions of watchfulness.

The outlook was not calculated to stir my spirits, except with the hope that a possible chance might be given me to open my heart and end my anxiety. But with this slight prospect my feet were quickened and I flew down the smooth declivity which ended at the river, my momentum carrying me far on its expanse.

Up the river I sped, skipping the great tidal fissures which broke the wide surface of the winding stream, the sharp cutting of the skates being the only sound. Finally, I stood panting and knocking at the door of the squire's house.

It was not opened, as was usual, by the squire, nor his sister, nor Dorothy ; but instead, as the two halves unfolded, I beheld no less a person than Lieutenant Bromfield.

Without moving, I stood blinking at him as though asleep, but he woke me promptly.

"Come in, come in, doctor! This is a pleasure I am prepared for, as we figured you would be due to-night."

Mechanically I entered, and without answering advanced into the sitting room, where I had always found the family assembled, but no one was there. Before I had made this discovery Bromfield followed me, closing the door behind him.

"Draw near the fire and warm yourself, doctor. You must be chilled, and I dislike to see suffering in a fellow-creature." As I made no reply and remained standing, he continued :

"Do you know that I should have been greatly disappointed had you not turned up to-night? It would have caused me to place on paper what I have to say. You may be aware how difficult it is to write words of appreciation and thanks ; speech is much more satisfactory."

There was no mistaking the irony of this, which was accompanied by a low laugh. His face was not clear to me, there being no light in the room save that which rose and fell from the fire, but I could fancy the maliciousness of his countenance. He seemed much the same as ever—no better nor worse that I could see, his voice and manner being suggestive of something disagreeable held in reserve. I had small fear of personal violence here, and feeling obliged to answer, I followed the meter he had set and said :

"Lieutenant Bromfield is always considerate, but I cannot imagine how he is in my debt when I confess to being in his. If he has anything to communicate I am ready to hear it."

"*You* in my debt, doctor! How so? I fancied it otherwise!" he returned easily.

"Oh! nothing beyond the glory of capturing an enemy," I replied as easily, shifting my back to the fire and facing him. "You must know it has its reward."

His eyes flashed a spark at this, but he seated himself.

"Ah, yes!" he returned. "My captor! That is another affair! We will cry quits later! I probably did you a favor by presenting myself at that time; but the matter in hand is different. What you did was in the way of honorable war; I would have done the same. You see I harbor no ill-will!"

"You are graciousness itself," I replied.

"You are complimentary. And how is the public health, doctor? Since your great success, I presume you have obtained a firm footing in your profession ; so firm, indeed, that you cannot find time to serve in the field the glorious cause for which you have so disinterested a love."

"I have served it fairly well at home, so far, as you will allow," I answered, without apparent notice of the sneer. "But as an end to this—what is Lieutenant Bromfield doing here? Is he aware of his danger?"

"There is no danger to an exchanged prisoner, doctor, if you bushwhackers pretend to honorable warfare."

"Ah! Then he has not obtained the coveted commission! How is it, lieutenant, that you have resigned the sea, without a firmer grasp on the army?"

12

"What the devil do you know of my affairs?" he said, scowling at me.

"Very little of interest or consequence to me," I returned, with a forced smile; "only it seems strange that you should have resigned and taken no part in your own pet scheme."

"To what scheme do you refer?"

"To that you proposed to the squire when I chanced to overhear you: that of murdering the inhabitants of Norwalk and forcibly abducting a young lady. Honorable warfare, of course!"

"Damnation!" he exclaimed, leaning forward as if to rise; "have you dared repeat this to her?"

"I have certainly not repeated it to her," I answered, without flinching, and looking at him defiantly; "though the 'dare' had no weight with me."

"The better for you, sir; the better for you!" he said, controlling himself and settling back again; "and that brings us to the point. For what sum am I indebted to you for your medical services in her behalf? I have much to thank you for in restoring her to us. To be mighty plain with you, I have no desire nor intention to have her placed in a position where you can draw on her gratitude, or of letting the account compound until you feel at liberty to draw on her affection. Do you understand me?"

"I understand your brutality," I replied, with a tightening of the throat. "I have called to see the young lady in question, and until I do see her I shall acquit her of all complicity in this insult. What is she to you but an acquaintance you are unworthy of, and by whose authority do you dare tender me payment for an act of humanity?"

"By my own authority, you miserable leech!" he thundered, standing up and losing control of himself. "I never knew one of your cloth but who thought more of his fee than his feelings. Name your sum and quit forcing yourself into this house—or, by Heaven! I will find a way to make you. It may help you when I tell you the lady is my affianced wife," he continued, lowering his voice to a thick whisper, "and I will attend to the chastisement of any of your image who tries to beguile her interest. This is my business here to-night and to-night will end it. Mark me well."

I felt that he was lying,—even the lowering of his voice carrying that significance,—but the possible doubt was to me like a blow on the head. As the life of a drowning man is said to drift before him in an instant, so did past events, tones, looks, and trivial incidents flash before me and make me find a solution for them in this. She *might* be his affianced wife. The incongruity of the characters never struck me. The fact that she might not be a party to this, and was ignorant of Bromfield's errand, had no weight. There was enough cause for the curse of jealousy, and it leaped on me in full force, silencing and staggering me. Had I not been deeply angered by his insults, I might have given way abjectly and left the house; but I was too thoroughly aroused to allow him to mark my defeat, so I answered without heat and without moving :

"Your reputation, sir, is not such as will permit me to believe you. When I have this from the lips of Miss Beauchamp, I shall feel bound to withdraw my attentions— not before."

"You confess you have intentions, then ? "

"I confess to *attentions ;* to no one have I confessed more. Give me conclusive proof that these attentions are unwelcome to her and they shall cease. That is all I have to say." And with this, I sauntered to the window and began boring a hole in the thick frost of the pane.

He had passed behind his chair, the back of which he grasped tightly with both hands. I felt his eyes follow me in hate as I crossed the room, but for a moment or two he remained silent, as though gathering his words. For one so impetuous, he controlled himself well, for it was with something like a low snarl instead of a shout, that he said:

"For a country spark, you carry a high hand; but if you think so insignificant a being can thwart my wish, you are a poor reckoner. My authority shall be the law in this. You make pretensions to gentility, and yet come unwarrantably between a lady and her desires. I appeal to your reason, you see, before using other methods."

"You have made no appeal to either my reason or my credulity," I answered, facing him. "You hint violence because I do not tamely accede to a wish as you express it, and which I have yet to find is shared by the lady in question. Let me be plainer. I have small desire to come between her and her wishes, but between you and your unjustifiable demands, I shall certainly stand—and as surely as I stand here. I presume I am safe from assault in this house. Give me one minute's conversation with her, and the matter will be final."

"That you shall not have," he answered, setting his teeth. "If necessary, she will be removed from your importunities."

"As would have been done long since," I ventured, "had her dissent not stood in the way. Do you refuse to allow me an interview?"

"As nothing to the purpose, I do."

"On what grounds and by what right?"

"Damnation!" he broke out. "On my own will! And, if you must have it, on her own expressed wish, so begone!"

He was trembling in anger now, and his face was as malignant as a devil's as he shouted the last words.

"Do you mean to say that she has expressed a wish never to see me again on any terms?" I asked, trembling myself.

"I do."

"Lieutenant Bromfield, you lie!"

His chair went down with a crash as he flung it from

him and rushed at me. I had barely time to spring behind
another and swing it over my head when the door opened
with a bang, and the squire rushed in and threw himself
upon the maddened officer.

"Bromfield! Stop!" he shouted. "I told you you
would gain nothing by your headlong temper if you
applied it to him. Let him alone, man. Leave him to me,
and for God's sake shut the door!" he said, as he pushed
back my opponent and stood looking from one to the other
of us in evident trepidation.

I still held the chair aloft and stood braced to bring it
down on the officer had he passed the squire and advanced;
but as though brought suddenly to his senses, he made no
movement forward. Instead, he backed slowly to the door
with his eyes fixed on me, and softly closed it.

The squire broke the silence.

"Put aside that chair, Anthony. Are you not ashamed,
gentlemen, to forget yourselves in this house and in this
manner? Bromfield, leave us alone; I will finish the subject with the doctor."

"Not until I have arranged matters to offset the insult
he has offered me," he said doggedly. "Sir Upstart, when
and where will you give me satisfaction? I have three
indictments against you now; we can settle them all at
short notice, and wipe them out in one meeting."

Lowering the chair, yet keeping a firm hold on it, and
speaking with my voice trembling with excitement, I
answered:

"Lieutenant Bromfield, I understand you well. But you
forget that I have no reason to give or demand satisfaction,
for with this evening's interview and events I am not ill-
pleased. You must credit me with wonderful magnanimity or unequaled idiocy if you think I would make myself
a target for your gratification. You overlook the fact
that I have naught against you, save that you are a Tory
and no gentlemen, and if, perchance, I had sufficient cause

to meet you on what you may be pleased to term the
'field of honor,' I should hesitate in this case, as I have
small desire to be murdered as you are reported to have
murdered the boy Bowden—you cowardly cur!"

This I said slowly and clearly, and with startling effect.
Even in the uncertain light of the room his face showed
livid. He took a step backward as though struck; then
with a cry of "Hell and damnation!" he stooped to leap
on me, but was met by the open arms of the old man,
while I again lifted the chair in defense.

There was a short struggle, and the squire's grasp and
voice prevailed.

"In the name of Heaven, Bromfield, would you ruin
everything?" he exclaimed, as he hugged the stalwart
frame around which he had clasped his arms. "Are
you mad—to resent a boyish taunt at such a time?
Settle your affairs elsewhere, but calm yourself while in
this house. Leave the room! For God's sake, leave the
room! Had you given me my way, this would never have
occurred. You will ruin me and mine! Suppose they got
wind of this above. Go, now; I will bring Anthony to his
senses."

So, urging and pushing, he finally got the door between
us, but not before the thwarted Tory had shaken his fist at
me, and, with many an oath, vowed a future settlement.

"And now, Anthony," said the squire, as he locked the
door and proceeded with shaking hands to make a light,
"I trust you will listen to reason. It was fortunate for
you that I came in in time to save you from the fury of
that madman."

"Exactly, squire. Fortunate and strangely opportune.
I feel you have condoned my sin of eavesdropping," I
replied, not in the least mollified by his suavity.

He straightened himself and looked hard at me for a
moment, but made no answer; while I seated myself away
from the fire, for though I felt somewhat calmed after the

late excitement, I was in a glow of heat and needed the influence of the cooler portion of the room.

"Though I am under your roof, Squire Beauchamp," I continued, as he maintained silence, "I need not apologize for what I am about to say, especially as I am perfectly aware I can never impose on your hospitality again, for an imposition it has undoubtedly been. I am to thank you for the events of to-night, and know from what has happened that Bromfield's presence is due entirely to you, although you are under oath not to communicate with the enemy. And I shall——"

"Hold! my young friend," he interrupted, in some haste; "you are at fault. He is an exchanged prisoner and not under arms."

"Precisely, sir. An exchanged prisoner—notoriously an enemy and exchanged; but not a paroled one on oath not to take up arms, and I happen to know that he is only waiting for a commission to be openly obnoxious."

"No! no! Anthony—no!" cried the old man, holding up his hands. "He is not on service and is harmless——"

"As a rattlesnake!" said I impatiently, cutting him short; "but it is of you I am speaking. 'Tis a thousand to one, Squire Beauchamp, that he was within the enemy's lines when you communicated with and brought him hither."

"Now, Anthony! now, Anthony! I protest! You are trying to get me into trouble." He came toward me, speaking with the persuasive patronage I so well knew and hated. "Bromfield came on a matter—no doubt he spoke to you of it—regarding my ward and niece. It is of this matter that I wish to talk with you—firmly perforce, but kindly if you will receive it in the proper spirit."

"I am bound to listen, squire," I replied, mentally apostrophizing the old hypocrite; "but I hope you will not open by insulting me with an offer of money for my services to Miss Dorothy."

"Did he do that? did he do that? I told him it were worse than folly."

"So the hay was cut and cured, and the ground plowed, was it?" I sneered, feeling mightily relieved somehow, by the knowledge that they had plotted—a fact I had hardly doubted. "And now, I presume, you will allow me a final word with Mistress Dorothy, that I may receive my dismissal at first hands."

"Anthony," said the old man, with an attempt to appear kindly impressive, and in his own slow manner, "let me explain matters. You are not aware that Lieutenant Bromfield has expressed his affection for my niece, and considers himself bound to her; in fact, it has been so considered for some time, they having been intimate long before the unfortunate occurrence which brought her to me. Place yourself in his position and consider how you would feel if—if circumstances—certain circumstances, prevented your immediate marriage, and you were aware that another was making overtures to gain her affection. So you see that I—*we* are not unreasonable in asking you to discontinue your attentions, your visits here. I am sure your good sense will lead you aright, and your growing interest, which has been all too plain to us, will easily be controlled and finally forgotten. I am sure your profession——"

"Confusion to such humbuggery!" I interrupted, cutting him short, as my patience gave out. "Will you, once for all, permit me to have this from the lips of your niece herself?"

"But, my dear doctor, my niece has retired for the night, and——"

"To-morrow, then?"

"I am afraid it would be to no purpose, and I cannot consent to more mischief being done. It could make no difference."

"No difference, if the lady denied an interest in that brute? I assure you, sir——"

"No, sir; no difference!" he interrupted, with considerable asperity. "If she is blind to her own future welfare, I am not. You cannot see her, nor do I believe she wishes it."

"Has she so expressed herself—exactly?" I asked, gradually beginning to heat up again.

"Well, she has intimated as much; but as to expressing herself in so many words, no; it were hardly necessary."

"I knew Bromfield lied when he said she had," I returned, feeling the full weight of the imposition put upon me, "and you abet him, and will allow the lady no choice. It is more than plain that you and Bromfield have been plotting, with a very slim foundation to rest on—the belief in my easy intimidation. Now let me clinch this matter and open myself as I have never done before. I love your niece in a way which your friend upstairs, or perhaps listening at the door, is incapable of feeling. I openly and proudly confess this fact, though I never dreamed I would first confess it to you or under this pressure. What is more, I shall not attempt to cover or dislodge such feelings until I hear from her own lips that she finds my love unwelcome. This is my right, the world to the contrary. Now, sir, as for *you*. For my own peace of mind, and possibly for the happiness of Miss Dorothy, I shall place you under conditions to this extent: if any attempt be made to move her from under your roof to a distance, without first granting me the interview I have demanded, I shall have you a prisoner to answer for breaking your parole. Give her wishes due consideration and you will not be molested through word of mine. I shall see her sooner or later, and be either accepted or rejected. But see her I *will*; if not here, elsewhere—*that* you may depend upon. I trust I have made myself understood."

And with that I picked up my skates and walked to the door.

While I was speaking he sat looking at me, his face

growing darker and darker as I proceeded. As I finished, and tried vainly to open the door, which I had forgotten was locked, he arose and took the key from the table, saying :

"Before you leave this house for the last time, my peppery young rebel, I wish to speak one more word."

There was nothing suave about him now, in face or voice. It was honest ugliness.

"Mark well that neither you nor yours attempt to cross my doorstep again. I owe you much for the indignities that have been put upon me, and for that reason alone I should forbid and prevent your alliance with my niece. Be assured I shall take such steps as will make your meeting impossible ; not by removing her secretly," he added hurriedly, as he saw I was about to speak, "but by uniting her with her lawful lover at the first opportunity. He will then have the right to protect her, and even *you* will not gainsay his right to remove her."

"I grant as much," I answered, with a sneer ; "but appearances indicate that neither you nor he have great faith in the strength of her affection for him, else you would not be afraid to trust her in the presence of one who has not been an avowed admirer. Under the circumstances, you will have some difficulty in forcing a lady of her spirit into wedding one of Bromfield's stamp. My knowledge of both shows nothing in common. I wish you joy in the attempt. Now, please unlock the door and let me out."

"Young sir, you will meet with your reward at no distant day, I trust." Then, in a loud voice, as I stepped out of the house : "Give my regards to your father, and a good-night to you. I will deliver your message." And before I could speak, the door was shut, and I heard the fastenings slide into place.

CHAPTER XX.

As I sat on the snow crust and bound on my skates, it was with a lighter heart than I had known for months. Shut out from Dorothy as I was, and about to be misrepresented (a matter plainly to be guessed from the squire's last remark), I was in no way depressed. His whole conduct, down to his farewell (given for the benefit of anyone who might have been within earshot), laid open his studied deceit, and was practically an avowal of its continuance.

His knowledge of Bromfield was an admission that he had lied under oath, and now he was about to give Dorothy a false message from me, the nature of which I was left to conjecture.

If their wishes met with her approval, deceit would have been unnecessary. I had but to wait for an opportunity to see her, though then I had no realization of the burden of the word "wait." Why my sentiments were to be feared, lest there was reason to fear their being reciprocated, was beyond my understanding. The squire's dislike of me could be no factor, else I should have felt its effects long since. No; it was to be an attempt at coercion, which they feared would be unsuccessful so long as I remained in the field.

As I reviewed the events of the evening as I sped homeward, I gathered hope. My jealousy of Bromfield went to the wind, and I only dreaded for my darling (as I fondly thought of her) the ordeal she was about to undergo, and which I could no more prevent than could any of the buried stones by the roadside.

The advent of spring was the point on which my eyes were now fixed. Beyond it I had no future ; no details planned when it should come. In some unknown way it was to be a climax. What it would bring and how bring it, I never thought upon.

Bleakness and sunshine alternated, but at last spring did come, and, in its way, was as impetuous as the winter. Almost like a transformation ice and snow disappeared, and the land was a flood of running water. Almost immediately the bosom of the hills and the fields showed out black and sodden. The season advanced in its strength and glory, and so rapid was the change at last that the meadows were green and trembling in the heat, and the forest soft and plumy, before I was well aware that my time to look for something definite was at hand.

During all this wait there had been no word from the squire's, nor had any knowledge been gathered as to the state of things under his roof. We knew nothing of the departure of Bromfield, and only through report did I know that Dorothy was still there.

Now that the advent of mild weather made it possible that I might meet Dorothy out of doors, I became alive to signs of activity about her house, and renewed my old method of watching from a distance. My passion had not been abated by time ; rather had it strengthened ; nor was I aware how I had idealized her until we finally came face to face.

It happened much as I would have planned it months before had I given my head to plans and details. I had lately taken to hitching my horse near the spot where we had dismounted on the night of our first attempt to capture Bromfield, and then making a detour of the home-lot ; keeping within the edge of the forest that I might see without being seen. Nothing occurring, I would remount and proceed to town, doing the like thing on my way home.

This system of espionage had continued for a week without my having observed anyone; but on a beautiful, warm morning, when I was later than usual, I tethered my horse as had been my custom, and struck into my path around the home-lot. It was the middle of May, and life, light, and happiness filled the air. Birds sung in the sunshine; the tenderest of green showed in all growing things; the full brook, brown with the recent rains, gave a noisy summons for all to come into the open air, and Dorothy had accepted the invitation.

The brook flowed under a rude arch in the stone wall, coming from the north and, cutting a corner from the lot, went its babbling way southward and out again. The space between the wall and the brook, which was here crossed by a small foot-bridge, was a triangle of some fifty feet each way. From the center of the close, level turf, sprang two great chestnut trees united near their roots, and between them a rustic seat had been constructed, though it was now in an advanced stage of decay. Other trees grew along or near the wall, and this spot, unblemished by underbrush, was one of singular beauty and had the added charm of seclusion. Screened from the road by the tangled growth that overran the wall, and from the house by the rising ground, although not distant from either, it was an ideal retreat for a dreamer.

A paradise it was to me, for there on the seat between the trees was Dorothy, her hands lying loosely, palms upward on her lap, and her dark eyes on the water of the brook, that bore away all manner of tiny, floating things— her own thoughts with the rest if I could judge by her listlessness. She did not look well. The paleness of long confinement indoors marked her face, and her attitude betokened weakness or weariness. There was no covering on her head, though the scarf which hung from her shoulders showed that she had used it as such. Her pretty feet were crossed and the lights fell on her like a caress.

I came upon her unawares, and stood looking over the wall with my heart in my eyes, as rigid as a hound that points his prey. I was under a spell, but it was broken by her lifting her head and gazing straight at me ; her eyes growing large and frightened.

In an instant I was over the wall, but ere I had taken a step forward she arose and drew her small figure to its full height, trembling while looking at me from head to foot before she spoke.

"Doctor Gresham has surely forgotten himself !"

"Dorothy——"

"Mistress Beauchamp, at your service," she interrupted, with a sweeping courtesy ; "and why have you seen fit to force yourself on me in this manner ? "

"Mistress Beauchamp, then, if you will," I answered, nettled at her attitude, yet vaguely understanding it all. "Why, in turn, have I lost the common regard which you once held for me ? You scarce treated me with this formality at our last meeting. Is it presuming too much for me to ask civility at your hands ? How have I merited this ? "

"Your own conscience should tell you, as it doubtless does, sir ; and to be frank, I am bound by my own promise as well as desire, to hold no further communication with you. As I am defenseless, will you not leave me and refrain from molesting me in the future ? "

For a moment this struck me dumb. It was a situation for which I was totally unprepared, and after the months of suffering I had gone through on her account, it seemed almost inhuman treatment. To obey and leave her was not to be thought of for an instant. An explanation must come now or never ; and mastering myself, I spoke :

"It would be untrue for me to say your conduct is all a riddle. I am aware that I have been vilified, but how and to what extent I cannot say. As a friend, I ask this information of you that I may set myself right in your eyes. I think I have a claim to this much."

As she made no reply, I slightly advanced, and holding out my hand, said :

"Mistress Beauchamp ! Dorothy ! Am I not to have common justice ? "

She repelled me by a step backward, but the coldness of her face was a little softened, and then as with an effort, she broke out piteously :

"Oh ! why did you come here ? Be generous and go ! Even as a man you must know what it costs me to stand before you to whom I owe my life, and feel the gratitude that is your due being smothered by the resentment that is my right ! You will not force me to be unmaidenly ! Why should you seek to renew a friendship you have thrown aside, and sue me to explain the cause of my attitude when you know it but too well ? "

"I know naught," I burst out, "save that on my last attempt to see you months ago, I was assaulted by that cowardly Bromfield, and forbidden the house by your uncle. I had tried to see you that night, but was thwarted, and am, I hope, too manly to force myself where I was plainly told I was not wanted."

"Assaulted ! And forbidden the house ! "

"Aye ! Not only myself forbidden, but Charlotte also. How could I set myself right but by seeking you thus ? —hardly expecting this reception to reward my waiting. The cause of the trouble, I care not to state to you now ; enough to say that my presence interfered with their plans. Oh, Dorothy ! " I exclaimed, holding out my hands, "if as a simple right you will not let me know how I have been maligned, I will appear ungenerous and demand in the name of my past good offices in your behalf, that you tell me how I have been belied. I have the right of defense. If then I do not explain away this thing, I will never molest you more."

Her hands were clasped now, and she was bending forward in eager listening.

"Assaulted! And by Bromfield!" she again exclaimed, in amazement and with knitted brows. "For what?"

"My candor will be in sharp contrast with your hesitation, if have it you must. Because I would not accept a fee for my services to you, as he wished to have his affianced wife under no obligations to a country leech."

"His affianced wife! His—— Ah, I see," she said, drawing herself up and blushing violently, her eyes dilating as she fixed them on me.

"And my uncle?"

"Abetted him in all, albeit he prevented actual violence. I was plainly told that your desire was to see me no more, and was threatened and finally banished because I doubted their words and claimed my—my dismissal," said I, bowing, "from your own lips."

"But—but the message you sent——"

I interrupted ere she could go further. "I sent you no message; covered or otherwise. *That* I swear as I stand here," and I removed my hat to give weight to my oath. "Your uncle has created a lie. Bromfield vowed vengeance at my crossing him, and the two were united against me principally because I dared demand to see you and ask you what I would ask you now. Dorothy, did you wittingly hold aloof from me that night, or ever say my visits were distasteful and that you wished them to cease?"

"*Never!*" she answered, looking me full in the face. "I was told you made no inquiries for, or mentioned, me except slightly."

"Slightly! *You!* My—— And lastly," I continued, controlling myself and looking away over the stretch of green that lay before me, "may I ask—if you be the promised wife of Lieutenant Bromfield?"

"*No!*" with vigor; "nor ever was nor ever will be. Leave me, doctor; leave me now and let me think. I have been grievously hoodwinked if all—if any part of what you tell me is true. Oh, I have been blind! I must act slowly. Please go for now."

"Dorothy," I said, with all my might holding my feelings in check lest I should betray my passion, "tell me that you believe me—in part at least; I will prove it wholly if you will but listen."

"Nay, nay, not now. I do believe you, yes, and I say it gladly, though sorrowfully. I have been troubled by many things. Do you not mark it? Do I look like your friend of a few months agone? I was unhappy enough then —but now—I might have known. Go, please go," she urged, glancing toward the house and holding out her hand, which I grasped as though I could not let it free. "You will see me again."

"When?"

"You are scarce forbidden the outside world, if you are the house," she answered, with the first ghost of a smile I had seen. "I shall be often here when it is warm and pleasant," and she withdrew her hand, gathering up her skirts preparatory to leaving me.

It would have been ungraceful and ungracious for me to have disregarded her wishes, which had more force in her appearance and action than in her words; and I backed from her as though in the presence of royalty, until I could back no farther. Then with a little nod to me, she waited until I had leaped the wall before she turned and crossed the bridge, and I marked her walking over the rising ground toward the house, slowly, and with head down as though in deep thought.

"Adieu, my love!" said I. "God grant the sun may shine to-morrow as it does to-day."

13

CHAPTER XXI.

THE PROPOSAL.

I was her lover still, but not an accepted one, and yet the tumult within me was one of extreme happiness. It may have been that her statement denying Bromfield's right to her was the cause; or possibly the simple fact of seeing her after so long an exclusion from her presence. It may have been something inherent in the hot blood of a lover; I cannot define the reason, but I could have dropped on my knees and prayed in very thankfulness.

My impatience so overran my judgment that I was at the wall the next morning, long before I had reason to expect she would venture forth. Moreover, beyond my intuition, I had no certainty of her coming at all and no right to believe she would expect to see me. As I seated myself where I could command a view of her approach and had recourse to my only solace—a pipe, I wasted a deal of brains in trying to forestall a possible disappointment in case of her non-appearance. There was everything in the day itself to keep up the spirits. The sky was clean washed and wonderful in its purity, and the sun, with a hint of summer fervency, sent a dancing mass of lights and shadows to enliven the prospect.

But there was no need of philosophy; for though I had sat, smoked, and thought for more than an hour, my staying powers had not been tested when at last I saw her coming over the rising ground. Before she had fairly set foot on the shaky bridge, I was over the wall and at her side. She gave a little start and a wan smile as she held out her hand, saying:

"Frankly, doctor, I did not expect to see you again so soon."

"And as frankly, Dorothy, it is none too soon, and would have been before had it lain with me."

"I doubt the wisdom of it," she returned.

"And why?"

"You know you are outlawed, and were I discovered with you, even this small stretch of liberty might be curtailed. My uncle is no friend of yours."

"You believe it now?"

"I have known it a day now, and had I not been amiss in my head, I might have marked it before. But it matters little; my punishment cannot be long nor severe."

"But long or short, I cannot let you suffer inconvenience through me," I replied. "The squire, I know, hates me with the hatred of his kind; yet what can he do to his niece to make her suffer because she will not share his hate?"

"Ah, my friend," she said, turning to me with an air of depression, but not attempting to seat herself on the bench to which I had led her, "what suffering cannot be inflicted by a caustic tongue or one unbridled! What misery and hurt pride may not come from being continually watched and harassed! I now know you were right in all you told me, and the knowledge has only made my life here harder; but at the same time it eases it by bringing it to an end. Pardon my frankness, doctor," she continued, with an appeal in the brown eyes that looked into mine, "it is best you understood; I owe you that much at least. I told my uncle that I had seen you, and faced him with the facts as you gave them to me, and though he denied them all, I knew by his manner you spoke true.

"Of course there were words I cannot repeat,—bitter ones,—but so it has been. It ended finally, in my determining to return to Norwalk, where I have friends who will doubtless welcome me. There, at least, I will not be constantly at war, as has been my lot here for a time past."

" Return to Norwalk ! " I repeated mechanically, aghast at the prospect of her departure.

" Yes ; Norwalk is my old home, and—and—I know "—with a little choking to her voice—" oh, it will be hard at first—so hard, but it is best; I cannot endure this constant pressure. I had rather you had left me where you found me, than to have been brought back to life—and—this."

Here the eyes that had begun to fill, overflowed, and, burying her face in her hands, she sank with a sob onto the seat by which we were standing.

Had I been caught in some flagrant crime I probably would have turned no paler, and will swear I would have trembled less than I did then at the sight of her distress and the aspect of blankness that overwhelmed me at the idea of her going to a distance. Hitherto, I had governed myself by restraint or a sense of the fitness of things; but now I was beyond my own control.

The sky might have been black instead of blue, and the breeze a thundering menace for aught I saw or cared. I was only aware that before me sat the girl I loved, and she was going away. The abject misery of the whole winter was forced into the few moments I stood there watching her, and I knew that at last I was to shake off its grasp or face the worst.

I had made no movement or sound up to the time she recovered herself and removed her hands. She was about to speak again, but as she raised her eyes to mine, something she saw in my face made her recoil and drop them, and then I placed myself at her side, while the torrent of my feelings boiled over.

My first words were in pity for myself, but what I said, and how spoke, I cannot tell. Indeed, such details are too sacred to transmit. I know that in some inexpressible way I caught encouragement from her face, though the head was drooping, and her eyes remained downcast on the

trembling little hands that lay folded in her lap. I know
what I saw added to my eloquence, and that I marked the
track of my love's life with all its happiness and unhappi-
ness, from the time I found her on the sands up to the
present moment. There were no soft endearments and
no clasping to the heart ; no knee worship or lip service.
God knows there were no flippancies, but only a man
pleading as though for life—aye ! and it was for life
and heart's ease. My voice was deep with feeling when
I ended.

"And now, my love, for my love you are and will be, I
am in your hands and at your mercy. Give me what you
can."

And she—God bless her—turned her sweet, brown eyes
on me for the first time, looking full into mine. Eyes
that were brimming with tears that she did not shame to
show, and from which the love light shone—a light I had
never known before ; and smiling like an angel, she lifted
her hands and placed them both in mine, and said :

"You saved my life, my love; it is yours to keep. I
was wishing it so—oh, so much ! "

I had won her. It was a blinding change from darkness
to light. My want was filled, my hunger satisfied; but
great as was my reward, I could no more have spoken than
though I had been stricken dumb ; neither could I express
my passion, save by bending my head as though under the
weight of a tremendous obligation, and humbly kissing the
hands that were not withdrawn from mine.

But humility is not an abiding thing in the heart of a
successful lover, and I soon rose above its level. There
was no affectation of coyness on the part of this pure girl
as she yielded me my rights ; but time is no laggard, and I
was startled to find the morning had flown, by the blast of
the dinner horn, that never sounded so prosaic as it did
when it came sharply from the house and brought us to
earth again. Then for the first time we were face to face

with reality, and there was scant time for Dorothy to make her flushed cheeks presentable before meeting the squire and his sister, so there was nothing for it but an engagement for the morrow and a hasty adieu.

When she had disappeared over the hill, and I had turned to and mounted my horse, the excitement of the morning gave place to a natural reaction. Not one that lowered my spirits, but it sobered me and prevented any excess of elation, though life to me that day had rounded into something near perfection.

I desired my family to keep the matter secret from all save Harry, until we had formed some line of action ; for stronger and stronger grew the realization of the obstacle we had yet to contend with in the person of the squire.

Well I knew that I could not at once marry, nor would Dorothy now go to Norwalk, unless her treatment compelled it. To remain, hold her secret, keep Bromfield and the squire at bay, and yet lead an endurable life, would be a delicate matter, and need the tact that only a woman possesses.

I now knew that the stress under which she had lived was due to the never-ceasing pressure brought to bear on her to marry the British officer; and that with a heart yearning for another's affection, together with a pride galled by deceit, and a hope stifled by disappointment, ere half grown, her life in the gloomy old house had become well-nigh desperate.

I pitied her in the telling of it, and hinted that an open avowal of our relations might aid her escape from further persecutions, but she had shrunk from the idea.

"'Twill but make matters worse, rather than better," she said. "You do not know my uncle as do I ; and as for Lieutenant Bromfield, he would ride post-haste on the news of it, and goad you into some act of violence. I know not what he might dare, or what might befall you ; he is a wicked man. No, no, Anthony! Grant me my first wish. Promise secrecy."

And I had promised.

It was not through fear of Bromfield that I had made this promise. I confess I shrank from another personal encounter with him, especially as he would be smarting under a sense of disappointment, and his fury would not be bounded by a spirit of fairness; but being confident of my ability to keep out of his way, I was uninfluenced by fear of his violence.

It was the squire, and the hell he would conjure up to plague the life of Dorothy, that gave me the most concern. The length of deceit to which he had gone was an index of his possibilities, and was shown in the character of the message he had delivered as coming from me on the night of our last meeting.

He had invented the one most likely to touch the pride and kill the love of such a nature as Dorothy's, and that without the saving grace of delicacy. He had stated that I had called to see him touching the payment of a bill for my services to his niece! On his refusing to pay the great sum I had demanded, he asserted that he had offered me what he considered a just recompense, which I refused, and my last words were to the effect that if he, knowing the worth of the lady, placed her at so low a value, it would be hardly worth my while to waste my time on her in future.

The coarseness of this should have been the best proof of its falsity, and she had doubted it; but as I had returned no more and all intercourse between her and my family came to an end, she gradually grew more and more indignant, especially as the influence of both her uncle and aunt was constantly brought to bear, and she finally came to believe it.

However, this had not influenced her regarding Bromfield, as they had undoubtedly hoped it would. Had she not withstood their efforts to force him upon her, and gain her consent to a union entirely repugnant to her, they might not have developed the later ugliness that took possession of them and rendered her a victim to every chance for petty persecution.

All this, and many other details, I obtained from her in our future meetings, sometimes brief, but often prolonged. Knowing the risk we ran in a trysting place as open as the home-lot corner, the nook was abandoned and our walks were through the forest, where, under the protection of its intricacies, we felt free from observation ; and apparently no suspicion was attached to her wanderings.

The change of her intentions concerning Norwalk went by unremarked ; the squire, in his stupidity, probably thinking her original determination arose from passing anger.

For us, the days slipped by with a speed known only to lovers ; but no happiness is perfect—for long at least, and though in a measure, life then held more than I had ever dared to hope, there was forever the consciousness that we were being ground between the nether millstone of our desires, and the upper one of the circumstances that held us apart.

Lower and lower had fallen the credit of the country and the finances of my family. A Continental dollar was now worth but two cents, and my income for some time past had been no more than one pound a month in good value, though I had no lack of practice. My poverty showed in my clothing. Instead of a certain spruceness I had been wont to affect, I presented a picture of one very low in the world, and the fact that I had many companions in misery was the only thing that salved my pride and made me bear my altered appearance with decent grace. In dress, I was anything but a beau. My shoes were coarse, heavy, and without buckles ; my stockings darned and re-darned. I had descended to wearing leather breeches in order to preserve the only presentable pair of cloth ones I had remaining, while my coat, waistcoat, and hat were shabby in the extreme.

To take a wife and throw her on the charity of my distressed father, who by his donations to the Commonwealth had reduced himself to extremities, appeared to me unmanly and not to be considered ; but this would have been necessary had I then married. The war—the eternal war that now seemed to belong to the natural order of things, was accountable for our state of grinding poverty. The whisper of actual hostilities came only from the south. Nothing marred the tranquillity of the northern colonies, save the ripple caused by two unsuccessful excursions of the enemy into Jersey.

But lights as well as shades are necessary to produce a picture, and though for the most part the sun shone merrily that summer, it was to be expected that clouds would fly across its face at times. And they did ; though happily not throwing a shadow that touched me very heavily.

CHAPTER XXII.

THE DISCOVERY.

THE natural depression caused by the stringency of the times had been of such gradual growth that it produced no shock, and we faced it bravely ; but suddenly there came an event which spread such a gloom over the whole land that men became panic-stricken and the end of our national hopes seemed very near. I speak of the treason of Benedict Arnold, the knowledge of which fell with an effect that paralyzed the community.

Though this shadow marked a broad streak in the history of the times, it had no bearing on me or those near me ; I was too thoroughly in love and too much absorbed in personal affairs to be sharply hit by a matter so general in effect. My own difficulties were enough ; and in regard to Dorothy, around whom they crystallized, matters seemed about to draw to a head.

The fall found us as far as ever from the object of our desires. Beyond the positive pleasure I obtained in meeting my love, and the rather negative one of hope for the future,—the last sentiment that leaves the breast,—life was deadly dull in those days. Had it not been for Dorothy I would then have joined the regular army, and doubt if I should have received much opposition from my father.

The years had used him well. On the breezy promontory of Hardscrabble animal life and health flourished. No changes had come to us save those of development. Charlotte had grown to be a woman for whom a man might well yearn, and Hal was showing a furtive discontent that I, better than the rest, understood.

As for myself, I was at the acme of physical health, and had but two cares : my love and my poverty. But love and poverty are distressing factors though they help to balance each other, and, while I felt myself hard pressed by misfortune, I was still capable of standing another blow.

At last came the day when the steady swing of my life was to be interrupted, and I should be near the hour that marked the lowest ebb of my fortunes. I have reason to remember it. It was a glorious afternoon and I had met Dorothy by appointment, all discontent vanishing for the time as I took her in my arms and lifted her from the wall. Through the forest we went, the fear of discovery having long since vanished; my happiness in my love as great as on our betrothal, albeit my spirits were not so riotous.

Hand in hand we wandered, the hours hurrying on as such hours do. We were returning and had almost reached the wall by the edge of the woods, when to my profound astonishment, I saw the lank form of the squire's sister standing by a tree, her eyes fixed on us with an expression there was no mistaking. She must have had us in view for some time, for the timber growth was open at this spot ; but, fortunately, Dorothy and I were then walking some few feet apart, and to an ordinary onlooker our meeting in the woods might have passed as an accidental one.

The spinster stood as motionless as the tree at her side, her skimp, black gown hanging loosely over her skimpier figure. Her bony hands, covered with half-mitts, each clasped an elbow, and her thin lips were drawn into a hard, straight line. She was as swarthy as a gypsy, her general squareness and hardness of outline making her an unattractive object at best ; but here in the woodland, and under the circumstances, she appeared entirely out of place, and to me was a hateful object. She spoke no word nor made a movement, nor for a second did her black eyes turn from us as we advanced, for there was nothing to do but continue forward and brazen it out.

I was decidedly shaken by her sudden advent, and could see that Dorothy was in a panic, for the color had at once forsaken her cheeks and she was trembling so she could scarce control herself. Not daring to offer her assistance, I walked on, my love trailing a few steps behind. As we neared the somber figure, I saluted with as much ease as I could command, but she made no return by as much as a sign. We continued on our way, I feeling like a culprit caught at a piece of villainy, and Dorothy looking as though she was about to faint. I could feel the black eyes boring into my back as I walked on, and I cut at the grasses with the stick I carried, knowing the while what a lamentable failure I was making of my efforts to appear unconcerned.

"Does that basilisk never speak?" I whispered to Dorothy, as I sidled near her.

"She will speak to me, and to the purpose," she answered, with an hysterical laugh. "I know not what may happen now! I confess to being fairly frightened! Oh, Anthony! what shall I do?"

"Do nothing unusual; only let me know if they increase their persecution and I will find a way out of it," I answered in desperation. "Let us know the worst first; perhaps we are both unduly frightened—it may pass as a chance and a few words settle it."

And so trying to comfort her with a possibility that I felt scarcely existed, I mounted the wall, prepared to assist her over.

It would have been wiser had we proceeded to the road and gone openly to the front of the house, by so doing giving the matter the flavor of an accident, but fate ruled otherwise. Dorothy had but just put her hands into mine when her aunt's voice broke on us. We had been followed by her at a distance, but she now came up.

"Dorothy, you may come to me," she said, in a tone devoid of harshness; then addressing me directly: "I will take charge of this lady, sir, and relieve you of further trouble. Get from the wall and good-day to you."

Except that she had spoken, there was no change in her. The arms were as rigidly folded, and the figure came to a rest in exactly the same position as when I discovered her. It was as though she had been moved along by a spring which had suddenly run down. That she had not been violent gave me some comfort, and not wishing to further compromise my darling, who promptly moved to her side, I obeyed, bowing myself away with my best grace and without making a reply.

The hopes I had of this incident passing unnoticed were doomed to disappointment; for though I received no message from Dorothy concerning her treatment (a thing I scarce expected unless they had gone a step further in their persecution), I saw nothing of her for five days, which seemed as many weeks, though I waited each day for signs of her, and this to the detriment of duties elsewhere.

I had begun to fear that she was confined to the house and all means of communication cut off, when on the following Sunday I approached my old lurking spot and spied her sitting beneath the chestnuts in the familiar corner by the brook. I had barely realized my good fortune, and was about to break cover and go to her, when I suddenly marked that she was under guard; for on the apex of the lift of land lying between her and the house, sat the old lady in a chair, so posed that she could command the house itself and have her eye on her niece as well.

This watch-dog of a woman suffered no discomfort in her vigil, for she had placed herself beneath a maple which was now a glory of color, apparently reading what was probably her Bible, feeling, no doubt, that she was fulfilling her duty to her God and her wayward niece at the same time. She was a keen-eyed old sentinel, and to have approached within earshot of Dorothy, unseen by her, was impossible.

I was brought up, therefore, with a "round turn," as the saying is, and betwixt anger and disappointment, came very near losing my head and discovering myself. But I fell short of the latter and took to thinking instead of fuming, and I there hit upon a plan to forestall the guard and get an uninterrupted conversation with my darling. However, my plan could not work till the next day, when I trusted Dorothy would return to the old trysting-place, and I strove to content myself with my eyes alone, looking at her a long time, but making no sign for fear of the sharp, black ones on the hill.

Finally Dorothy closed the book that she too had been reading, and, with a backward glance, returned to the house. On this, the aunt picked up her chair and followed after, and I now knew that the episode in the woods had resulted in the tightening of the bands that would make the days of my betrothed an unbearable misery if continued.

The simplicity of my scheme to see her recommended itself to me on the first thought. It was to climb the very chestnut under which she was in the habit of sitting, before she arrived and while the way was clear, and there, perched a few feet above her head and protected by the foliage, which had not yet greatly thinned, we could talk to our hearts' content, if the old lady would remain at her distant station.

Therefore, the next day, with my wits on the alert, I was in the brave old chestnut before the chill of the morning had fairly gone. My elevated seat commanded the door of the house, which I watched with an intensity born of the fear that I might watch in vain. But the same hope which stirred me prompted Dorothy to the old spot at the old hour, and I had correctly surmised her probable action.

She came finally. In each step she took down the hill I noted by the bent head and helpless look the weight she was carrying on her heart. My pity went out to her until

I could have cursed myself for my inability to relieve her distress, and I vowed that a different state of things should exist ; though to cut the knot of the difficulty by marrying, and leading her into poverty, would be but shifting her suffering to a fresh spot.

She dreamed not of my presence, but I knew she would brighten under it for a time at least, though now she was listless enough. Before she was halfway to the brook her aunt came from the house with a chair, and, placing it on the golden carpet made by the fallen leaves, took up her watch.

She was well out of ear-shot if I spoke low; and, as Dorothy came under me and cast a look over the wall, I softly called her name. The work she held dropped to the ground in the start she gave, but quickly recovering herself, she took her seat, and leaning against the trunk of the chestnut like one aweary, answered with evident relief :

"I felt you must come to-day, Anthony, and knew you would devise some plan."

"Aye, to-day, and each day, so far," I answered guardedly. "But this thing cannot go on forever. You are hugging our secret for my sake, while I would sooner take the old man by the throat and abide by the consequences than to have you suffer, as it is all too plain you do and will."

"Yes, my love, I do, and will and must, if I stay here," she answered sweetly, though like one exhausted. "Even if I dared overstep their last commands and leave the home-lot, I would be followed and watched, and pay the penalty in a torrent of words. I shall never be free from my aunt's eye again. I must leave here, love ; I must go, and we must both be patient, though I know 'tis a wearying thing. Never, never could I pass through another such winter as the last. I have wished so to see you and say this, dear; for it will kill me long before my time if I am obliged to remain where I am, shorn of all independence and respect."

She spoke with a pitiful air of dejection in voice and manner. I could make no immediate reply, but was forced to remain silent by the inward struggle I was undergoing, the like of which I had never experienced.

I bent low as I dared when I had mastered myself to answer, and could see the tears trickling down her cheeks. The sight of them, with the knowledge how surely the canker of melancholy would eat away her health, only strengthened the determination to which I had just come.

She should go to Norwalk for this winter, and I would join the army. Not as a recruit, but as a surgeon, as I felt amply qualified for the office. This I had determined upon as next to the last resort, the whole matter coming to me at once with the force of wisdom. The hour for sacrifice had arrived, but the sacrifice should not be one-sided.

How I longed to take her in my arms and comfort her no words can tell ; but worse than a wall kept us asunder, and I could only use barren words to hearten her as I unfolded my plans to the poor thing, who was now sobbing beneath me with a violence I feared would be noticed from the hilltop.

But she consented to the plan. There was no other feasible thing to do. When at last she had controlled herself and left me, and the watch was withdrawn, I descended from the tree, it having been settled that in a fortnight she would depart to Norwalk, and I offer my services to the regular forces, then lying along the Hudson River and in New Jersey.

The summer campaign had closed, and as there was no demand on the colony for recruits, it looked as if I should be obliged to journey alone to the American camp, a prospect for which I had but little liking.

Harry's patriotism became blunted when I proposed his joining me, and there was nothing for it but to set off by myself, or wait an uncertain length of time for a batch of volunteers to be gathered and forwarded.

But at this juncture Jacob Moon arrived from the east and put an end to my embarrassment. The old man was overjoyed at my determination to enter the service, and a week after his arrival we started together, our destination being White Plains.

There had been heavy rains for several days, but now it had cleared into the perfection of crisp, autumn weather. The dust on the roads had been well laid, and the air washed clean of all haziness. The genial companionship of the spy was a foe to depression, and from the liveliness caused by constantly changing scenery, the motion of riding, and the prospect of honorable activity, my spirits quickened into something like their normal condition.

During the natural flow of our conversation I retailed the course of events concerning Dorothy and myself, to which the old man listened with a serious face, many ejaculations, and many questions. When I reached and described the encounter with Bromfield the previous winter he slapped his thigh violently, shook his head, and frowned.

"I would I had been there, my son; I would I had been there!" he broke out. "Ye should ha' brained the infernal villain with the chair while ye had the chance, and choked the old man into a sense o' what's proper. I believe in the choke; 'tis salutary. Well, well! between the two black Tories and the old cat, the lass had a hard spell, no doubt."

Many a time he shook his head and muttered to himself as we rode along, and I knew it was of Dorothy and her troubles he was thinking.

CHAPTER XXIII.

THE "DEBATABLE GROUND."

As we approached the western boundary of Connecticut, we made a detour to the north to escape possible contact with the British, whose detachments were constantly scouring the region between White Plains and New York. This brought us into the southern portion of the "Debatable Ground"—the section of country along the banks of the Hudson between the outposts of West Point and White Plains. In a general way, this strip of country was considered occupied by the American forces, but the posts were few and far between ; the intervening distances being common ground for two distinct factions known as the "Cowboys" and the "Skinners."

They were semi-military banditti, the first supposed to be attached to the colonial interests, the latter to the British, and while each was at war with the other, they both preyed alike on the private property of patriot and loyalist. These bands of freebooters were composed of the most desperate of the off-scourings of society, and, as they generally worked in small squads, were without principle, discipline, or responsibility, and under no authorized command, their advent, which was always as sudden as it was unexpected, was a terror to all.

It was late in the afternoon of the last day of our journey, which had thus far been made without mishap or adventure. We had struck into a comparatively disused road, in order to turn south again without the roundabout trip to North Castle, which lay some fifteen or twenty miles north of our destination. As Moon calculated, we were then only twelve miles or so from the American camp at White Plains, which we hoped to reach ere a late hour. The section we had lately been traversing was the most attractive I had yet seen; the frost effects on the foliage being exquisite, and the country itself all that a lover of nature could desire. Our change of road, however, shut out extended prospect, as it led through a forest whose somber grandeur was in sharp contrast with the undulating and open country we had just left, and we pushed along hoping to get through and onto the main road before dusk. Small paths extended from the way and ran into the depths of the woods that surrounded us, the evidences of habitation becoming more and more infrequent as we progressed.

After a long and silent ride that had taken us deeper and deeper into this wilderness, we came to a narrow stream of considerable depth, that was crossed by a bridge, the blackened timbers of which appeared to be in the last stages of rottenness. Here Jacob pulled up his horse and knitted his brows.

"In trying to shorten the trip by crossing country instead of sticking to the known way, I fear I have lost bearings," said he. "I fancy we'll have to take the back track and make for the detachment at North Castle for the night. Ye be lighter than I, lad; dismount an' pick your way over the bridge to yon rise in the road, an' see if ahead ye can make an end o' these woods. They bother me, an' we be not as safe here as within a fort—that I tell ye."

Without knowing why, I felt the latter fact myself. The forest was already becoming gloomy as the sun sank to a level with the west, and we were in the country infested by the lawless bands before mentioned.

I dismounted in haste and advanced upon the bridge, when its condition immediately arrested me.

"The bridge has been fired, Jacob, and recently. It is

no rot that has blackened it!" I called back; for the timbers and planking still clearly showed the comparatively fresh char of the wood. "But 'tis too weak to ride over," I continued, noticing the shaking of the structure as I walked.

"Then keep your voice down, my lad," was the reply, in a low tone. "There's been some deviltry here. Hurry on an' get back."

I walked rapidly up the slope to its top, which might have been forty or fifty rods from the bridge, loosening the pistols in my belt as I went. Once there I cast a hasty glance about. The road continued as straight as an arrow, but on either side for a space of perhaps a dozen or more acres was a clearing. In the center of the opening to the right stood the blackened ruins of a burned house, with nothing left standing but its stone chimney, and across the road were the remains of a partly consumed barn built of logs. The land around showed signs of recent cultivation, and as I walked forward to satisfy my curiosity I saw the tangled growth of what was once a flourishing garden, now giving evidence of having been trampled by horses.

The field to the south had been reaped, and by that I guessed the conflagration had been since harvest time. But if I had a doubt of the recentness of the date, it was soon set at rest and in a horrible manner.

As I approached the house to gather further details, my attention was attracted to a tree which stood near the ruined building, its foliage blasted and its trunk charred by intense heat; and there, at the end of a rope thrown over its lowest bough hung the body of a man, his flesh on one side baked to a crisp. The few remaining rags of clothing that clung to the revolting object were scorched and blackened, though enough was left to show that when alive the victim had worn the scarlet uniform of a British soldier.

I quailed at the sight. Accustomed as I was to death, I

had never seen it in this form. The profound silence surrounding me, the gloom of the coming evening, and the evidence of tragedy before my eyes, presented a combination for which I was unprepared; and without daring to look into the ruins of the dwelling, I turned and hurried away. Making straight for the road, I was about entering it, when I detected a movement in the wild growth that bordered the highway. There was barely time to wonder at its cause, for the air was still, when the figure of a man partly rose from the tangled mass and turned toward me. So ghastly a face on a human being I have never seen. It was livid. Across his forehead appeared the gash of a recent wound, and both mental and physical suffering showed in the large, deep-set eyes and hollow cheeks. His hair hung about in the wildest disorder, and his lips were blue and swollen.

The figure was but half clad and appeared a skeleton in its thinness. He was on his knees with his hands clasped in abject supplication, and spoke in a voice so weak I could make nothing of what he said. As I halted involuntarily and marked these details, he fell forward onto his face.

Friend or enemy, there was nothing to fear from this pitiful creature, and I was at once by his side. He made no movement as I turned him over, and for a moment I thought he had expired; but he soon opened his eyes and from his lips came the word " Food ! " By looking at him I might have guessed the man was starving, but now I knew it. Lifting him bodily and with but slight exertion, I carried him to the road and laid him on a strip of grass, then with a word of encouragement, I turned and ran back to Moon.

While I hurriedly ransacked the saddle-pack for food and brandy, I retailed all I had seen, and asked the spy to return with me.

" Gladly enough," he answered. " But I must get the

horses over. Had ye an idea I would leave them beyond my ken ? Will not the bridge bear at a pinch ? "

" The risk is great ; I am afraid of it."

" Then hie ye back alone, an' I'll try for a ford. Failing that, I'll swim the animals across an' soon be with ye."

Hastily dipping a cup of water from the stream, I made my return to the poor fellow as quickly as possible. He lay as I had left him. Raising his head, I first gave him water, which he took with avidity, and followed it by a liberal dose of brandy. Watching him closely to mark the effects, I gave him the yolk of a hard-boiled egg mixed to a paste with spirits and water, and then a sliver of cold chicken ; for our haversacks had been well stocked at our last stopping-place.

Not a word did he utter during the while I was feeding him, only looking up at me with the calmness of one who is helpless and puts his trust in another.

" How came you in this plight, friend ? " I finally asked.

His only answer was to lift a trembling hand and point to his feet. My attention being drawn to them, I saw they were wrapped halfway to the knees with the remnants of a shirt, and carefully removing the covering, I discovered that both legs were broken above the ankles, the bone of one protruding through the skin, which showed evidence of gangrene.

I had hardly finished my examination and determined the hopeless condition of the sufferer, when Moon arrived, and, from his saturated breeches and the appearance of the horses, I knew he had been forced to swim the stream.

" Well, my son," he said, after an inspection of the starving man, " we can do but little for him—more's the pity. We must ride for North Castle an' get help—'tis the nighest spot I know. But how can we bestow him in the meantime ? he is far past traveling ! "

" There's a long journey for him soon," I remarked,

knowing Jacob would understand, but the prostrate man had caught my meaning.

"God bless ye for your kindness, who e'er ye be. I'm nigh my end, I know it."

It was the first sentence he had spoken, the words coming feebly and with effort, but seeing that food and stimulant were having their effects, I gave him more brandy and was soon able to get his story.

It was short enough. He was a victim of the Skinners, though a leaner toward the king, his son having been in the British army, and it was the body of his son that hung on the tree. The murder had been committed by the gang, because the young man, who chanced to be at home, resented some insult offered his mother. The band, which consisted of about a dozen, having once used violence, carried it to greater lengths. The house was ransacked for booty, and as little resulted from the search, they became possessed with the idea that the farmer had a hidden hoard somewhere in the vicinity. The poor fellow before us, who had seen his son and his wife murdered, but was powerless to interfere, next occupied their attentions. In the endeavor to force from him the whereabouts of his treasure (which to us, with his dying breath he denied having), they had resorted to torture ; first breaking one leg and then the other, by blows with a fence rail. Finally firing the house and barn, they had dragged him to the edge of the woods, and there left him, after giving him a parting cut on the head. When he recovered consciousness it was raining and the fires were out. He managed with infinite labor to drag himself to the edge of the road in hopes of seeing a chance passer, but, until we came, no soul had appeared on the lonely highway, save three of the band that had worked the destruction, and to have attracted the attention of these would have meant instant death. For a week, as he guessed, he had lain there without food or drink. They had stripped him of coat, shoes, and stockings, but with his shirt he had bound up his wounded legs.

Little by little we got the story, and now it behooved us to provide for him in some way, and then push for assistance, though I doubted if he would last till it reached him. The remains of the barn was the only thing like shelter, and thither we carried him, laying him on the floor under a portion of the partly fallen roof.

The charred hay, soaked by the recent rains, made a stench I could scarce abide, but I fancied it troubled the dying man but little. Putting food and brandy within his reach, I again filled the cup with water, and spreading my cloak over him, bade him keep up hope. As a last word, Jacob bent over him and inquired the nearest way to camp.

"North Castle," he whispered, in answer. "On—the way ye were going." Then speaking louder with a great effort: "Five miles through the woods—north—the first road for two. God bless ye both ! Look to yourselves— the way is unsafe. Curse the war ! "

He fell back at this, and having done all in my power for the dying man, I turned and left the place, Moon quickly following, and we were soon mounted and going rapidly on our way.

By this time it was dark in the forest, though the road was plain before us, being lighted by the yet brilliant sky. We had traversed perhaps three miles, neither of us speaking, and doubtless both engrossed in the same thoughts, when out from the woods ahead stepped two men. The light was too uncertain to make out their characters, or if they were armed, but we immediately pulled up our horses.

" 'Tis what I've mistrusted all along," said Jacob. " Go slow, now ; follow my lead an' mayhap we can pull through. Be ready for aught that happens, but don't shoot unless driven to it—'twould be but a signal to the rest. Keep your eye on me, an' if I use violence, ride down the other chap. Have no fear for me. I'll ne'er strike unless I am sure o' my man."

He spoke quickly and quietly as we walked our horses forward. We had approached within a rod of the two, when one of them called a halt. He wore a common army hat with the black and white cockade of the American forces, but no other part of his dress bespoke military partisanship. His companion bore no distinctive mark about him.

As they advanced to meet us, I saw both were armed with pistols. Their faces showed their desperate characters, and I had but little doubt they were pickets to a larger force; but had no time to go deeply into surmises.

"Who be ye?" said he who had stopped us, advancing and laying hands on Moon's bridle rein.

"Friends to the cause, an' peaceable men when unmolested," was the answer. "Take your hand from my rein, my man; 'tis an offense."

"Ho! but ye have a free tongue," returned the fellow without loosening his hold. "I know not what ye mean by 'cause.' Are ye for the king or for congress?"

"Trust me for being no king's man," said Jacob easily.

"I think ye be!" was the rejoinder. "I'll not take your word, whether or no. I shall hale ye to the captain for a search; and if so be ye have vallables about ye, ye had best first hand them to us for safe-keeping, for the captain has had a dry hand o' late. Do ye mark the hint?"

"Aye, I mark it," said the spy. "Move on; we'll follow."

"Ye'll not follow. Ye will get from the horse an' go before; but first, what have ye?"

"Aught I have is in the saddle-bags," said Jacob, with the air of one submitting to the inevitable. "If it must be, it must be; but ye are only to hold them in safe keeping."

"Safe enough, I'll warrant ye," said the other, with a broad grin at his companion, who had not yet spoken. "Drop off, now; an' ye too," said he to me. "Move lively!"

Like one stiffened by infirmities, Jacob began slowly to dismount. As he threw his leg from the saddle, his eyes met mine, and I knew that the instant for action was at hand. He had no sooner reached the ground, than like lightning his manner changed, and he jumped for his opponent, grasping him about the body in a way that pinned the outlaw's arms to his sides.

I looked for no more. It was the signal. Driving my spurs into my horse, I put him full at the other man who was standing in front and about ten feet from me. He was not taken entirely off guard, for before the animal struck and bore him to the ground, I saw the flash of a pistol, and my temple felt as though a hot wire had been laid along the flesh.

My frightened horse bore me some distance before I could check and turn him, but when I did, I saw that Moon had his man down and was putting his choking theory into practice. The other had struggled to his feet and was about going to his companion's assistance. Before he had fairly taken a step I was upon him again, riding him down as before, but as I went over him this time, I dropped from the saddle, and, drawing a pistol from my belt, with its butt I dealt him a blow on the head that stretched him lifeless in the road.

With the exception of the pistol shot, there had been but little noise and no shouting. The action had been too sudden and violent to permit of signals. From the fact that there was no immediate attempt at rescue, I judged that the fight had been without outside witnesses, but as Moon arose from his now unconscious enemy and we stood together in the gloom, I distinctly heard the hoof beats of a body of horses coming from the direction we had ridden.

Though for a long distance in the rear the road was straight, the waning light did not permit of an extended vision, but the ear soon told us they were approaching rapidly and were in considerable numbers.

"Our work was done with dispatch," said Jacob, after an instant's keen listening. "But now we have the whole pack on us. Our pattern is cut. We must ride for it, lad."

With a last glance at the two lying motionless in the road, we at once mounted and put speed to the horses.

"I fail to fathom how we got between the main body an' their outpost," he continued, as we sped along. "There's something strange in it. The more I think o' it the more I fancy 'twas not the shot that roused them— they were too distant to hear it. What e'er comes now, we must ride over—there must be no stopping. God give us luck this night!"

CHAPTER XXIV.

A DASH AND A DISASTER.

MY wound did not trouble me. Though the blood was running down my cheek and soaking into my neck-band, I felt it was nothing serious, the pistol bullet fired by the man I had ridden down having but plowed the flesh of my temple. I could feel with my hand that there was no depth to the cut, but it had been a narrow escape.

For half a mile or more we went at a great rate, the horses warming to the work as we progressed; the sound of our pursuers, if such they were, being lost in the noise of the hoof beats of our own animals.

I had little fear of being overtaken at the pace which we were going, and was congratulating myself on the certainty of our escape, when we came to where the road finally turned. It showed us that danger was ahead as well as behind.

By the side of the road and some twenty rods before us burned a huge fire, around which were a number of men, some standing, and some lying or sitting. We came into view so suddenly and acted so quickly that I caught no details of the group, but I saw we were marked almost at once, our speed having made cautious approach impossible. There was a general commotion and springing to feet as Jacob shouted :

"Spur on, lad, spur ! 'tis our only chance."

Driving in the rowels, I pulled a pistol and we dashed ahead. Possibly their ignorance as to whether we were friends or foes saved us from instant misfortune; for they stood still and fired no shot until we were well abreast of them and going like the wind. Then a wild shout arose, and a volley was sent after us as we flew past.

I felt my bridle arm jerk up convulsively and then drop helpless. At the same instant my horse gave a terrific bound and seemed to double his speed, nearly unseating me as he sprang forward, and I knew that he, as well as I, had been hit.

Stuffing the pistol back into my belt, I took the rein in my right hand and looked around for Jacob. He was close behind, and safe so far as I could see—but that was not much, it being now quite dark. The speed with which I was going kept him a little in the rear, and thus we went for a matter of three minutes, when, without warning, my horse suddenly went down, sending me flying over his head.

I know that I turned a complete somersault in the air before landing. I know there was a horrible sense of snapping and crushing as I struck the road, and then I knew no more.

When I recovered consciousness I felt no pain, but, instead, was overcome by a numbness more unendurable. It was black darkness I awoke to, but in a moment I found it was because I was in the woods, for on looking up I saw the faint radiance of the sky through the limbs of the tree beneath which I was lying.

The misery of the deadness that possessed me was so keen that a groan broke from my lips. It was immediately answered by the voice of my companion.

"God be thanked! ye are yet alive! My poor, poor son! God be thanked for this! I thought I had lost ye! Where do ye suffer?"

"Nowhere—everywhere," I groaned, trying to move, but finding it impossible. "What has happened?"

"Your horse fell, my dear lad; an' mine in its speed rode over ye before I could check him. Were ye struck by a ball? There is much wet on ye—is it blood?"

"The left arm only, I think, Jacob. Were you hit?"

"Nowhere, lad; nowhere—nor the horse, but yours lies dead in the road."

"Where are we?"

"In the forest hard by the way—— Great Jehovah! Hark!"

As he spoke, the sound of a rattling volley of firearms came on the still air. It was answered by wild yells and irregular shots that plainly told of an engagement; and then for a space silence fell, only to be broken by an occasional report or a distant shout. Presently a horse approached, dashing along the road at full speed. It was followed by another and another, as though in flight, and as the sound of hoofs were lost in the distance, an unbroken quiet settled over the forest.

The minutes which ensued were filled with expectation, but nothing happened to cause further alarm, and after the brooding silence had lasted for a space Jacob broke it by saying:

"I fathom it all now. That scrimmage was a fracas 'twix the Cowboys an' Skinners. One was behind us, the other before. We were not the game of the cavalry in our rear; 'twas the gang we flew by that they were after. Mighty Heavens! To think that we could have slipped quietly into the woods an' had ye saved all this! But the way is clear now. Do ye think ye might make a shift o' riding if I carry ye to the horse?"

"Not to save both our lives," I replied. "My arm is broken—and a rib or two, if not more," for as I took a long breath and spoke, I became conscious of a dull, sickening pain in my chest. "You must leave me, Jacob, even as we left the poor fellow awhile back. Ride to North Castle and get help; I can no more stir than though impaled."

"Ye poor lad! Are ye maimed so badly? How can I leave ye here alone?"

"You must—and the sooner the better," I groaned, as

sharp pains began to shoot through me. "There is no other way; only make haste and return."

With this he moved off, but soon returned bearing a saddle, which he placed beneath my head; then getting the horse-cloth under me, he tucked his cloak snugly about me, and after a few words left, and I heard him galloping away.

I either fainted or slept soon after, for of that night I remembered nothing. When I awoke, it was broad day and the forest was full of woodland noises, though in the active misery I then experienced, I wonder that I marked them. The sun was shining, but it must have rained heavily during the night, for I was wet through and chilled to the bone. At first I was absolutely rigid, but soon found I could use my right arm and both my legs, though they were exceedingly stiff. To shift my body an inch was impossible, and what between the uncertainty of Jacob's fortunes (for he might have been stopped on the road), and my own plight, made desperate in case of his ill luck, I was as down-hearted as was possible. My state and that of the outraged farmer might become parallel, and I had about succumbed to utter hopelessness when I heard the distant tramp of horses, and shortly after, Moon, followed by half a dozen dragoons, burst through the underbrush.

Never in my life have I been so glad to see a human face, nor ever was a mother more tender of her child than was the old man, albeit I promptly fainted when they moved me to the horse litter they had brought, and knew nothing of his doings until afterward told.

Then there was a wait; for half the party had been dispatched to the barn to rescue the unfortunate man we had left there. It was more than an hour ere they returned and reported the wretched creature dead. They also reported that one of the two men we had encountered lay dead in the road, and the locality of the bivouac was marked by four bodies—undoubtedly Cowboys; while the surroundings showed indications of a sharp fight. The neighborhood was a dangerous place in which to linger, and our cavalcade moved slowly forward.

Of these latter facts I then knew naught, nor very little of anything for days after. The fever that seized me and which was due as much to lying so long on the wet ground as to broken bones, brought me so low that my living became a question of endurance. It had soon been discovered that besides the slight wound in my temple, the jar of the fall and the contusions caused by being trampled by Jacob's horse, I had a shattered arm, three fractured ribs, and a broken collar-bone.

The bones of the ribs and collar knitted fast enough, but the arm became a problem to the surgeon, and for a time the question of whether or no I would lose it, hung in the balance. But my youth and general good health conquered, and the limb was saved, though the winter had well-nigh half gone ere I was pronounced out of danger.

Then came the tedious up-hill climb—and slow enough it was. I had plenty of friends and as good care as any army post could furnish, but it was dreary to wait and wait. Jacob had been forced to leave long since, promising a speedy return ; but thus far I had looked for him in vain. Letters there were, both from Dorothy and from home—coming like little gleams of sunshine through a leaden sky. They brought no bad news, though Dorothy was already dreading the spring, when she must return to the squire's ; doubly dreading it as she saw no chance of my being near ; but no other spot on earth could she claim as home.

It was not until the winter was over, and a new campaign about to open, that I took to mending rapidly. Then I was little more than a bag of bones,—a wreck of my old self,—and barely able to sit up in bed. It was early in April, and land and sky were full of promise when I finally left the hospital ; and no baby learning to walk

tottered more. I was forced to admit that my services as
an army surgeon, or in any other capacity, would be worthless for a long time to come. My sole desire was now to
get home, and as I had never been "sworn in," there lay
no difficulty in my way, save a lack of strength and means
of transportation.

The latter might be easily remedied, as my credit would
procure me a horse, but the first bid fair to keep me
anchored in North Castle for an indefinite period.

But Fate always turned kind to me when she had me
fairly " betwixt the devil and the deep sea" (for which I
am under obligations to her, as she throws so many to the
one or to the other), and this will be seen in more than
one instance if my tale is perused to the end.

It was late in the month. The leaves were budding and
the beauties of the season rapidly unfolding, when Moon
unexpectedly arrived.

" I have good news for ye, lad," he said, after greeting
me and hearing my wail, " an' will bear ye company the
way back. I'm for Providence this time, an' in no press o'
hurry. Well, the Lord's will be done ! but I am getting
over old for much more o' this traveling."

No strengthening draught could have had the tonic
effect on me that came with the knowledge of the possibility of having the old man as a traveling companion ;
and with no more delay than was necessary for me to prepare an outfit, we set off for the east; this time keeping
to the most direct and frequented roads.

Dorothy was still in Norwalk, and thither we directed
our course; but owing to my feeble condition, our progress was slow and by short stages. Though slow, to me
it was not tedious. Each day brought a marked improvement in my strength, and by the time we arrived at Norwalk I was able to keep the saddle without an almost
hourly stop. As we approached the town, Moon left me ;
for I was determined to seek rest and comfort in the pres-

15

ence of the one person who could best minister to my necessities. He could not be prevailed upon to stop with me, but promised to return by way of Hardscrabble and be my guest for a few days.

It was not without a shock that Dorothy noticed my changed appearance, but the joy of again being with her did more for my health than aught else could have done. When after three days I left her, I jogged homeward with something more than mere good spirits, as the Gordian knot had been cut at last ; for, deeming the old life impossible, we had decided to be married at midsummer, letting come what might. It was easy for us both to argue that it were better to suffer poverty together than heart-ache apart, and we agreed that our secret should continue to be kept until the banns were called in church; then our immediate union would remove her from the control of the squire, and perhaps, in the face of the inevitable, he would decently sanction what it was past his power to prevent.

It may be advanced that we might have done this before, but we had not had time to digest our experience; now, nothing else seemed possible. Before my arrival it had been determined that Dorothy should return to Groton within a week, and I had narrowly missed seeing her ; therefore no suspicion arose from the fact that our home-coming was so nearly coincident.

I might dwell on the days that were passed at this period, for I remember them clearly; but no salient point presents itself, and to recount them would only lengthen my tale to no purpose. It is enough to say that Dorothy had nothing to complain of in her treatment, save that the old watch was regularly put over her, and as regularly made useless by my taking to the tree after the fashion of the fall before.

It was a little exasperating, but we could well afford to wait the passage of the few weeks that intervened before springing the mine under the squire, and now, with my

rapidly increasing strength and spirits, I was looking forward to a period of mental rest and all the happiness a
man has a right to expect.

But instead of peace and mild activity, I was on the
threshold of events beside which all my previous adventures paled. My former experiences seemed to repeat
themselves with double force and wonderful coincidence,
and to follow in a quick series of misfortunes that threatened, and came nigh, to overwhelming me. But the details
shall come in their proper sequence.

CHAPTER XXV.

THE LAST TRYST.

IT was the middle of July, and the weather, which had been intensely hot, had eased in point of temperature, though the air remained close and sultry. The sky overhead was as uncompromising as a sheet of brass, but blurred away toward the horizon, and there was a thick, murky haze portentous of something threatening. The indications were toward one of those summer gales known as "smoky sou'westers," the strength and duration of which there is no guessing ; but as it was a matter of little interest except to those who follow the sea, I thought nothing of it ; only praying for a break in the drought and a breeze that might come from any quarter, if it would change the atmospheric conditions.

It wanted but a fortnight more and notice was to be given to the parson to publish the banns, and to this event I was looking with feelings of mingled trepidation and delight.

And then Moon put in his appearance. Though tardy, his welcome was warm, but I noticed that he carried an air of fatigue and despondency that was unusual with him, though I thought the cause his long journey and the depressing effect of the weather.

"I know I come late, lad," said he, as we sat on the stone wall the first evening of his arrival. " 'Tis many a day since I knew what it was to shake a free foot, but I hope 'twill not be many another. I'm getting too near harvest time to endure much more o' being under orders, an' I fancy this will be my last trip. I will e'en try to make it so, an' ask for an honorable discharge ; then, my lad, methinks I will come hereabouts an' settle hard by ye, for I know o' none to whom my heart clings more than to ye here. Here I can well wear out my remaining years in peace."

He paused a moment and then resumed :

"I trust ye'll see me soon after the matter I have in hand goes through ; then near ye I'll sit an' play dry-nurse to your children, lad, if ye won't meet my wishes by an objection, an' finally lay my old bones where I know they'll not lack respect, if only for the good wishes they bear in them now."

He spoke like one wearied out, as he undoubtedly was ; but it was the first time I had ever heard him give voice to low spirits. As though marking it himself, his manner immediately took a new turn and he spoke cheerfully.

"An' how's affairs between ye an' the lass ? "

I freely told him of our plans, and he expressed a hearty satisfaction at the way the matter was to be brought about, and all traces of depression vanished in the laugh he gave as he fancied the impotent fury of the squire.

"But, lad, ye might do me a great favor an' let me see the little lady before we go. Can ye not manage it ? "

"Before *we* go ! Where ? " I exclaimed, turning to him in open wonder.

"Well—by the Lord ! " he ejaculated, bringing himself up suddenly with a stare and slapping his great hands together. "Here I've rammed home the ball without the powder to drive it out. Faith ! 'tis a sign of age, an' high time for me to quit. Let me make amends. I must let ye into a state matter, for I have this right when I feel the need, an' count on your help.

"List, now, an' keep it close ! When I left ye at Norwalk, I was for Newport, after the Frenchman o' the fleet there—but the name bothers me."

"De Ternay ? " I suggested.

"Nay, nay. T'other one with a Frenchier twist to it."

"Rochambeau?"

"Aye, by the mark! Roshamby—that's it! He was to meet Washington at Wethersfield,—such was my message,—an' I was to quit an' come here according to promise. Well, well! I had to go back with them to point the road, an' that's what made me late. But to be short. Instead o' being let go, I was held there until the talk was over— an' a time it took. Betwixt the chief an' the Frenchman there was hatched up some scheme to bother the British, but o' it I know naught. I was given a dispatch to deliver to the red-coats, so that it may appear to have fallen into their hands by accident. 'Tis but one o' many that will be sent out for the same purpose.

"Now the matter in it is this: Washington an' the whole army, with the French, are to sit down around New York an' starve the enemy out; a regular siege, mind ye, an', by the same token, as this is a false letter *that* won't be done ; though what *will* be done I have no mind, as I was not honored with their confidence, an' my guess is neither here nor there.

"'Tis a plain job, but one o' the hardest I've had laid to me, though I've half a plan an' wish ye an' your boat to carry it out. Now ye have it at last."

"When do we go?" I asked, my spirits falling in the face of the thought of leaving Dorothy at this stage.

"In three days at most—time enough to ease the good-bys o' the lass."

"Where, and for how long?" I asked, with unusual unreadiness.

"Why, lad! ye be quizzical!" said he, looking hard at me and laughing outright. "But I understand the state o' affairs. 'Tis but a trip to Huntington Bay, where I can put the paper into the hands o' a friend who is a red-coat or a buff jerkin as occasion may warrant. His is the head for fine twists o' this sort. He an' I together may hatch a plan, for this letter must get to Clinton by way o' Brooklyn an' their rear on Long Island. Mayhap I can leave the whole business in his hands an' be free. 'Tis just a pleasant sail, an' a quitting o' four-an'-twenty hours or more. There can be little risk. Are ye for it?"

I still hesitated. There was no excuse for refusal, but an indefinable dread of possibilities took possession of me and made my answer a lingering one, but I decided.

"Well, Jacob, as it lies in the line of duty, 'tis beyond me to refuse you," I answered, "but we will take Bailey, as one more in case of mischance, and is that all?"

"All," said he, with evident relief. "The matter's settled, an' now for your lady. As I told ye, I'm fain to meet her at close quarters. I have never beheld her since she lay senseless in the cabin. 'Twas on that trip with me, two years agone, ye found your fate; I would I could find mine on the trip to come. But my mind's easy, my son. Your going sets me right; after that, a long rest."

During the interval of our further conversation (for the warm night kept us long out of doors), I had been casting about how to get Dorothy and Moon to meet; but of my plans, all lacked reason save one, and that was to place myself in the tree and tell her my old friend, of whose history and services she well knew by this, was over the wall. Then she might walk toward it without creating suspicion, hold a brief conversation, and possibly allow him to get a fleeting glimpse of her; but the latter I would leave him to manage. It was an awkward expedient, but I saw no other way to gratify the old man, and he readily took to the idea with great good humor.

Therefore the next morning saw us early mounted and away for the squire's. The weather had changed during the night, and from the southwest was blowing a brisk wind that promised to grow in force. It was warm enough, but the looked-for gale gave a breath of life which was welcome after the long stillness of the air.

The sun was murky, one being almost able to hold the bare eye on it while it was yet low, for the smoky conditions were unchanged, and nothing but rain would clear the sky and give the blue its proper brilliancy. There was a brave rustle of leaves in the forest, and on the moor the long grasses bent and sprung in the sweep of the wind that drove over its unbroken level. As we got further inland the gale seemed to abate, but it was only because the shelter of the woodland flawed it, and caused it to come in violent puffs.

"Now, this is pleasant," said Moon, as he settled down on the grass under the wall and lighted his pipe. "Shin ye into yon tree an' let us wait; but mind ye be not too free with the love on your tongue, as ye will have two pair o' ears to take it in, instead of one. Aha! 'Tis many a day since I lay in wait for a lass, an' never before with a gooseberry to keep matters straight. Give me the word when ye see her break cover, lad; I wish time to get rid o' my pipe."

It was early to expect her, especially as the wind might make it a trifle uncomfortable for a seat out of doors; but I had not been on my accustomed perch five minutes when I saw her come from around the house and start for the brook.

"She is coming, Jacob!" I sung out, loud enough for him to hear.

"Aye? 'Tis a short shift she makes o' delay. An' is the old cat about?"

"Nay, but there's a flaw in the wind," I remarked, more to myself than to him, for her unusual mode of leaving the house, and the hurried way in which she advanced, showed me that something out of common had happened.

The fact, too, that her aunt had not appeared gave color to my belief, and thoughts of sickness at the house came for the moment as the probable explanation of the slight change in her usual procedure.

As she came rapidly on and crossed the bridge, I noticed the paleness of her face ; then, without taking her seat, she appeared to be looking over the sod at the foot of the tree, as though searching for something lost.

"Anthony," she said softly, without lifting her head, "Bromfield is here. I watched for you from my window, and have slipped out to tell you."

"Bromfield ! Here again ?"

"Yes," she repeated hurriedly, "Bromfield is here. He came late last night. I have kept my room, and must go thither at once to lock myself away from him. He has begged to see me, but I have put him off. I think he goes this evening. I shall not meet him if possible to prevent it. Come to-morrow, dear, and if he is yet here something will hang from my window to let you know. Oh, love, I am so frightened, and shall be until he goes ! I am afraid of him and fear for you."

I confess I was vastly disturbed by this. I had now little anxiety for Dorothy and less for myself, but his mere presence gave me a feeling akin to that which is felt when close to a snake—a mingling of hatred and disgust. It would have been much the same had he been near me, though caged ; for his individuality was more than disagreeable, and made itself felt even at a distance.

His being there was a fact, however, and the wisest thing for both Dorothy and myself appeared to be retreat. Since he knew the risk of being in the neighborhood, his stay would not be protracted, and my love could avoid meeting him by a temporary sacrifice of her liberty. It exasperated me to be pinched, in any way or for any time, by this black Royalist, but policy came to my rescue, and caused me to take a practical view of the situation.

For the nonce Moon and his errand were driven from my head by the news she had brought, and I had told her to return to the house until Bromfield had gone his way, and was about proposing a plan to protect her in case she was driven to extremities, when I spied the officer himself making his way toward us with a rapidity that made it impossible for me to descend from my place of concealment without immediate discovery.

Dorothy was still bending over in her pretended search, and did not mark his advance until I suddenly exclaimed:

"By thunder! Here he is now! 'Tis too late for me to escape."

There was no time to say more, for he came over the grass to the footbridge with a speed that was all too lover-like.

I never had a better illustration of the feminine resources, or a woman's ability to play a part when forced, than at this juncture. Instead of starting in fright, Dorothy circled away from the tree, and continued searching the ground, as though absorbed in the occupation. It was not until Bromfield had removed his hat and saluted her with "Good-morning, Dorothy!" that she looked up in well-feigned astonishment, and answered in a voice from which all hurry had vanished:

"Ah, good-morning to you, sir! A boisterous wind, is it not? I have been looking for a thimble I fancy I dropped here yesterday, but the hunt is fruitless, and it must be elsewhere. I will look further in the house."

She made as if to pass him, wearing a little smile of apparent good will, for I could see her face, as she had moved some distance from the tree.

"Nay, Dorothy," he interposed; "let the thimble be and spare me a moment. Seat yourself for a space. I desire a word with you before you go."

"Nay, sir, in turn," she said, with a pretty laugh. "'Tis far too windy here for me. Will not your words wait? I am busy this morning and have no time."

"I warrant you, my words will be well worth your while. Spare your pretty fingers and listen; this is a chance to be alone with you that I have hoped for, and one not to be lightly lost. The wind is warm; come and sit."

He had blocked her way before, and he now took her hand and attempted to lead her to the rustic bench beneath me, but she caught it from him, saying :

"Pardon me, but I hardly need assistance. What is it that will so much command my interest ? "

" Will you not sit ? "

"Aye, if you will have it so," she returned, and walking to the bench she seated herself with an air of determination that one less blind than he might have seen boded no good to his cause, let it be what it would. "And now what is your further will ? " she continued, as though forcing to a head what she feared was to come.

"Ah, Dorothy," he began, dropping close beside her on the seat, and bending to look into her face, " why do you harden your heart against me ? Have I not proved to you by words, and will yet by deeds, how I love you ? I have even in this journey, which was taken solely for you, incurred some little risk."

"Nay, no risk for me, sir," she answered quickly; " I have asked none ; you have come and gone ere this and have been unmolested. If it be a risk, why should you take it ? It will hardly pay you, if for me. You are in no position to be successful. I regret it if I wound you, but I must tell you that I know your story, your devotion, and what you call your love for me ; but it is to no purpose. My uncle knows it. See him ; he can convince you. Now pray pardon me and let me go. I have much work to do."

She arose, and dropping him a courtesy, took a step toward the bridge ; but he was instantly on his feet, and grasping her hand with some vigor, drew her down again.

" Listen, Dorothy ; listen to me," he said, with something less than his previous smoothness. " You might have been right in saying that my position was one in which I could not hope for success—right the last time I saw you, but not to-day ; and you are wrong in thinking that the risk of

coming among these rebels is the one to which I referred.
Of that I have no fear. Let me give you a plain tale, my
love, and you will change your manner toward me."

Now, this was mighty pleasant to me, as can be imagined.
Within a few feet of me sat the man I hated, making open
love to the girl whom in a month I hoped to call my wife ;
and there I was, bound by every consideration to remain
quiet and listen. My blood boiled. I would have dropped
on to the broad shoulders that were exactly beneath me,
and fought him, tooth and nail, with the best will in the
world, save for the sufficient reason that nothing would
have been gained thereby, and I should surely have been
worsted, perhaps killed by him in his blind fury at being
overheard and overcome in the field he held the dearest.

I was therefore compelled to listen, as was Dorothy
also ; for the hand he laid upon her arm was meant as
much for a detaining force as for a caress. Without an
interruption, he continued :

"When I was here two winters since, I was wild for fear
of the constant coming between us of that impudent young
quack ; who, after all, did me a great favor in finding you.
My own affairs were then under a cloud, and his miserable
arrogance wrought me to such a pitch that when I saw you
I no doubt pressed my suit awkwardly enough. But I
loved you none the less,—before or since,—for, sweetheart,
you have filled me, heart and mind, since I first knew you
as my sister's schoolmate, while visiting us in New York.

"Two years ago I was nothing, holding no position and
with only a possibility of getting influence to help me to
something better than I had held. This tied my tongue,
Dorothy, and made it impossible to use the arguments I
have now at hand. I could give you no position in society,
no wealth, no brilliancy to gladden you, and no hope for
the future ; not even could I have given you much of my
presence, for I was taken up in the ceaseless matter of
acquiring influence for the end I have at last attained.

"Your uncle wrote me that he had effectually disposed of that young doctor, with whom, by the way, I have a heavy account to settle. That relieved my mind to some extent, and then at last, but recently, I received my longed-for wish. Dorothy, I hold a commission of a major in His Majesty's Regulars, and am now on my way to join my regiment. I should have gone at once from New York to Brooklyn, where they are stationed, but could not forbear a journey to you to lay this new honor at your feet; this, with the position and wealth it will bring ; for I shall not long be inactive, I assure you. Hence, the risk I run is disobedience to orders. I was due two days since, but they will condone the offense, or I will gladly take the punishment, which will be light enough at the price of this dear hand."

There was a momentary pause as he laid his palm on the back of her hand, but not a word did she speak, nor made any sign, save to draw away a trifle. Presently he resumed :

"I shall return by the rear of the line, crossing the Sound to Huntington Bay, and if I bear with me your promise to become my wife, I swear the honors I gather shall be reflected to you. It will give me a strong hand to deal with these rebels, for a strong hand is necessary. And now, my love, for my love you are, and will be——"

"Nay, nay, sir," cried Dorothy, starting up and putting both hands to her ears at the words which I had used when on that very seat I had opened my heart to her, and which, womanlike, she had treasured and I remembered. "Nay, sir, no more, I shall hear no more. Had you position, wealth, or all the world could bestow, you lack one thing—my affection. You know but little of me or my sex, if you think we can *all* be bought. So, sir, no more. As your errand is fruitless, it is therefore finished. You had better be gone to your new duties and not trouble my peace."

She had stepped away from him now, leaving him seated and looking at her in evident astonishment. On either of her cheeks burned a bright red spot. Her eyes were wide open and flashing, though her voice was not raised.

It was pure self-control that kept her at this height, and never had she looked more bewitching than in her suppressed excitement. But now the whole tenor of the man changed, and his real character came to the surface. He strode toward her, and taking her wrists in his hands, peered closely into her face for a moment, and then slowly and suspiciously asked :

"Have you seen that fellow again? If so, by——"

"What fellow?"

"That d——d doctor. Have you seen the man?"

"The constant and insulting watch kept upon me is an answer to that. Please let me go!"

"Aye, true enough!" he said, dropping her hands. "But is there no one to whom I owe my defeat? Give me but an inkling and——"

"There is no one but yourself, Major Bromfield—for that is now your title. Were I free to meet your wishes, my nature could never mate with yours. Your need is more for a woman of the world, and though I feel highly honored, I shall decline further intercourse."

Again she swept a courtesy over the short grass and essayed to cross the bridge ; but again the major interposed with a still more violent manner.

"*Were* you free! Then you are *not* free! By Heaven, Dorothy! you will drive me mad! Tell me your heart is wholly untouched, and I shall still hope. Tell me, tell me!"

He had gone to great lengths now. With one hand he grasped hers, and the other was passed around her waist while he drew her to him in a close embrace. The girl turned away her head, and struggled in a vain endeavor to free herself, but nearer and nearer he bent his face to hers.

This was too much for flesh and blood to bear. I was nearer to going crazy than I ever was before or since. Had I been armed I should have committed murder by shooting him as he stood. I saw nothing but Dorothy struggling in his arms, and heard nothing but Dorothy and her piteous prayers to be let free. In an instant, and with consequence far out of sight, I swung from the branch and dropped to the ground within a rod of the villain.

CHAPTER XXVI.

MOON MASTERS THE SITUATION.

THE proverbial clap of thunder from a clear sky, or the coming of an angel from heaven, would have had no more startling effect on the major than did my sudden advent. Unloosing his hold on Dorothy, he stepped back a pace to take the measure of the interloper. For an instant he failed to recognize me, as the two years since we had met had doubtless altered my appearance, and he gazed at me in wonder ; while with a premonition of a tragedy, Dorothy flew to my side as though to protect me. It took not many seconds for the situation to dawn upon him, and his face became a picture of hate.

"And this," he snarled, between his teeth, "is how the squire has been hoodwinked. And 'tis you, you sneaking dog, to whom I owe the debt. By the devil and all his angels, we are well met ! And here and now I will settle the score I owe you. By the Eternal ! if you escape me this time, I deserve branding ; so prepare yourself. I will kill you—you cur ! Dorothy, turn you aside that you may not see me break your lover's back, for as I'm a man, you shall never rest in his arms and he breathe. I say you are mine and not his, and here's the proof."

The man was a maniac for the time, and murder was plain enough in his eye as he walked slowly toward me. He was evidently unarmed, as he drew no weapon, but as he came forward Dorothy uttered a shriek, and threw her arms about my neck.

"Unloose me, love—quick !" I cried, as he drew toward us, and putting her off as he came up, I threw all my

232

strength into my right arm, and dealt him a blow in the face, springing beyond his reach as I did so.

The blow staggered him, but did not bring him down, and while I was vainly casting around for some means of defense, he tore off his coat and made a rush at me.

At that instant there interposed between us the square, squat form of Jacob Moon. In my excitement I had lost thought of him, but I was in his debt from that moment, as he undoubtedly saved my life.

"Avast there, ye hot-headed loon!" he shouted, as he pushed Bromfield back from the embrace with which he had caught him. "Would ye kill a boy o' half your years an' weight, or are ye still up to your old tricks? There'll be no back breaking here—save I take a hand. Look to the lass, my lad, I'll tend to our friend; faith! I thought ye would never make a move."

I ran to Dorothy, who had sunk to the ground, and was staring before her with glassy eyes and lips apart, like one distraught. Even my call to her and my touch had no effect at first. The shock from fright had dazed her brain for the moment, but as I put my arm around her, and lifted her to the seat, while a terrible fear struck me, she turned and looked at me, and putting her hand over my face as though to be sure of its realness, she suddenly took to sobbing violently; then I knew at least her mind was safe.

The reaction from this little episode shook me more than that which had gone before; and sitting with my arms around her, I turned my attention to the other two.

Bromfield stood glaring at us over the shoulder of Moon, who stood betwixt him and the tree. His hands worked nervously, and his face was white as chalk, save where a large spot, from which trickled a few drops of blood, marked the impact of my fist. Some few words had passed between them, which I do not clearly remember, but the Royalist had come to his senses, in a measure, for he looked more like an angry man than one bereft of all

16

brain control. Moon, whose back was toward me, stood braced as though to take up the shock of the onset that appeared imminent ; but instead of immediately flying at his opponent, Bromfield spoke violently, and as though in answer to some remark.

"Then stand aside and let me give him his deserts. Let him fight if he be a man. Stand off and see fair play, if you will—I have an old score to settle with the fellow."

"So?" returned Moon. "An' I have an older one to settle with thee, ye heartless, man-lashing bully. Ye have made my blood boil on the deck o' the *Dragon* many's the day, an' ye may thank the Lord ye are now dealing with a man o' conscience an' not one o' your own kind, else ye'd be lying face skyward, by this. Fair play, is it? Nay, thou roach, it lies not in ye—for see the difference between your bodies."

"Give us arms, then," was the answer; "anything that he may be my equal and I get my right."

"Aye, an' see him killed by thee? Faith! I should think ye would fear the crossing o' swords might fetch the ghost o' young Bowden to blast ye."

"Curse you!" yelled Bromfield, "what devil conjured you up at this time? Hold your infernal tongue, or by—— "

"Nay, then," said Moon, lifting aloft his hand and interrupting, "no devil—but the Lord raised me to smite the Philistine." Then with a change of tone and manner, "An' by that same Lord, my humor is getting short, an' as an end to this—Major Bromfield, I make ye a prisoner in the name o' Gin'ral Washington, an' to your old berth at the fort ye'll shortly go. Leftenant, take the lass to the house, an' then ride to Colonel Ledyard an' ask for a handful o' men."

This was the last straw to the baffled major. As the old man spoke he half turned to give the order, while the officer, with the eye of a trained athlete watching to take his opponent off guard, sprang at him with the quickness of a cat, and seizing him with the under-hold, tried to throw him. Then began a terrible struggle. The stocky form of Moon fell back a few paces at the shock, but he had turned in time to meet the charge breast on, though at a great disadvantage. The two were instantly locked in close embrace, and sway as he would, Bromfield failed to immediately drive the spy to the ground, as by the rush he had undoubtedly hoped to do. It therefore became a wrestling match with life and death for the prizes. They had turned in the struggle so that the face of Moon was now toward me. Fury was on his countenance and he seemed to be holding his breath. His head was bent, but I could see his teeth set over the upper lip, and the great veins swelling on his forehead, as, with a force slow but irresistible, he tried to bow his broad back away from the strain of the brawny arms that encircled him, and I saw his hands working slowly downward over his opponent's back; while the officer strove to lift him till the muscles in his neck stood out in broad bands, showing the fierceness of his exertions.

Together they tottered over the smooth turf, a magnificent spectacle of human strength in battle, and one that held me spellbound. There was no sound made by either, save the short quick breathing of the officer, and the breath of Moon, which was let go with a sudden blast only to be caught again and held. Neither seemed to be able to obtain the mastery. The play of the trip was made entirely by the Tory, whose attempts to interlock were frustrated by Moon with a jerk that sent the officer's leg back "to brace," and the contest became one of brute strength.

There was no telling what the end might be, but such a terrific strain could not last for long, and I had witnessed the combat fully a minute before I realized I had a part to act.

At the onset, Dorothy had turned and hidden her face against me to shut out the sight, but recognizing all the significance of the overthrow of Moon and fearing his possible injury, I put her aside, and springing to the rickety foot-bridge, tore up a loose plank and advanced on the infuriated men.

I was too late. I had not taken six steps toward them, when there came a quick change of position, a lightning-like shifting of hands and legs, and the feet of the Royalist flew into the air while his body shot over Moon's shoulder, landing heavily, back down, on the grass.

Before it had fairly settled the latter was upon him, and with his knee ground into his chest, he gripped the bare throat with both hands.

"Now may God keep me from killing ye as ye lie!" he thundered, as he settled his weight on the prostrate body. "But if ye don't give token o' surrender I'll choke ye till your face turns the color o' your black heart; by the Mighty Power above me, I will!"

As nothing but an effort to rise came from this threat, the hold tightened until the legs of Bromfield were flung wildly about, his eyes bulged from their sockets, his tongue hung from his mouth, and he grasped the wrists of the old man with both hands in a vain endeavor to loosen the vise-like grip that was killing him.

"Throw up your fists as a sign, an' I'll ease!" said the spy, as I noticed an ashy hue creeping over the officer's face. There was life and sense enough in him to understand this, and he tried to lift them aloft, but they fell limply to the ground. Moon immediately relaxed his hold and got to his feet, where he stood looking down on the fallen man, who gasped for breath, but made no attempt to rise.

He was in sore distress for a space, and all fight was gone from him; but he finally succeeded in raising himself and resting on his elbow, and was rubbing his throat and gazing about like one recovering from a stupor, when I saw the squire coming down the hill on a tottering run, closely followed by his sister. Hatless and out of breath he crossed the bridge, bristling with anger and excitement as he advanced upon us.

"Who has had the temerity to assault my guest?" he vociferated, as soon as his access of wind would let him. "Begone from my land, you interloper! What brought you hither? Who is yon fellow?"

Before a reply could be made, he turned to his sister, who had gone directly to Dorothy, and said authoritatively: "Abigail, take her to the house; this is no place for women." Then stooping to Bromfield, he helped him to his feet. "What cowardly conduct is this, my friend? It shall be paid for dearly," he continued, glaring at Moon, who was standing a pace or two apart, his face gathering darkness as he looked at the excited man, while he combed back with his fingers the long hair that in the tussle had fallen over his forehead.

Something in the spy's look evidently changed the squire's policy of brag, for he said somewhat more quietly to the officer, "Come, Bromfield, you are hurt. We will return with them." And he took a step to follow, but Moon's voice abruptly called a halt.

"Ye'll stir not hence—no, an' neither will the lass. Your sister I have nothing with; she may go."

"What is the meaning of this?" demanded the squire, in wide-eyed astonishment. "Do you dare——"

"Aye, I dare!" said Moon, interrupting him; "an' I'll brook no interference from ye, though ye be the squire o' this land, an' ticklish ground it is on which ye be standing. Your guest, as ye call him, is my prisoner, being a major in the king's army by his own confession, for I heard each word o' it; an' squire though ye be, ye are under a ban an' have broken your parole. But little better off are ye.

Guest, is it? A guest yourself ye'll be, an' o' the fort yonder."

The squire's white face had become a shade paler at these words. He turned a blank look on his companion, saying:

"Bromfield! Bromfield! Is it, indeed, so? How came it about? Have you ruined me at last by your violence and temper? How came you in this plight? Answer me as we go." Then with an effort at dignity, he said to Moon: "Let us pass, sir, or you shall suffer."

"Shut up, you fool!" was the ungracious reply of Bromfield, who for the first time found his voice; "the man is armed."

"Aye, armed I am!" said Moon, to my great astonishment drawing a pistol from out his waistband. "An' had it not been for that ye might have come off better through the scrimmage. But he felt the weapon when he hugged me," said he, turning to me in explanation, "an' 'twas his loosening his hand to get it that gave me the hold I wished when I tossed him. 'Twas murder he was after. He might ha' thrown me finally had he not given me an opening. 'Twas your advance, lad, that hurried him, as I hoped it would, for I knew he felt the iron an' would strive for it."

There was a grim smile on his face as he spoke, and he paid no attention to the implied threat of the squire, but said firmly:

"Ye will bide where ye be till I finish." Then still further relaxing his countenance until it assumed its old benign expression, he advanced to Dorothy.

"An' now, lass, I have but detained ye to speak a word to ye; for first an' foremost, ye it was that brought me hither. I came to greet ye an' say good-by at once. Have no more fear for your sweetheart. 'Twas I who asked him to bring me hither this morn, that I might see your sweet face, an' that ye might know me again as a good friend; an' little I recked o' what would fall out, but 'twas the

Lord's will an' a grand, good thing. Go ye to the house now an' forget not the name o' Jacob Moon, or that he will stand by your lover an' ye through thick an' thin, an' may God bless your pretty head."

These words, uttered in a way that might have won a stone, brought the angelic disposition of my love at once to the surface. Albeit, pale and shaking, as she still was, she put her hand in his, saying :

" I do not know you, sir, save by what I have been told and what I have just seen, but more I owe you than ever will lie in my power to repay. You are a good man—you are a good man ! " and lifting her sweet mouth, she kissed his rough cheek before he fairly knew her intention. He stepped back a pace in astonishment, and his face, weather-beaten though it was, showed the blush that came over it, while the quick tenderness that lit his eye told how completely he was won by the caress.

As his look followed her while she crossed the bridge with her aunt, he said to me :

" Go, my son, go to the house with her, an' then hie to the fort. I can hold the two here, without doubt. Faith, 'tis a gentle ending to a broil."

In an instant I was at Dorothy's side assisting her up the hill without any objection being interposed by the spinster, who had spoken no word from first to last. Dorothy clung to me with a nervous force that told how she had been shaken and yet felt the effects of the scene of violence she had witnessed. Still the little woman bore herself bravely, though with great effort, as I could see. We had just arrived at the top of the slope when a loud shout from Moon caused me to turn in haste, but there was no cause for alarm, for he simply made a sign for me to return.

Bidding my love adieu, I went back to the old man who, seated on the bench with pistol in hand, was watching the two who stood at a little distance in close conversation. His face had grown stern again, and as I came up he said in a voice far from genial, and in tones that were evidently intended more for them than for me :

"I have changed my mind." Then rising he approached his prisoners, and addressing Bromfield, said : "Look ye ! I will give ye a choice o' two things ; nor need ye bless me for a change o' heart. Either ye go to the fort on your old footing,—where ye will lie an' rot before your friends trouble more about an exchange,—or ye will consent to mount an' ride out o' town within the next quarter o' an hour, an' swear on your life to return no more, or molest those ye have tried to come between. Think quick, now ! As for *you*," he said to the squire, "I leave ye to the marcy o' the doctor here ; he can do with ye as he wills. Now, my son, there's your man. See him hanged if ye like ; he's yours, an' ye have enough to hang him on."

This sudden change in the determination of the spy took me aback. 'Twas from no feeling of tenderness, I felt sure, for voice and face belied that.

"Why do you let him go ?" I asked.

"Because it suits my purpose ; perhaps to let him gather rope to swing himself with ; anyway, he's my prisoner, ye will allow, an' I do as I list."

This he said harshly, and I felt hurt at the reply; but before I could demand an explanation he blurted out to Bromfield :

"Come now, be quick ! "

"Give me my luggage and let me be gone," said the officer. "I promise on my honor."

Moon looked at him for a moment and then burst into a laugh.

"On your honor, is it ? Well, but I have small faith in your honor. I would as soon look for comfort with cold feet as for honor an' ye to be housemates, but 'twill do for this time. Show the lad his traps," said he to the squire ; and turning to me : "My son, go through them for arms an' papers, then come to the barn, but let not the squire from your sight the time ; after that we'll to horse an' ride this devil out o' town."

At this we moved away from the brook, Moon, with pistol still in hand, following Bromfield in the direction of the barn, while the squire and I went toward the house. As we walked on the old hypocrite became abject in his pleadings for me to spare him.

"I'm a ruined old man, Anthony, and my life is in your hands. If you give me up it will be my death. Have mercy on me ! I will withdraw all opposition to your union with my niece ; I knew not matters had gone so far. I have been no enemy to the colonies in all this; I'm a victim of appearances. 'Twas all for what I thought the good of Dorothy, but now I know how you have made my wishes barren. No good can come to you—no good—by giving me into the hands of the authorities. They will have no mercy ; I am a doomed man if you show me none."

He wrung his hands and clutched my sleeve in his endeavor to detain me and exact a promise, but I only looked at him from the corner of my eye and made no answer.

In this fashion we entered the house, and ere long I had gone through the major's effects. There was a brace of pistols, both loaded, and a number of papers, among them being his commission as a major in the Royal army. His clothing I put in his saddle bags ; the pistols and papers in my pocket, and without apparently noticing the continued pleading of the squire, told him to go to the barn, which he did, I following with the luggage.

His man Matthew, in utter ignorance of what had happened, and seemingly with little curiosity, was saddling the major's horse, and having finished, was dispatched for the two we had left fastened by the road. In the interval of waiting, Moon went over the papers, and giving back to me all but the commission, he handed it to Bromfield, saying :

"Ye would be lame without this, an' so ye may have it."

I could make no head nor tail of his actions, and not until afterward did I understand his apparent generosity, but I felt there must be a purpose beneath it all, so held my peace. The horses having been brought, without as much as a farewell to the squire, who looked as though the his world was about ending, Bromfield climbed into saddle at the command of Moon, and with a "Come, my lad," from the spy, I followed suit, and we three filed into the highroad.

It was getting toward noon by this time, and the wind was still blowing merrily as we took the way to New London; Bromfield riding ahead, Moon, with his pistol still uncovered, and I following close behind. Many were the eyes that showed curiosity as we crossed the ferry and rode through the town; but Bromfield never turned nor spoke, and but for Moon's weapon we might have seemed valets riding behind a master. 'Twas a strange procession even for the times, and had I not been recognized as part of it I doubt if we had been unmolested; for to see a stranger riding through the town with an armed man at his rear was a sight that would have commonly required explanation there and then. Once well through it, however, we rode rapidly for a mile or more, and then Moon ordered a stop.

We were on the brow of a gentle hill that sloped to the west when we came to a halt, and the spy, turning on the officer, said:

"An' now, here we part. Ye have met me twice; beware o' the third time. Ye may go your way alone to do your worst in the service ye disgrace, but it behooves ye to do your best to mind your promise; an' this I say—if ye *do* come back, come well armed an' with as many eyes in your head as has a peacock in his tail, for if the war be still on at our next meeting, I'll kill ye at sight. Now go!"

Without a word the Tory drove his horse into a canter,

and was soon hidden by a curve in the road. As we saw him disappear, Moon turned to me with a radiant face and a complete change of manner.

"Ride now, my son," said he, "for we must be off to Huntington Bay as though life lay in the getting there. Yonder innocent will bear my mail to Clinton."

CHAPTER XXVII.

THE START.

As we sped back, a dim understanding came to me as to his motive in letting his prisoner go, and, during the delay in crossing the ferry he unfolded his plan, which was simple enough.

"I owe ye an apology for the short way I took ye up when ye spoke a while since, but I had a cause. How to be sure to get this letter to Clinton has been a sore bother to me, as in the end I might have been stumped when I got to Huntington if my man was not ready with a way. But here was a messenger bound straight for their lines if I but chose to open my hand. An' now to get there before he has time to cross, an 'twill be given him as though just taken. Do ye see the p'int ? Then, again, to have it sure I make no mistake, I am telling ye the war is well-nigh over, though I say it not abroad. I have reasons for so thinking, an' little good would it do to lock him up for a few months, when I could use him. Neither would I be hard on the squire, were I ye, though he deserves all he would get. I turned him over to ye that he might feel the need o' your mercy an' do your will by the lass. Hold it over him. But I think we pulled his fangs this day, an' things be in good shape. An' now," said he, as we mounted on the other side, "stop and bid good-by to your little lady while I press forward an' pick up young Bailey an' get the nigger to the boat. We must make a start, an' if this wind holds 'twill be quick work an' the last business for Jacob Moon—God be thanked!"

We rode rapidly until we were abreast of the squire's,

and, telling Moon I would join him at home in an hour, I turned in and saw him post on at full speed. I was evidently looked for, as the squire promptly came to me when I dismounted at the door, and began, in a cringing way, to ask what he had to expect at my hands.

I cut him short by a demand for Dorothy, for I had little time to waste on him, and it disgusted me to see the old man, who had hitherto carried his head so high, become servile to one so many years his junior.

" Dorothy is in her chamber," he said, in answer to my question.

" Call her at once, then."

" I am afraid she is ill, Anthony, and will be unable to descend."

Hearing this, I brushed past him into the house and up the stairs two steps at a time. I knew the location of her room, and, as the door stood wide open, I immediately entered.

She was lying on the bed, with her aunt in attendance, and at once I saw that the difficulty lay in the nervous shock she had received. Giving the spinster directions to procure certain remedies that might be found about the house, I took advantage of our being left alone to explain to my darling, who lay and listened with flushed cheeks and dry, bright eyes, the necessity of my temporary absence, telling her just what we were about to do. I had little time to stay by her, and it went to my heart to leave her ailing, though I thought a rest of a night and a day would make her right again. I left, therefore, bidding her be of good cheer, as the squire would make no more trouble; telling her to think nothing of what had passed, but to try and sleep. I kissed her sweet lips and went from her side with a word to her aunt that the fate of her brother would depend upon how they treated Dorothy. E'en at the doorsill I stopped and looked back and saw my dear girl close her eyes in obedience ; but the little start, and their quick opening again, made it too plain that she would live over the scene of violence and terror time after time, until her bruised nerves were rested. Having great faith in my prescription, however, I heartened myself and turned downstairs again, and without paying attention to the squire, who still waited and at once began his prayers anew, I leaped into the saddle and was off.

As I galloped on, the wind I was facing roared at me ; but I judged it had not increased in its force, as I thought it would in the early morning, for in the way I was riding my ears would have hummed in a dead calm.

I was glad there was no increase to it, as a gale of great strength would have stayed our progress on the water instead of hurrying us on our way. 'Twas something more than a whole-sail breeze at present, but though not fair for our course, would well serve ; and as I had had scant sailing that season, I looked forward to getting onto the broad waters of the Sound and feeling the pull of the wheel and bound of the swell.

As was usual, there was not much to do to the little vessel itself, and though there was no bustle about her, there was plenty at the house, and I was at once set upon for the story that Moon had but partly and too modestly told. The wonder of it was how completely the air had been cleared by the storm, and the only dissatisfied one was Harry, who cursed his fate for always being adrift somewhere when a ready arm would have been of use. He took to the matter in hand with all his heart, but had little to do with the preparations, as Charlotte seemed to have mysterious reasons for getting him away from the rest. But e'en lover's partings drag to an end, and the hours that appeared to hang for Moon, who was all impatience to be off, doubtless went at speed for the two who made such an ado when we came to say " All's ready ! "

It was more the distance we had to go than the mission itself that made the undertaking a serious one.

Huntington Bay is across the Sound almost due south from Norwalk, and, as the crow flies, about seventy-five miles from our anchorage ; but with a wind that might hold from the southwest for two or three days, as these smoky gales are apt to do, and our course lying almost in the wind's eye, the distance to sail would not be short of an even hundred and fifty, though the getting back would be but play and would be done in about half the time it would take to beat up the wind.

Huntington at this time was in the line of a great high-road for the British, and was the point of departure for many of their vessels, a small detachment being posted there to keep open a supply line from the Sound to their lines in the rear of Brooklyn. To the east of the bay at the head of which stands the hamlet of Huntington, the Long Island coast is a barren beach of beautiful white sand and pebbles, broken here and there by a cove that might give shelter to a small vessel, but in those days devoid of habitation save for an occasional rude dwelling in the woods hard by the water ; and even now the forest skirts the shore with the aspect of an unbroken wilderness. Five miles to the west, there is a long arm to the Sound, called Cold Spring, that runs inland and bends so that the head of it almost meets the head of Huntington Bay, and ends not more than three miles from the town of Huntington. Into this arm of the sea it was Moon's intention to slip and make his way overland to the cabin of the party to whom he was to deliver the bogus communication, if chance favored his finding him ; while he (Moon's friend), acting as though in the interests of the British, would intercept Bromfield upon his arrival and deliver the message into his hands. Such was the raw plan, that might demand a change later. To get there was now our single object.

I figured that with the present aspect of wind and weather it would consume all of three days before our return would be made good, and as it was evident that the approach and landing must be under the cover of darkness, it behooved us to make a start during the evening of the day we were on, that we might fail to arrive the night following. Well armed we were this time, with a rifle, a fowling piece loaded with slugs, three brace of pistols, and a cutlass, to say nothing of Rod's spear and the knives we carried. We had naught else aboard to excite suspicion in case we were halted, but even in that event we still had the paper from Howe which I had once used and which might still prove effective despite its old date. As a last resort there would be four to fight, but I think none of us looked for any difficulties save those of approaching shore by night, the uncertainty of finding the party Moon was after, and the possibility of Bromfield getting over and on his way before the plan could be straightened out for practice.

It was nigh onto six o'clock before the last thing had been made ready, and much time had been lost too, for the tale of the events of the morning had to be told and re-told and talked over and tossed this way and that and wondered at. Charlotte was to go to Dorothy the next day, which helped my heart not a little. My father showed anxiety, though he would not tell the cause, but the grace he asked at the supper table was of more than usual fervency and length, and was answered by the deep "Amen," of old Moon.

After this it was a short shift to get aboard, and when we drew out of the river's mouth and were bearing south on a long leg to windward, under jib and mainsail only, we could see my father and sister waving to us from the height of Hardscrabble, as they stood in the yellow haze of smoky light made by the lowering sun.

Even then a fear clutched me ; but it was not for myself, and I took it to be a qualm at leaving Dorothy, wishing myself again ashore and on my way to her instead of putting miles of water between us.

It was uncanny enough outside. Even in that light the waves had black hollows in them and broke with a hiss that might try the nerves when darkness drew on ; but the plow had been grasped and there was no turning back, so I steadied myself at the wheel and minded me of the four leagues of water due south, over which we must travel before we could make a tack for the west and an inch on our real way, and it seemed a never-ending distance.

As the sun went down and darkness came on apace, I felt a shivering sense of loneliness I had not marked since I was a lad. There was the violent motion of the vessel, and the snapping hiss of the water in the blackness of the night was made more grewsome by the phosphorescence that was in the sea, for the foam of the wake had a radiance that gave no light. Anon, some huge wave greater than the rest would break hard by, but out of sight, with a roar that made me think of rocks and gave me a "turn," though I knew there were no rocks near. Overhead, a few stars struggled through the haze, but it was a black night—aye, a black night to be on angry water and close to it, as in a small vessel ; and it makes a sight of difference whether one be so near the treacherous stuff that by bending, one can thrust one's arm into it to the elbow, or one be raised above it on the high deck of a stanch craft and feels a sense of security from its very distance.

There was no light shown save in the little binnacle that glimmered under my eye. Rod lay on the heel of the bowsprit in a shower of spray, keeping a lookout, while the others sat silent near me. I have no doubt that Hal was impressed by the darkness, the rush of wind and water and the roar of both, but Moon would sometimes put in a word and show by his easy manner that his nerves were not affected.

At ten o'clock, having been four hours at the wheel, I gave the helm to Moon, after coming about and laying a course a little north of west, so as to fetch into the lee of

17

the Long Sand Shoals that lie off the mouth of the Connecticut River.   By so doing we would have some miles of
comparatively quiet water when we struck there, and
knowing Moon was safe to find the way, I took a big
draught of rum and turned in, leaving them to settle as
they would, on the watch for the night.

The day had been a hard one for me, but, tired as I was
(and my arms ached from the strain of steering), I could
not readily sleep, but lay listening to the thump of the
waves, or their hissing as they tore along the run of the
vessel.   Everything was a-creak and a-rattle, and when I
did finally lose myself, it was to get uneasy dreams, the
worst of which woke me in terror; but I slept again, and
when I at length came to myself it was glimmering day,
and I was thankful the night was spent.   The old man lay
asleep in the bunk opposite mine, his face as peaceful as
that of a child.   His white hair fell about it like a circle
of light, and he was a picture of a man whose heart, mind,
and health swung in harmony.

Harry, all dressed, was lying along a transom cushion;
and this, with the easy motion of the boat, told me we had
gotten into quieter water ; probably inside the shoal.   Rod
was steering when I got on deck, and, sending him below
to rest, I took the wheel.

We were then abreast of Cornfield Point, or just by the
mouth of the Connecticut River.   As we sailed close
ashore, the land looked lovely in the growing light, but.
the prospect to the south was angry beyond telling.   The
wind still held, or was a little heavier, I thought, and the
way the seas broke over the bar that guards the river was
a sight to behold.

This streak of shallow water, that has forever been and
will forever be a menace to the mariner, is known as the
Long Sand Shoal, and is the result of the ages of deposit
brought down by the great river and dropped, in the *delta*
fashion, a few miles off its mouth.   The tides have cut

and shifted it, until it is piled into a long, narrow bank, shaped like a hog's back, the water deepening gradually from the center to the ends. For its entire length it has no hole or opening, and there it lies, and ever will, from three to five miles of grim death, hidden by the sea. The inside, or north side, is pretty steep, owing to the wash of the tide east and west, and between it and the land there is almost a harbor, the bar so thoroughly breaks the swell from the south.

It was through this narrow strip of water we were now speeding, and I had determined to again tack south for an offing, when we should clear the west end of the shoal, but it was close sailing, for the wind seemed to back and head us off. There was no change in the aspect of the sky, which still remained blue at the zenith and went all murky as the eye came downward, but I was pleased to know the weather would hold, for now that light was over the water, the face of things was better and my vapors of the night blew away, though the ash-colored tumult we would soon run into was not encouraging.

We were drawing dangerously near land, and I had shaken the sails a dozen times in trying to claw off, when Moon came up.

" Ye may get over the end o' the bar now," he remarked, as he saw where we were. "A whole day o' this is bad, but thank God 'tis the last, an' we will make the bay soon after dark."

He was in the best of spirits, and I turned the wheel over to him while I took the glass and tried to see if aught was in sight, but nothing showed anywhere, so we hauled on the wind and came about, pointing now due south, and were soon plunging into the raging water to the windward of the Sands. There was not enough violence to the wind to account for such a tumult, but it had been blow ing steadily for thirty-six hours now, and had piled up a swell that on the Shoals created a rumpus that was well-nigh sickening, and we were not in the worst of it either.

The strain of the little ship was great and she labored heavily. I was fearful of the gear, for my poverty prevented my buying a single new rope, but fortunately all seemed in fair condition, and if nothing carried away in the next few miles, we should get easier as we reached the lee of Long Island. The pitching of the sea had at last rolled Harry onto the cabin floor, and he came on deck with a sleep-hungry look in his eyes that was laughable. Rod still slept below in the galley, and thus we held on until after sunrise, making small progress against the blows we got, but gradually drawing away from the roughest of the muss.

The sun was well above the horizon before we saw it, and then it gave no brightness to the day, but hung in the haze like a ball of blood and cast no ghost of a shadow. There was no beauty to sky or sea ; only a pale blue, without clouds, overhead, and a dust-colored tumble of white-capped waves all about. Despite the season, it gave me almost a chill to see the bleak desolation that encompassed us ; the never-ceasing heave and toss of the water and the blue outline of the land we were again leaving.

Breakfast heartened both Harry and myself, as Rod had come to life again and prepared the meal, but the old man seemed to stand in no need of spirits, and was the youngest of us in his gayety and lightness of heart, being like a man about to wed. He was constantly talking of the one less mile we were to go, or laughing at the prospect of having Bromfield carry the letter which he (Moon) had on him even during the fight.

But time told at last, and we pounded along until finally I could see the Long Island coast and noted that the waves were a bit less spiteful as we drew toward the land. It was then that Harry, who had the telescope to his eye, said :

"There's a craft yonder and coming east."

"What is she?" asked Moon.

"A schooner is all I can see," was the reply; "but she carries a yard on her foremast, though no cloth to it—or 'tis furled. She's far off to be sure of her."

"Perhaps she's a fisher hugging the lee of the land," I suggested.

"Aye! 'tis possible," put in Harry, "but she's not cut like a fisherman. Mayhap she is out of Huntington."

"Faith! I hope not," said Moon quickly. "Give me the glass."

He took it, and swaying with the boat, looked for a full minute before lowering it.

"She's too distant, an' the muck makes her unsartin," he said, as he handed the glass to me and took my place at the wheel.

I got a bearing on her, but she bobbed in and out so rapidly there was nothing to be discovered beyond what Harry had seen. It was plain she was in no hurry, as she had on no upper cloths, and, try my best, I could not make out aught of her colors; so I gave the tube back to Moon and resumed the helm.

"Do you think she sees us?" I asked the old man, who with knitted brows seemed mightily interested in the vessel.

"I know not. She makes no sign that I can mark, but I take it there's no use o' beckoning trouble, an' if we hold our course we'll close on her. Ye had better get about, lad, an' if they have a curiosity about us we'll find it out soon enough."

Singing out to Rod, I put the helm hard a-lee, and again we were facing west by north and making for the center of the Sound, which here was nigh its greatest width, and save that the seas were shorter, it differed in no wise from the aspect of the ocean.

CHAPTER XXVIII.

THE WRECK.

As I altered the boat's head and put the stranger forward of the larboard beam, I felt a sudden return of the depression of the night before. It seemed premonitory of immediate events, and though there was no reason for it, I had a feeling that there was trouble in store.

Our course was now almost parallel with the schooner, but in the opposite direction, and she might have been three or four miles away, being just discernible to the eye through the hazy air.

We had not been sailing on the new tack for three minutes when I saw them come about also, and head to cross our bows.

"Ha! They scent us," cried Moon. "Now, what the devil does that mean? I wish I could see her nearer an' yet be further away. I've a notion that I hate to be stopped an' have to explain."

"What need we fear?" I asked, though I had plenty of fear in me as I spoke. "We have nothing on board, and, should it prove a Britisher, we still have Howe's pass. Perhaps we had better lay to and let them come up; it may ease matters."

"There's no call to do that till we're asked; but I like it not—I like it not. Could it be by chance they make to cross us? A Yankee would know us no enemy by our size. By Jehovah! I know not whether to run an' lose time, or to keep on at a risk. I'm fairly stumped."

His face bore an expression of deep perplexity now, and it was contagious. Harry looked at me and I at him, but neither spoke as we waited for the old man, on whom we both depended, to determine what action should be taken. Again Moon took the glass, and getting on one knee, made a bracket of his arm on the cabin top, and with the telescope thus steadied, looked long at the schooner that was by this well off the larboard bow and rapidly crossing us. I could make out that since she had changed her course she had set her maintopsail, and was about to remark it to Hal, when a round puff of smoke broke from her bow. The sound did not reach us through the noise about, but a little speck went aloft to the peak at the same time, and I knew it was a summons to heave to.

It acted like magic on Moon. Jumping to his feet and closing the glass with a snap, he shook his fist at the boat and shouted :

"Aha ! ye blathering whelp o' the devil ! I have it— I know ye now, an' I'm not to be caught by chaff. Up with the helm, Anthony ; they have the weather gauge o' us ; hard up an' show them your heels."

"What is it ?" I asked, as I put the wheel over hurriedly, while Hal paid out the main sheet until the great sail was broad to the blast.

"By the Lord o' Israel ! 'tis fate in the shape o' the *Dragon*, an' ye may know what that means unless your memory has failed ye. If I don't take the throne from Jonah for bringing ye bad luck on the sea, may I be cussed ! I know her now, I know her now ! an' she hoisted the colors o' the colonies, union down, to coax us. The *Dragon* it is ! Aye ! 'tis a fit name for the scaly pirate ; but Jacob Moon's no fool, an' we'll lead her a dance. 'Tis a starn chase, ye black imp," he said, again shaking his fist, with a scowl, and speaking at the schooner, which was now on our starboard quarter, "an' I'll let ye into the length o' it. We're not your game yet. Ye need have no fear o' their guns," he said, as he turned and almost smiled on us, for he doubtless read the consternation on the faces of us both.

"In such a jump o' sea they could never hit a speck like this, though they were at easy range. They may try later if they close up, which misfortnitly, I fear they'll do. Forgive me, lad," he said, laying a hand on my shoulder, "I never dreamed o' risk like this. We might ha' cozened nigh everything else they have afloat, but now 'tis a lost cause an' we must run for it."

I felt all his words implied. Though naught but a chance shot would compel us to heave to and surrender, there were more hazards than that against us. She was coming on, two feet to our one, for as I swung my head over my shoulder, I marked them set the fore and mainsails wing on wing, and spread the square sail on her fore-topmast. With this spread of canvas, a few miles would bring them on us and they might fairly run us down or drop a solid shot into us at close quarters, though I knew their wish was to take us entire, and little they guessed what a find they would have if we fell into their clutches as prisoners. It was a great pyramid of canvas that bore down upon us, and she looked twice her size the way her sails were swung.

After his first outburst, Moon stood silently gazing at her, while Hal, with the instinct of fight in him, went below and began to load the rifles and pistols. For a space the old man stood studying the distance of the oncoming vessel, which was now visibly gaining on us, and then of a sudden he said :

"She's coming like a white squall, but there is one more move ye can make an' ye must chance it. Set the tops'l, an' then clap on your preventer backstay an' h'ist the outer jib ; 'tis all ye can pull even if your sticks hold out against it. Ye must then make for the Shoals an' run over as near the top as ye dare—they will fear to follow in the water ye draw. They're bound to go 'round, an' ye can slip up river to Saybrook, where they durst not chase. We are safe to get off, so be it nothing carries away."

The plan was wise and as plain as day. The Long Sand

Shoal we had left at dawn was scarce ten miles to the north, and by skipping over it where there was but enough water to float us, we would gain an hour on them at once, and long before they could get around the bar, we would be up the Connecticut River and out of reach. The addition of the topsail would tend to drive us down by the head, but the outer sail, or jib topsail, would lift us, the two balancing. It meant putting on every rag we owned and trusting to Providence that nothing broke, and the increase of speed would make a problem of their ability to catch us before we got to a safe haven. Therefore, there was no time lost in getting out the backstay to take up the extra strain, and setting the sails. Then altering the course to due north, so that every stitch was drawing, I set her for what I thought was a point halfway between the middle of the Shoal and its eastern end. A terrible strain it was we were under, and an unsailorly way of carrying canvas in such a wind ; but life hung on it, and the effect was at once felt.

The gale, which was like a living thing while we were facing it, now seemed suddenly to fall to a calm as we fled before it, but the steering was a thousand times more difficult than it had been. We yawed fearfully as the waves passed under us, and it took all my strength to keep the helm up, under the increase of sail ; but we were beating the seas, and with the loss of the deafening roar of the wind in my ears, I got a grip on my nerves, especially as I watched Moon's face and saw it clear a trifle as he noticed our increasing pace. The backstay that ran from the topmast-head down and backward over my left shoulder to a bolt in the deck by the taffrail, was as taut as a bar of iron, but as it had rarely been used I was little afraid of its letting go, and so long as it held, our upper spar was safe.

If there had been the least doubt of the schooner's intentions before, it was now set at rest. As soon as I had put the sloop's head to the north, she swung her mainsail to starboard and followed, now lying down to the pressure of her immense spread of canvas in a way that showed the intensity of her purpose to overhaul us, and despite her errand, was a thing of beauty. The seas to her were nothing as compared to us. Time and again our bowsprit speared a billow ahead before we rose to it, and the roll of the little craft was so great that frequently the end of the boom drove into the water, and I finally got Rod to take a pull on the topping-lift to keep the sail from being swept in and gybing, which would have meant immediate destruction.

Onward we sped, the seas growing greater as we neared the shallow water. A look of anxiety was coming back to the old man's face, and his jaw had a firm set as he watched the enemy, who in spite of our increased gait, was gaining rapidly upon us.

" 'Tis getting to be an even chance," said he, " but the odds left are yet in our favor. Can we but keep well at long range an' they hit us not by luck, we are sure o' supper ashore."

It was almost impossible to use a telescope to advantage, but Moon was constantly at it, and little was said among us until we were within half a mile of the boil of the bar and the *Dragon* about half that distance behind us. It needed no glass to see them now, and all that was going on.

As it had become a sheer impossibility to hold the wheel alone, I had called Rod to my aid, and thus eased, I frequently took a backward look. Five minutes more would find us over the bar, and as though they knew we were about to escape, they began firing at us. Above all the roar of the sea, I heard the report of the brass piece they carried forward, but the shot must have flown very wide of us, as I saw no sign of it. The next shot passed through the center of the mainsail and was a lucky hit for them, as the hole it made tore wide with the pressure of the wind, and reduced our speed.

"They'll not have a chance to be doing that again," burst out Moon, as he marked the rent, "for by the powers! there's none too much water under us, an' they must needs look to their own necks an' sheer off or they'll ground, an' the good Lord help the craft that grounds here this day."

But try it again they did, and it was wonderfully good work they made of it when the conditions were considered. They evidently trained their gun on us and then waited until we both rose, when they fired, for this time the shot plunged into the sea so near us that it splashed water into the cockpit. At the same time there was a *spat!* and a rifle bullet tore a furrow in the mahogany rail and slapped into the woodwork of the cabin.

"Faith! that's a game I'll take a hand in myself," said Moon, with a grim smile, as he gripped his way down the companion and reached into a bunk for the rifle. Harry, who had his gun with him, having brought it on deck some time before, threw himself onto his stomach along the cushion, with one leg out as a brace, and waiting for a heave, fired and turned on his back to load just as another bullet struck us; but I know not where, only hearing the slap of it. He looked worried as he lay there, for all his fright, if he had felt any, was gone, and while he rammed home with all speed, he roared out:

"Tony, they be trying to pick off the man at the wheel. Can't you lie down and steer? I hate to see you make such a mark for them!"

"It's impossible!" I shouted, "and 'tis only for a minute more." For now we were on the hog's back, and the surf was something terrible. Sea after sea lifted us and bore us on at its mercy. The boat was like a mad animal, or a runaway that had taken the bit in its teeth, and for an instant I forgot the danger that menaced us behind, so absorbed was I in the contemplation of the fearful war of waters around us.

Our escape was now to be measured by seconds, and an hundred feet would clear us. They could never follow, for I was sure there was less than a fathom of water beneath us, and they certainly drew ·twice that. It was strange to me they had dared to pursue us so far ; but now there was no time to think of them or aught but the howling vortex in the midst of which we were reeling.

Moon, who had primed below, had crept up the steps and reached the deck, on which he stood braced against the end of the cabin, with legs wide apart to balance himself for a shot. There was a smile of triumph on his lips as he looked at the almost baffled enemy, but while I gazed into his face to read it, there came a *zipp!* close to my ear. I saw a quick tremor to his eye, his jaw dropped, his gun fell from his grasp, and, clapping both hands to his chest, he pitched backward, head foremost, down the companion.

I uttered a cry of horror at the sight, and Harry, dropping his piece, leaped after him. For a brief instant I saw him bending over the prostrate body, and then we struck with a sickening jar and a cracking of timbers, and hung. It was but for a moment. There was a sharp report close to my ear, and I felt a paralyzing blow on my left shoulder. I saw the topmast bend and sway like a whip, and then break off with a crash just above the hounds, while the falling spar pierced the swollen jib and tore it from top to bottom. But the wind was at us, and down we came lower and lower, until we lay almost on our starboard beam's end, the mainsail on the water for half its length. It seemed complete destruction. Turning to look for what I knew would be the next blow, I saw a huge, green sea making at us.

It struck us fairly on the counter, and leaped aboard with a deafening roar. In a second I was knocked from the wheel, and, together with Rod, jammed against the cockpit locker and buried under the weight of the vicious roller.

I was not unconscious in the sense of being stunned, but I lost complete control of my wits, only feeling that the end was at hand, while through my head, like a flash of lightning, came the thoughts of Dorothy, my father and sister, the quiet of Hardscrabble, and being found dead on the shore.

I thought the rush of water would never end, and through it all wondered when I would lose consciousness and how it would feel to drown. Perhaps I had been lost for a second or two, for when at last I came to myself, it was like waking from sleep. I found I was still on the boat, with my head out of the water, and we were on an even keel, lifting heavily, and with our nose to the wind.

The first thing I marked was Rod scrambling up the companion stairs, down which he had been washed. Over the floor of the cabin was more than a foot of water, that drove backward and forward violently with the motion of the boat, which was so logged that she barely rose to the swell.

Harry and Moon were jammed under the table, the former trying to pull himself free; while the body of the latter lay like one dead, alternately covered and uncovered, as the water rushed this way and that.

It took mighty few seconds for me to catch a long breath and determine the situation. Leaping into the water below, I got Harry by the legs and hauled him, half smothered, to his feet. He gave one wild look at me, but said not a word. Together we laid hold of the body of Moon, and, dragging him from under the table, laid him on the transom, which was just awash. I then sprang to the deck, with a yell to Rod to ship the pump, and, calling Harry to follow, drew my knife and ran forward to cut away the wreck of the top-hamper, that was thumping the life out of everything in reach, for I feared it would part the jibstay or standing rigging and let the mast go by the board.

It took but a few moments' reflection to come at the bottom of the disaster, and this was what had happened : In the first place, we had struck near the inner edge of the shoal. Whether I had miscalculated the spot, or the tide had carried us west, I will never know, but I had entirely forgotten to make allowance for the trough of the sea. We had been let down onto the hard sand as a wave passed under us, and, together with the lack of water beneath us and the force of the wind, we were thrown on our beam's ends. As we stuck fast, something had to go, and it proved to be the preventer backstay bolt that drew from the deck, the iron striking me a heavy blow on the shoulder with the recoil of the rope. Then came the following sea that pooped and well-nigh wrecked us ; but its volume was great, and while washing over, it lifted and flung us from the edge of the bar into deep water, where we had righted. Somehow the main sheet had become entangled in the wheel, so that it was drawn home, and the little vessel, relieved of all pressure forward, owing to the slitting of the jib and loss of jibtopsail, had flown into the wind, and lay heaving to the swell in the lee of the Long Sand Shoals, a wreck aloft, and probably in a sinking condition from the blow received when she struck.

Worse than anything that had yet chanced was the fall of Moon, who, I had no doubt, lay dead below, hit probably by the last shot they had fired before we went aground. But there was still a fighting chance for the rest of us if we could keep the vessel afloat, for even the comparatively smooth water here gave no help to escape in the small boat, for the dingey was gone, having been washed away by the sea that had struck us, and the davits on which she had swung were bent almost straight, showing the force of the resistance with which her tackle had held.

I had turned sick at the fall of the old dispatch bearer, but the events that followed so rapidly shifted thoughts of him into other channels for the moment ; and now, with the instinct to save life where life remained, I turned my sole attention to the safety of the vessel. The water in the cabin was from the sea that had swept in, and it must be gotten rid of first. With a natural impulse, I had set Rod at the pump, which was made to fit to an eye on deck, and led by a pipe to the well. He was fitting it while I was forward cutting and slashing with all my might to free us of the *débris* of rope, sail, and spar that cumbered us. Harry had not followed at once, and I shouted for him. As I swarmed up the larboard shrouds to get hold of a line that still held the wreckage, I cast my eye toward Rod, who was now working the brake of the pump with all his might. Even as I saw him he stopped his stroke, and, with one arm pointing to the Shoal and eyes bulging, he shouted:

"Fo' de Lawd God! Mars 'Tony, see yonder!"

The cry had an intensity to it that brought Harry to the deck, and in the few intervening seconds it took me to slew myself around to get a view, I saw him stop and stand spellbound. The sight I beheld made me forget all else. The loose wreck thrashed about me, but I felt not the lash of the whipping ropes' ends. The torn mainsail thundered in the wind, but I heard it not, and we might have settled and gone down then and there without my remarking it, so absorbing and heart-sickening was the tragedy under my eye.

The *Dragon* had grounded! grounded, I imagine, some three hundred feet further out than where we had struck! Whether they considered our mishap as the result of a chance shot, or whether in the excitement of the chase they had neglected their pilotage, or the whole was due to ignorance on their part, will never be known; but grounded she was. They had evidently discovered they were in shallow water and had attempted to claw off, for she was partly thrown into the wind; but the discovery came too late. When I first sighted her her foremast was gone, and the wreckage hung over her side and bows, a mass of confusion. From where I was hanging, using both arms and legs to hold on, I saw her people running backward and forward along the deck, but there seemed to be no united effort at any point. A number sprang into the main rigging and made aloft as though to get out of danger, for the rush of water that broke over her threatened each moment to sweep clear her decks.

As I looked, a huge wave toppled over her, and she broached to, broadside to the sea; another lifted her with a sidelong lurch, and as she came down the mainmast went by the board as quickly and easily as though it were a twig, carrying with it those who were in the shrouds. She was hard aground her whole length now, and the wild rollers, meeting an obstruction, went clean over her or spouted high in air, their tops blowing away to leeward like smoke. She was partly on her side, but the next lurch tipped her deck nearly up and down, and I saw her guns and all the loose gearing, together with a mass of struggling human beings, slip into the sea. The maddened waters seemed as hungry as they were merciless, and wave after wave opened and closed like great mouths.

For anyone to live in that wild tumult of water and wreck seemed utterly impossible; but, as though to take no chances, there came a mountain of green that met the hull, and lifting it, carried it twenty or thirty feet further onto the Shoal, dropping it with a crash that could be heard above all else. The sea following turned her fairly over, with the keel in the air, and the *Dragon* lay like a black rock, the surf going over or pounding on her in a way that showed she would be driftwood long before her loss could be known to the enemy.

It had taken but a few minutes to accomplish the complete wreck of the schooner, which an hour before had been like a living thing. A beautiful menace she was a short time ago, with victory in her eye and triumph in her heart,

but now, a black hull, bottom up, and of her crew not a
soul remained alive—or at least not for long. One man, I
saw, who had escaped the mass of wreckage and was clinging to a spar that drove toward us, but he never got within
our reach, for though I could see his head from time to
time as he rose, I soon saw the spar floating barren, and he
had gone the way of the rest.

CHAPTER XXIX.

THE DEATH OF MOON.

LIKE one in a reverie I still clung to the shrouds and looked at our late enemy. 'Twas hard to believe my own eyes, but I was called to my senses by Harry, who finally turned to me as though he had suddenly brought to mind something forgotten. Drawing a long breath, he said:

"Get below, Tony, there's life in the old man yet, but that sight has knocked aught else out of me. Thank the Lord we're safe so far, and I take it we can keep the water down and reach land with him. Mayhap you can save him; I marked him breathe and could find no wound."

There came a sudden gleam of hope in me as I heard him, and I slipped down the shrouds to the deck, leaving him in my place to finish the work of clearing away the wreck, while I hurried below.

The cabin looked but half its height, owing to the depth of water in it, which swashed to and fro against the old man as he lay on the transom. Through it all was a mass of floating cushions, camp-chairs, and bedding that were being flung hither and thither. To heave some of the stuff out into the cockpit was the work of a moment, and, safe from their battering, I went to the side of Moon. At once I knew there was life in him, and knew too that his senses had been knocked out by the fall down the companion steps and not by the shot, as his breath was coming now, but in the stertorous heaviness that plainly indicated a violent blow on the head. He was still unconscious, but I opened his shirt and found the wound, the first glance showing me that the man's days were numbered, and he would get his discharge from above. A small, bluish hole near the heart marked the spot where he had received the bullet. There was no outward show of blood, but the internal hemorrhage was the worst possible feature of such a wound.

Without delay, I waded through the water to the china locker, and was met by an avalanche of broken crockery as I opened the door; I doubt if a whole piece remained. Grubbing through the mass I found the rum bottle, smashed, it is true, but still holding about a quarter of a pint. Using the bottom of the bottle as a tumbler, I made shift to get some of it down Moon's throat, and little by little I gave him all. Putting some soaked pillows under his head to raise it, I stood watching him for at least fifteen minutes, and at the end of that time noticed that the water in the cabin had gone down perceptibly.

Slowly the labored breathing ceased, and presently he opened his kind old eyes and looked at me, and then, with a half smile, closed them again and shifted his hand to his head. There was naught to be done. I stood looking down on him with a great tenderness surging through me like the waters through the cabin. The tears blinded me as I realized the helplessness of the once powerful man, and for him to die without one more word to me seemed worse than cruel.

It was all so sudden, so hard to compass—Jacob, dear old Jacob, the memory of whom even now moistens my eyes as I write.

Outside the steady thumping of the pump still asserted itself over all other sounds, and inside the water gurgled and splashed. Anon the mainsail was lowered, and its folds shut out the day from the smashed skylight, and I heard Hal stamping overhead as he got the canvas in stops. A moment after, the eyes again opened and the hand moved from his head and groped for mine, which I gave him. His first efforts to speak were pitiful, but by getting my ear to his mouth I heard him say, with a sigh :

" 'Tis all over, lad."

"Aye, old fellow, 'tis nearly over," I said, with a choke, but it was too much for me, and dropping on my knees in the water I put my face in his great hand and sobbed aloud.

He evidently mistook my meaning, for he opened wide his blue eyes and, bringing his other hand to rest on my head, he said, still feebly :

"Forgive me, my dear son, forgive me ! I could not ha' guessed it. When will they get aboard, lad ? "

It was plain, then, that he thought we were taken and knew naught of what had happened, as how could he ? It made me frantic for the moment to think that we were safe while he was slipping away. I managed to get my arm about his neck and put my face close to his.

"Nay, man ! You have no need to ask forgiveness from me. They will never board us now. The *Dragon* lies a wreck on the Sands and all aboard are lost. The boat has escaped, Jacob—aye, all but you." I choked again and then burst out : "But you, you dear old fellow, you were shot and fell, and, God help me ! how can I tell you ? "

"Aye, aye. Is it so ? I know now, I know now. Say no more. God's will be done. An' ye were not scathed? Aye, 'tis all right, 'tis all right. Weep not for me, lad. I knew something was far wrong with me here, but 'tis an honorable discharge, though I thought not to come by it this way."

He lifted his hand and laid it over the wound, then closed his eyes again and remained silent. As I still knelt by him I heard the anchor let go and the chain rattle through the chock. Then the pump ceased its thump for a moment as Harry relieved Rod, and soon after I saw the negro splashing around the galley and finally crawl to the deck again.

Anxiously I watched the face of the old man, whose end was not far off, for I marked on him that peculiar look I had seen so oft in others as they neared the threshold. It broke my heart to think he was to go out in this fashion, lying in soaked clothing with the chill of lowering vitality on him ; for with the reaction from all the excitement and my lack of present exercise I felt the cold of the water, which was up to my hips as I knelt, creeping all through me. But there was not a dry thing aboard, from the stump of the topmast to the keelson, and naught could be done for his comfort. To move him to the deck meant death at once, so by him I stayed and waited. He was not suffering, for which I was more than thankful, and his strong hold on life let him linger longer than I had looked for. After a space he opened his eyes again and turned them on me, saying in a voice stronger than he had yet used :

" Well, dear lad, I have fixed it all. 'Twould not have been many years, anyway, for I am an old man an' I might ha' been a burden to ye had my plan hung ; but I did hope for a bit o' quiet near ye an' the lass, an' the children, mayhap. Well, let it bide. Send to headquarters the way o' my taking off. There's nothing in my hiding-place now, an' there be but two things more, an' ye promise me not to say them nay—promise, lad."

" I promise aught in my power, Jacob."

"Aye ? Then my traps ashore an' all that's in them be yours. I have no kith or kin to mark my going, so ye see I was for a lonely old age, saving ye an' those that belong to ye. 'Tis not much ye'll find, but a trifle o' saving in gold an' silver I had always by me. 'Tis not much, but with it goes the blessing o' Jacob Moon, an' 'twill make a small dower for your lady if ye be loth to touch it."

He stopped, for his breath was getting short, and for some minutes he lay with closed eyes as though gathering strength to continue.

Still went the pump with hardly a moment's rest, and now I noticed that the water was low. With the swoop of the swell we tossed with more motion, and at times as we pitched a small surf ran from one end of the cabin to the other, leaving bare for an instant a portion of the floor. And with the water was going the life of the old man.

Slipping my arm from under his neck, I stepped on deck to speak to Harry, who was working for dear life at the little brake, the sweat standing on his forehead in great drops. A glance showed me that we had drifted away from the Sands, and the anchor had been let go to prevent our getting on a lee shore. Forward was Rod, and on going to him I saw he had a needle and palm, and was roughly closing the rent in the jib. The wreckage had been cut loose and was piled in a confused mass of canvas and rope close by the mast. It had all been done while I was below, and showed quick work and clear heads, and, seeing that as soon as the water was out we could make for home, I turned to descend again, giving word to Harry to be ready for a call, and in that event to turn the pump over again to Rod.

For the minutes I had been on deck the old man had not moved, but as I went down into the darkened cabin, he again opened his eyes and groped for my hand. He took it between both of his, and looking at me, said, as though there had been no interruption :

" Ye promised me, lad, but perhaps the next will be harder. I ask ye to bury me at sea."

I gave a start at this and looked sharply at him, but his mind was clear enough, for he continued :

" My trade has been blood,—but not innocent blood, thank God!—an' I have seen the terror o' death around me times enough. 'Tis not death I fear, my boy," he said, with a weak smile and a caress in his voice, as he feebly patted the hand he held ; " but I have a horror o' the dark hole an' the foulness o' corruption, an' the wind an' rain, an' being all alone ; an' I would fain be launched into the cold brine, an' it all be washed away. Somehow, it seems not so far from life an' light."

He sighed heavily, paused for breath, and in a moment went on :

"It strikes me not so black, an' what odds is it that my bones be not marked ? 'Tis best, my son. I always loved the sea ; it will take care o' me kindly ; an' ye promised—ye will promise again ? "

His eyes were fixed upon mine beseechingly as I shifted my glance, for I could not at once make answer.

"Ah, lad ! I know it goes hard, but ye'll not say nay to the only favor old Moon will ever ask. 'Tis getting short—'tis getting short—ye will promise—will ye not, my son ? "

Words were beyond me, for the piteous tones and the look he gave unmanned me again, and I could but bow in promise to his strange request, which seemed less strange the more I thought of it after.

He sighed, and made as if to nod, and then said :

"That's well ; I know now—'twill be done. Call your comrade."

I quickly put my head up the companion and called Harry, who at once got Rod to relieve him and came below. The old man took his hand and placed it in mine, where he held them both.

"Ye two be friends," he said, with evident effort ; "see to it that ye stick fast while life remains to ye. Lay not your love aside in anger—for I tell ye—there be but little that's more God-like than true friendship. Prop me higher,—lads,—I feel—choked."

He made as though to help himself, but the exertion brought on a fit of coughing that forced blood from his mouth, and he sank back, while I placed another wad of soaked pillow under the poor old head.

For the space of a minute he was still, then said in a firm voice :

"An' now,—Almighty God,—take—me—when ye list."

They were his last words. He seemed to collapse and become unconscious, albeit the breath failed not to come and go.

We stood over him, our three hands locked, and the minutes swung by in silence.

Lower and lower sank the water. The cabin floor was free, and showed the soaked carpet littered with a strange mass. Down in the well I heard the first faint suck of the pump that meant the last of the flood, and, as I heard it, Jacob unclosed his eyes for the last time, and with a wandering look caught mine, and there fixed them. There were two or three quick heaves to the broad chest, and then all was over. Moon was dead; but his honest blue eyes were yet wide open, and looked into mine as though from another world.

I know not how long we stood looking at him before Harry broke the spell by saying :

" 'Twas a noble nature he had, Tony ; and 'tis a fitting end. Better than being blighted by disease at last." His eyes were full and his voice trembled as he continued : " Go you on deck, old boy, and leave him with me for a time. Send Rod down."

He bent reverently and closed the old man's eyes, while I went above and sent Rod to the cabin ; then, seating myself on the heel of the bowsprit, I looked over the wide water and tried hard to realize all that had happened.

Just twenty-four hours ago the man who now lay dead below had stood between me and probable death. Over me came the recollection of my strange fears in the hours just preceding our danger ; the premonitions of coming disaster, for what else could they have been ?

'Twas some such matter as this, that has since grown on me, that kept me gazing in seeming blankness over the sea for I know not how long—an hour maybe, and then Harry's voice called me. I went down again, and saw that the cabin had been cleared of the greatest of the litter, and the body of Moon had been laid on the floor with a sheet, from which the wet had been wrung, spread over him. The soaked carpet sucked under the foot like a quaking bog, and little streams of water still trickled beneath the doors of the lazarette, as the moisture drained from the mass of rope and dunnage inside. Into a corner had been swept a heap of broken glass and crockery, among which lay the cabin clock and the brass work of the smashed barometer. The bunks had been stripped, and the bedding piled on the top of the cabin house (though I had not noticed its being done), and the little cuddy, once so bright and comfortable, looked dark and barren ; while the still figure under the sheet gave it a strange air of solemnity.

These things had been accomplished while I was on deck far away in the blues, and showed Harry's consideration in sparing me. Seated on the bare transoms, with the dead body of the spy between us, I told my companion of the last request of the old man, and my determination to have it respected, and together we decided that the best thing to do was to return to New London and put the matter in the hands of the authorities at the fort. There seemed to be nothing more on hand but to get up anchor and sail for home, and we went to work in silence.

It was past high noon when we got under way, and a for-lorn-looking craft was the *Will o' the Wisp* as she bore east. The torn sails were but roughly mended, and when the wind struck them, gaped widely between the stitches. The wet drained from the mass of stuff on the cabin house, and the confused pile of wreckage by the mast, the bent davits with the broken gear, together with loose rope ends and the stump of the topmast, gave her a dismantled appearance as the bright light of the sun, now comparatively clear in its height above the horizon, flooded and brought out all the scars she had received.

As we first rounded away before the wind I had taken the wheel, but dropped it at once as the strain gave my shoulder a twinge, and I realized I had been injured by the blow of the backstay bolt. Sharp pains about the ribs also bothered me, and on examination I found I was hurt from having been washed over the spokes of the wheel when I was struck by the sea that came aboard. My wetting had not tended to help the stiffening muscles, so I was well content to lie along the bare locker of the cockpit—for the cushions had gone—and let Harry steer us home.

The wind held strong, and it would take us but three or four hours to return to the spot from which we had been nearly eighteen in coming. There was nothing to eat and nothing to smoke, though I craved both food and tobacco, and the only resource was the fresh water which the metal tanks had held inviolate. As it drew toward late afternoon, the sun became veiled by genuine clouds, and the horizon held a darkness of a different character from the haze, which plainly indicated a change of weather. It was five o'clock, I imagine, when we dropped anchor off the town, and I was beginning to experience a used-up feeling ; for the excitements of two days had been crowded on me with little chance for proper rest. There was no need of hailing a boat, as our appearance raised curiosity to such an extent that half a dozen were on their way to us before the anchor had touched bottom. I was in no mood for story-telling, so our condition was partly accounted for by a tale of running on the Shoal, and as the cabin doors were bolted and the slide drawn, none of our visitors had an inkling of the extent of the disaster or of what lay below. Leaving Rod on board to wait word from me, I asked to be put ashore with Harry, and we were soon at the fort.

Great was my distress to find the colonel away ; but a messenger was dispatched for him, and in the interval of his absence I found my fatigue growing on me to an extent that told me I had about reached the limit of my physical endurance. When the commander finally arrived and heard our story,—which was mostly told by Bailey,—he was shocked ; but by this time my brain was so befogged that I scarcely remember the details of the evening. I do recall that the colonel listened with an absorbed look on his face, which I see now as through a mist. I remember, too, the upshot was that Harry should ride home and report the manner of our return, being back early on the morrow, while I was to spend the night at the fort, the officer himself taking off our hands all arrangements for the final disposition of the body of Moon ; and so, with the numbness of exhaustion on me, I went to bed.

CHAPTER XXX.

SICK and sore I was from top to toe the next morning, but my rest had been sound and dreamless, and I no longer felt faint and jaded. My chest was a mass of black and blue, as was doubtless my shoulder, the muscles of which I could barely move; but up I got, feeling none the worse for so doing, and was honored by the colonel's invitation to breakfast with him.

It was a dreary morning. During the night it had rained heavily, and now, though the downpour had ceased, the sky was banked with dark blue clouds that lay fold on fold to the horizon, and an east wind gave promise of still more rain. However, the air was washed clean to the edge of the ocean and the wind was light.

"Well, Anthony," said the colonel, when we were left alone, "as you will wish to take the sloop to her anchorage to-day, I have decided to allow the body to remain aboard. It can be cast over off Fisher's Island, which will be in the line of your run home. Had the old man been willing to be buried ashore, I would have given him a funeral with military honors; but I fancy he was not a character to care for much ceremony, and the simpler it is the better, perhaps. I will read the service myself, and we will start as soon as Bailey returns; everything else has been attended to."

But notwithstanding that Harry came shortly after, it was nearly noon before we left for the sloop. The rain still held off, but the threat of the sky remained. We were soon aboard, and I was grateful when I saw with

what care the matter had been arranged. Across the
bunks, from side to side of the cabin, was a litter of two
planks cleated together, and on it lay the body of my old
friend sewn in canvas, with a cannon ball from the fort
fastened in the foot of this rough shroud. Over all lay
the gay colors of the American flag, which from that day
to this never covered a more faithful or patriotic piece of
clay. At the bow of the sloop sat two old sailors sucking
at their pipes, while two men from the fort, with muskets,
were near them on the edge of the galley hatch. Rod,
who had been ashore, came off in a boat as we got aboard,
and, with no confusion and few words, the anchor was
weighed, the sails gotten up, and the sloop, now a dilapi-
dated catafalque, turned out toward the Sound. As we
reached the mouth of the river we met the swell that came
in from the sea, the result of the recent blow; and here
I saw the completeness of the instructions given by the
colonel, for at the first toss the sailors disappeared through
the fore hatch and presently came struggling up the companion, bearing the body which they laid, litter and all,
across the top of the cabin house with feet to starboard;
then, stationing themselves one on either side, steadied the
silent form as the menacing heaves threatened to roll it
from its resting-place.

There was not wind enough to make rapid progress;
but the swell strained the vessel and opened her weakened
seams. On Rod's going to the well to sound it, it was
found nearly full of water, though it took not many strokes
of the pump to clear her again.

It was a marvel to me that we had received no more
damage below, but the completeness of the sloop's construction was doubtless the reason for her stanch standing of the shock caused by the drop on the Sands. A blow
like that to a weaker vessel would have resulted in her
foundering. But Fate had no more trials for the *Will o'
the Wisp;* for ever after she saw nothing but life and light

hearts aboard, though to-day she crawled like a hearse and
her appearance was in perfect keeping with her mission.
Behind her towed the flat-bottomed punt that Rod had
brought off, and it slapped itself through our small wake,
making a sobbing sound that was fitting enough, though I
had not noticed it until Harry spoke of its quality.

We bore along at a snail's pace until well south and
west of Fisher's Island, when the colonel, standing up,
said : "Here we will have the burial service. Haul on
the wind and lay to."

The boat was thrown into the wind and the jib hauled
over. As we gradually lost the little way we had, the
colonel, mounting the cabin house, stood by the mast and,
taking from his pocket a copy of the service, began to
read in an impressive manner. Everyone rose and uncovered, and while we tossed on the smooth swell, save for
the occasional slatting of the halyards and the gentle beating of the reefing points, there was hardly a sound to
interrupt the words : "I am the resurrection and the life,"
with which the service began.

With a hand against the mast to steady himself, the gallant soldier, who was so soon to follow the one for whom he
was performing the last office of this world, read the dig-
nified service, while all about not a sail was in sight, and
overhead the somber sky hung like a pall. As he reached
the words, "We therefore commit his body to the deep,"
the litter, which had been drawn over until the head alone
rested on the cabin, was quietly lowered at the foot, and
the body of Moon shot from under the flag, and parting
the swell, disappeared from sight.

The drops raised by the splash had scarce fallen, it
seemed to me, when the colonel closed the book and
uttered the word "Fire !" and from the muskets of the two
soldiers came a report as a parting salute to the old spy.

It was all over; and even before the smoke which followed the shots had blown away, with the alacrity spring-

ing from the reaction which follows the burial of the dead, the sails were swung and we proceeded home.

Before we were halfway there the rain began again, and we were well wet by the time we got ashore.

It may be supposed that I was in a strait when I would forego a visit to Dorothy and take to my bed; but this I was forced to do, and received a coddling at the hands of Charlotte such as I had never known before. She had been to the squire's that day, and pronounced Dorothy quite herself again, but greatly grieved at the death of Moon and the failure of our mission.

My sister had nothing to complain of in the reception given her by the squire, who had greeted her like an old friend; though he might not have been so cordial had he known of the loss of my strongest ally.

Much to my surprise and more to my comfort, the next day brought Dorothy. It made me proud to see her assert herself in the sick-room and in her sweet voice demand this or that for me, while her cheeks flushed at the openness of the avowal of her right; and I fancied she was a bit proud of it too. Then I had to recount all that had happened since I left her last, and saw the soft eyes fill with tears as I described the death of the old man. I loved her better, if possible, for the sobs that she tried to hide; but the sobs would come and the tears had to be gotten rid of—which was done in lover's fashion.

Thus two days passed in a state of convalescent comfort, which only those who have been in the same situation can know aught about. In bed though I was, I had brought to me the saddle-bags which Moon had left me as a legacy, and together Dorothy and I went through them. They contained nothing besides the money, save some few 'clothes and a little ammunition.

In gold and silver there were seventy pounds (a noble sum it seemed to me), together with a wad of Continental notes which aside from their face value might have been two pounds more. We reverently put the things back where we had found them, placing the whole in security for future disposal.

Of the ten days I was in bed I did not see Dorothy for the last three. This probably did much to help me to my feet, for I notice a man will take his sick-room confinement easily only when far in love with his nurse. But for these three days I hungered for her, and then got up, and by the afternoon of the next, pulled myself feebly on to my horse and started for the squire's. Though Charlotte made fun of me and called me a terrible "case," she put nothing in my way, and quit her jokes altogether when I told her there never had been such an idiot as Hal when he first fledged as a lover.

I had a long talk with Dorothy alone that day, directly after which together we sought the squire, and finding him at the barn told him we wished to marry with no more delay, asking that the banns be published the coming Sabbath.

He was taken back at this, begging for a month more, in order, he said, to make better preparations and show how much he was in sympathy with our desires. It was all too sudden, he avowed, and assured me that if the banns could be delayed until the last of the month, the marriage might follow two weeks after, and in the interim he hoped to have a surprise for us both. He did not pester me for mercy regarding himself, as I had expected, but looked anxious as though fearing I would broach the subject. Had I but had an inkling of the matter which must have been even then boiling in his brain, I would have choked the heart out of him on the spot; but as it was, I was almost convinced of the sincerity of his saying that he would not have our relations (meaning Dorothy's and mine) other than what they were; and Dorothy looked at me and I at her, and glad to have things smooth for the future, we consented to wait; so in just one month from that day—Wednesday—we were to be wedded.

Heaven knows that death alone would have been small punishment for the squire for the hours of agony he caused us later as a result of the delay—but I will not run beyond the pace of my tale. We were not losing many days after all, and the matter being settled, we talked of other things, and then I went home.

It struck me as strange afterward that he mentioned neither Moon nor Bromfield, though his silence concerning the latter might easily be accounted for. He had spoken of my illness and had expressed a ready sympathy for me, but now I know that in his black heart he wished I had died; all his present decency being from fear that I might drop the hand I held over him.

In my subsequent visits, there was that about him to which I gave little heed at the time, but of which I knew the significance later. He greeted me well enough, but had little to say, though I often caught him watching me from the corner of his eye, which look he would shift away when I turned on him. He also took long walks after dark, and though I knew naught of their point or distance, his absence was a relief to my love and myself.

On the day the banns were called the face of my betrothed looked like a full, pink rose as she received the congratulations of the neighbors (mostly women), who flocked around her as though she had shot out a third arm or a pair of wings, or was in some way curiously different from the damsel they had known so long. The squire tucked her under his arm and bore her away, with the remark that this was not the time for publicity; her wedding-day, *when it came*, would be more fit; and left me to bear the brunt of the questions, for it was a surprise to all. For fifteen minutes I was more popular than I had been since the day Bromfield was brought home a prisoner, but finally got away, giving the gossips enough to talk over, from the short notice of the wedding, to say naught of the match itself.

19

I was somewhat surprised when later I heard that the squire had disposed of a horse, and was said to have sold his library and several heavy pieces of furniture. I remember thinking that perhaps he was raising money as a dower for Dorothy, or in some way it was to have relation to the surprise at which he had hinted; which latter it was, indeed, but in a way undreamed of by me.

The humor that was in me bubbled to the top in those fair days, and I was forever teasing Charlotte, who was almost as tickled as though it was to be her own splicing; but Hal was a trifle downcast, albeit that he swore they would not be far behind us.

I know nothing of the state of the weather at this time, which is strange, as it has always had a powerful effect on my moods, and through life I have associated the appearance of the sea and sky with events. But of the latter half of that month of August I know not whether it rained or the sun always shone, for the days were bright to me and not a film of a cloud passed over my spirits, save when once in a while I thought tenderly of old Moon in his unknown resting-place.

But there comes sharply to me the aspect of nature on the evening of the first day of September. Harry and I had been late in town; he on some matter, and I to attend a sick woman. He had waited for me to be free that we might go home in company, and we were walking our horses slowly over the moor when he drew my attention to an arrow-shaped ripple on the flat stillness of the river that spread as the object moved; just as a water-rat will leave a broadening wake on a still pond; and it passed as silently. We soon made it out to be a boat rowed up the stream, but without the sound of oars in the tholes, and the time and silent manner of passage marked it as peculiar. The sun had been down some time, but the air was dead, and the full stream reflected the last of the rosy hue from the west as though its surface was glass. Not a cloud was in the sky; but stars there were in plenty, blinking through the velvety blue overhead. We halted our animals and watched the object disappear up the stream, then spoke in wonder of what it could be ; but no thought of evil crossed my mind, nor am I now sure there was evil in it, though I have reason to suspect it.

The peace of the hour struck me as though I had just awakened to it. It was a lovely night,—a lover's night,— and, suddenly thinking I might yet pass a few minutes with Dorothy, I bade Hal good-by and turned my horse back. I had not gone far when I saw the boat coming down the stream, but gave it no thought—or, if I did, the thought was put to flight by my suddenly overtaking the worthy squire, who was abroad alone, walking with bowed head, and hands behind him, as though in deep reverie. He started when I hailed him close by.

"Ah, Anthony," he said, with an uneasy laugh, " it is you ! You frightened me. A lovely night. I was enjoy- ing it out of doors. Are you for the house ? "

I answered that I was, and apologized for leaving him, but as it was late, said I would hurry along. He made no reply as we parted, and while I was with Dorothy I heard him come in and go to his chamber.

If I am right in what I now suspect,—and some spirit had whispered plainly in my ear the nature of the silent object,—it would have saved many a brave soul and spared many a heart from agony; for even then the spread of the ripples made by the mysterious boat might have been from the fanning of the wings of the Angel of Death as it hov- ered over the town ; for I surely think that he then unfolded them, and one, at least, knew of what was in store, and that one the squire.

CHAPTER XXXI.

THE BEGINNING OF THE END.

It was on the fifth day of September—I well remember the date—when Charlotte told me she was going with Dorothy to New London to assist in making some small purchases. As she would return to the squire's for supper, she asked me to call and bring her home at night. As though hardly an evening fell that did not find me there with Dorothy, and those that did perchance get by without that happiness, discovered me putting some touches on my aunt's old room, which would soon be ours. Though the preparations were not great, they seemed so to me, and I thought the fittings good enough for a queen, as much of the best furniture of the house had been given over to beautify this apartment. I consented to Charlotte's request with a groan, as though the going would break my heart, and had my ears boxed, and was kissed and driven away, taking myself to town with a heart as light as the down or a thistle puff.

How lovely the world looked! There was as yet no touch of autumn that the eye might note, save, perhaps, a mellowness to the green of some of the trees when compared with others, or the little blood-colored splashes on the leaves of some of the creepers. It was all stillness, beauty, and warmth, though the masses of late meadow flowers and the yellowing of the standing corn plainly told the story of the season. The quiet of the town, too, was as of midsummer, and the dark, green arch of foliage over the streets, showing only spots of blue sky, was as welcome as during the fervency of early August.

. That evening, just before starting to fulfill my promise to Charlotte, I went, as usual, to the headland and scanned the sea. A strong wind had risen, blowing from the land, and the offing was clear of the smallest sail ; so, returning the glass to its well-worn slings, I proceeded on my errand. Had I but lingered I might have seen creeping up from the west the danger I had long been looking for and fearing.

I did not have Dorothy alone that night, owing to Charlotte's presence. The squire was in a very unusual state of agitation, and was constantly in and out, frequently asking me if I heard aught in the air, and acting in a manner that led me to believe the old man might be going daft ; while his sister, who always had about as much life and entertainment in her as a graven image, seemed to have caught his nervousness and, excusing herself, went out also—and stayed. There they were both standing by the gate in the warm night wind when I passed out later with Charlotte ; and as we rode along we laughed at them, they looked so like superannuated lovers saying the last words of their leave-taking for the evening.

Their behavior had been out of the common—but everything else seemed out of common to me in those days of waiting, so that I barely noticed it ; but the light laugh that came now so readily would have been changed to something deeper had I known for what the old couple were on the watch ; had I but known that their expectant ears were listening for a cannon shot that had been promised, and would have come, during the dark hours of this night of September 5, had it not been for the providential gale now blowing from the north.

It was not late when we arrived home, and my father dropping his book for a while, we three sat and talked. There was no sign of danger anywhere. It had but just become known to us that Washington had broken camp and was on his way south, all indications pointing to his re-enforcement of Lafayette at Yorktown, and that was the topic that held us talking; for an authentic report of the movement of the army always brought a discussion of its object and probable success.

How little we guessed, as we sat in the light of the flaring candle (for the night was warm and the draught that came in at the open door constantly shook the flame), that opposite us, along the Long Island coast, at that moment were sneaking the ships of the enemy, bound on an expedition which they hoped would be the means of turning the direction of the American army, and withdrawing its menace to Cornwallis. By and by the talk waned, the house was closed for the night, and we all retired.

As I broke the sound slumber of the night's rest and fell into the light drowsiness of gradual awakening, my dreams were strangely mixed with sounds of talking in loud voices, in which a half shriek mingled, and I was fully aroused by a thunderous hammering on my door.

I sprang from bed and hastened to open it, but saw only Rod, whose black face had been turned to a sickly green by excitement and hurry.

"Get up, Mars Tony ; get up, fo' God sake ! De Britishers hab come—dey is in de town."

"What do you mean ?" I demanded fiercely, for I thought he had gone crazy.

"Deys in de town, Mars Tony. Deys come at daylight, an' Mars Bailey am downstairs mos' daid. Dere's de cannon now—an' now—an' now——"

He was interrupted in his speech by Hal, who had made his way upstairs and saw me standing in my night clothes looking aghast at the negro. He was not nearly dead as Rod had intimated, except for loss of breath ; instead, there was an intense energy in him as he grasped the boy by the shoulder and panted out :

"Get the horses ready !"

Rod disappeared like a shot, and as I hurried into my

clothing Harry pulled himself together and in disjointed words told me what he knew ; while at intervals came the jarring sound of heavy guns that made me hasten action with excitement until I nearly lost my head.

He had been aroused by a messenger sent to alarm the country-side, and without taking time to catch and saddle his horse, which was loose in the field, had run from his house to ours. He had been told that a fleet had anchored off the mouth of the river and landed a large force near the lighthouse. They were advancing on Fort Trumbull. The inhabitants, with the exception of those who remained to defend the town, were flying to the woods, and that there seemed but little organized effort to stop the progress of the invaders. The last words of the messenger were to bring every man and arm available. Harry was equipped with all but the means of getting rapidly to the scene of action, and I had little wonder at his breathless condition. I managed to dress somehow, and strapping on my sword, into the belt of which I stuffed a brace of pistols,—the pair I had taken from Bromfield's luggage,—I made an armful of the rest of my weapons, got downstairs and ran for the barns. Both George and Rod were there and four horses were being saddled.

" De nags will be ready mighty quick," said George, as he hurried. " Ise goin' too, Mars Tony."

" You are a brave fellow," I replied. " You and Rod follow after us. You will find arms in the dining room. Bring the animals to the house."

It had been with a hope to get him to join us that I had gone to the barns. I knew that Rod could not be kept away, and with a last injunction to them to hasten, I hurried back to the house, where I found something of a scene taking place between Charlotte and Harry. The entrance of my father put a stop to a repetition of the parting of two years before, and an explanation of what had happened was again given.

During all this time the shots had sounded at regular intervals. There were always three guns, the signal of danger averted ; but the knowledge that the enemy was present made the signal of little importance to me, though it had a different effect on many others. Later there came a succession of irregular, heavy shots that told of a battle in progress, and it was afterward known that the enemy had become familiar with the arrangements for warning the people, and when two shots (for danger) were given from the fort, they fired another from the ships to disguise the import of the signal.

"You must be prepared to get to the woods," I said to my father, as I hastily filled my pockets with bread. "There is no knowing how far they will carry this raid ; to defend the house would be useless, so you had better be ready to leave at the first warning. If possible I will send back tidings of the state of affairs."

"Leave it to me to arrange for our safety," he answered, speaking without excitement. "I never felt my crippled condition more than at this time. It is for you I fear."

All was confusion. There was running to and fro, calling and tears, in the midst of which Aunt Freeman stood whipping her apron and wringing her hands, praying the Lord to save us all. In the excitement our two horses were brought to the door. After a quick leave-taking, Harry and I were in the saddle, and with the last words of my father to the effect that if perchance the house was threatened, they would go to a point in the forest indicated by a spring we all knew, we were off.

As we went through the barnyard, I saw the other two horses tethered at the gate, and knowing the negroes would soon follow, we urged our animals down the steep, stony hill, and once at the bottom, spurred them into full speed. On we flew through the tongue of the forest and over the moor, the heavy boom of cannon always in our ears. We met but two or three as we turned into the main road, but I accounted for it in our late start, and fancied the militia were already assembled.

As we tore past the squire's house I saw no sign of life, not even an open door, and with a fleeting thought of Dorothy still sleeping and unconscious of the tragedy hard by, we drove ahead. The little hope I had that the enemy might be held in check until a sufficient force had gathered to combat them, was dispelled as we approached the scene of the conflict ; for above the trees, and while we were still distant, could be seen clouds of smoke caused by the conflagration usually indulged in by the British before they began their open rapine and plunder.

When we neared the fort we dismounted, and, leading the horses some distance into the woods, tethered them, then cut across the open ground to the fortifications. There was not a sign of military preparation in sight, but several hundred men, women, and children were gathered on the high ground that made a point of vantage from which to view the drama then being enacted on the opposite side of the river.

The scene was exciting, for the British had compelled the evacuation of Fort Trumbull, and already had possession of New London, while from a number of ships and storehouses a great volume of smoke was rising, broken by the unchecked tongues of lurid flame. As yet the town itself had not been fired. Up the river some small vessels were flying to escape the range of the guns from ships, which for the most part had entered the mouth of the harbor and were anchored in plain sight. I counted fourteen vessels in all (though there were more outside), and saw at once that a crushing force had been sent against the town.

Near the edge of the river I could see small bands of red-coats running hither and thither through the streets, and once in a while a faint volley of musketry bespoke a skirmish back in the village.

We stopped not long to mark these sights, but proceeded

to the fort, as from the ramparts I concluded we could get as good a view, and at the same time be ready for instant call. Hardly had we entered the open gate, when Colonel Ledyard arrived from Fort Trumbull on the opposite side, bringing with him the handful of its defenders who had remained uncaptured in the flight across the river.

Fort Trumbull was little more than a breastwork closed only on three sides, and the weight of the British column that advanced upon the slight works was too threatening to be endured, so with a volley or two at the invaders, the guns were spiked and the band had retreated to the stronger defense of Fort Griswold.

So far the loss of life had not been great, though there was every indication of a bloody day. History only can serve me as to the events previous to my arrival on the ground, and to history the reader can refer, for it is my province to give my experience only, or such matters as bore directly on my fortunes. Beyond assisting in the defense of Fort Griswold I had no dream, and that I should have a personal interest in the fight, save as a unit in a force, I could not conceive. But the day had dawned that was to try my soul to the utmost, and held an interest that lay deeper than patriotism.

When we arrived at the fort the confusion of preparation (not of fright) was at its height. There were few cowards within those walls that day, I swear, and each one felt that the enemy would not allow the guns on Groton Heights to pass without attention.

Before I had gotten any information of what had occurred, the strength of the enemy, or their purpose and demands, the colonel entered the works. He was hot and flushed, but full of life, and gave his orders so clearly and directly that all forms of confusion at once ceased. Little or nothing of military regularity took its place, though the officers gathered around their leader and the men fell into something like order.

At this time, having resigned from the regular army, I was neither officer nor private, but simply a citizen who was lending his arm ; and feeling free to move, I questioned Colonel Gallup, who was standing on the outskirts of the group, and was informed by him of the great strength of the British; also of the startling news that they were land-ing a large force on the beach back of Pine Island and on the Groton side of the river. He was beside himself owing to the small force that had gathered to defend the fort, and observing that he had matters on his mind too weighty to admit of long conversation with me, I went to the gate to see if the negroes had yet arrived.

As I approached the sally-port, I was overtaken by an officer with the word that Colonel Ledyard wished me to report to him at once. As we retraced our steps toward the group I saw the colonel was talking rapidly and earnestly, pointing his speech with forcible gestures, while those about him silently listened. I caught no word of what he was saying, for as we came up, he abruptly ceased and turned toward us, the group opening as he took a step forward.

"Ah, doctor," he began, somewhat hurriedly, "are you here for service ?"

"Undoubtedly, colonel—but only to fight in the ranks. I now hold no commission."

"'Tis a small point on such a day, sir ! We are all in commission ! Perhaps your lack of an official one is for-tunate just now. You will do well. I wish a man of intelligence to carry a message to New London ; will you risk it—under a flag of truce?"

"Certainly, sir ! "

"Very good ! Go to my quarters—I will immediately join you."

I at once turned and obeyed, but had not been in the col-onel's room more than a minute when he hurriedly came in and, seating himself at his desk, began to write. His hand moved rapidly over the paper, then hastily dashing it with sand, he folded it and seemed to notice me for the first time since his entry, although he must have been aware of my presence, for he swung around and addressed me.

"Doctor, we seem to be in a hopeless position. New London is lost to us and the enemy in force will soon beset these works. I have in this letter made a proposal to the British commander, which if acted upon, will prevent a useless effusion of blood. Having obtained control of the town and cleared the river, Fort Griswold is as valueless to them as to us, but as a soldier I cannot tamely surrender it —nor will I. Who their leader may be I know not. You are to find him, deliver this, and return with an answer; but on no account reply to questions tending to gather information.

"I have selected you for this duty partly because holding no commission and unenlisted, you are supposed to be a non-combatant and are not liable to molestation, especially as you will carry a white flag; but principally because I know you as a young man of sense and equal to an emergency. I have nothing to add, except to say that unless the terms in this letter are complied with, the fort will be held and obstinately defended. Do you require anything further?"

"Nothing!" I replied.

"Then go, and good fortune follow you! It will be some hours before they can form to attack us from the south. By hurrying, you may save numberless lives. You had better go unarmed."

At this, he rose from his chair, and as nothing could be plainer than the instructions given me, I placed the letter in my pocket and hurried out.

CHAPTER XXXII.

FACE TO FACE WITH BENEDICT ARNOLD.

I FOUND Harry at the gate talking with George and Rod, who had just arrived, the former carrying my fowling-piece, the latter armed with my old pistols and his inevitable spear. I was comforted by the information that the family was already preparing the loose valuables for flight, and with the feeling of thankfulness for once that Dorothy was under the roof of a Tory, who would be unmolested in case the country was overrun by the enemy, I imparted the nature of my errand to my friend and, leaving my arms in his care, turned toward the river.

Avoiding the road and its longer route to the ferry, I made straight for the water's edge, crossing the open field in the rear of the low outwork with its two guns projecting through the grassy embrasures. I wondered that no provision had been made to man them or even to make them useless by spiking, but giving the matter no further thought, I plunged into the strip of shrubbery that grew along the river's edge.

As many had escaped from New London to Groton during the earlier hours, I had the idea that there would be a number of small boats abandoned along the shore, and this proved to be the case. Cutting a stick, I tied my handkerchief to it, and throwing it into the first boat that was handy, leaped aboard and was soon in mid-stream. The tide was at full flood and carried me up, as I desired. No other boat appeared on the river except down toward the enemy's fleet, where a number were passing between the ships and the shore. The heights of Groton looked peaceful enough, and but for the fort, with its fluttering flag breaking the sky line, and the crowds assembled on the hills, there was nothing to hint at what was taking place.

I was well aware I would not lack a reception on the opposite side, nor was I disappointed. As I drew near I heard shouting, and a shot was fired that struck in the water near me, and turning, I marked a number of red-coats who were making signals for me to approach them. Ceasing to row I lifted my white flag, fixing it in the bow, and pulled on, touching land at the foot of the main street. As I stepped ashore I was accosted by one who wore the uniform of a petty officer.

"So you cut and run for it, hey? but you were d——d lucky to get away with a whole skin. Were you in the fort yonder?"

"I am no deserter," I replied, picking up my flag and pulling the boat high on the land that the rising tide might not carry it away.

"What the devil are you here for, then? Are you after protection? Where do you live and what do you want?"

"I am under a flag of truce—as you see," I returned, "and bear word from Colonel Ledyard to your commander. Where can I find him?"

His only answer to this was a long stare and a shrug of the shoulders, but with something like respect he bade me follow him, which I did, the squad trailing behind without order. The town had not yet been fired, and except for the lack of familiar faces and the number of red-coated soldiers, there was little change in the appearance of the streets. In the distance I heard an occasional shot, but my attention was soon turned to a British officer who approached and halted us.

"Whom have we here?" he asked, after an interchange of salutes.

"Someone under a truce, who wants to get a word with

General Arnold in behalf of the rebel captain over the river."

"What is your business, sir?" said the officer, addressing me.

"As your sergeant stated—I bear a letter from Colonel Ledyard to the chief of your forces."

"Do you mean General Arnold?"

"What! Is it Arnold the traitor—Benedict Arnold?"

"You call him so, I presume, but you were wise if you curb your tongue, though you *do* come under the white flag. General Arnold leads us at present; he is in the tower of the church, surveying."

He spoke without temper or even ill-humor. I liked his face at once, and was well pleased when he ordered the sergeant to return to the river, saying he would take charge of me. For a moment I hesitated about going further or delivering the letter; for I was well satisfied that Colonel Ledyard would not have attempted any treaty with one who had placed himself beyond the pale of military recognition. I was about to so express myself, but quickly realized that my orders gave me no discretion in the matter, and therefore determined to fulfill my duty as it was laid down.

With a curt, "Come with me, sir!" we turned, and after a short walk, I found myself in front of the church, around the door of which were gathered a number of officers resplendent in gorgeous uniforms. I guessed it was the general's staff awaiting his descent from the tower, and presently there was a movement among them as three others emerged from the building.

For a moment I was uncertain as to which was the famous renegade, but soon picked him out by the formality and deference shown him.

My escort, asking me to remain at a distance, at once advanced to the group, speaking to another officer, who in turn went up to the commander and said something, pointing in my direction. A few words passed between them, and I was immediately beckoned to approach, when, stepping forward, I found myself face to face with the most colossal traitor of modern history.

He was a tall man, clad in the brilliant uniform of a brigadier-general. His face was strong and fine-looking, as faces go. The eyes were dark blue, and the complexion swarthy as though much exposure to weather had darkened it. Despite the regular features, his expression was not prepossessing, as the brow bore a scowl that looked to be habitual, and the mouth was too firmly set and sour. With a quick glance at me, he said :

" Who are you, sir ? "

" Dr. Anthony Gresham of Groton—late lieutenant of militia," I replied, with no notion of lowering myself to the level of a non-combatant on that day.

" You have a message from—from the fort across the river. What is it ? "

I gave him the letter, touching his hand as I did so, immediately stepping back a pace. He opened the paper, reading it with knitted·brows, and then asked sharply :

" What is your rank now, young man ? "

" I have none. I am but a volunteer for the time."

" Well, by G——d, gentleman ! " he said, with an angry rise of voice, and turning to those who had gathered around : " this is enough ! Here we have a simple civilian sent by the colonel of the fort, and through him, who is without rank or responsibility, we are expected to treat. Has he not enough brains or bravery among his officers, from whom to select a commissioned envoy ? " he asked, suddenly addressing me.

" He has plenty—and to spare," I answered, with considerable spirit ; " but doubtless thought he could better afford to lose a citizen than one of rank."

This was a clean blow at the dishonorable action of the British, who on several occasions had imprisoned messengers bearing flags of truce ; and it was recognized as such.

"Have a care, sir; have a care!" he repeated, in a warning voice. "Show less bravado." Then seeming to search
me through with a long, steady glance, which I as steadily
returned, he asked: "Can he make no better showing
across the river than he did here? Has he men enough
to work his guns? What is his force?"

"As for that," I replied bitterly, "the attack was as
unprepared for as it was unexpected, and who should
know the spirit of the people of Connecticut better than
yourself? I am only empowered to say that the fort will
be stubbornly defended in case of necessity; beyond this,
you can expect no information from me. I am simply acting as a messenger—not an envoy, and was ordered to
request an immediate answer."

"You shall have it, sir," he said suddenly. "Tell your
Colonel Ledyard that General Arnold, who commands His
Majesty's forces, now in possession of New London, refuses
to treat with him except in person or through officers of
rank. I consider his conduct an insult—though perhaps
not a deliberate one. Your ignorance in what you have
undertaken will protect you until you return." With this,
he swung on his heel, showing me his back; and calling
an aid, said: "They are strongly fortified. Send Major
Belcher to me; I wish to get word to Colonel Eyre."

As I stepped back, for I considered the interview as
over, he turned abruptly and said:

"You may tell your commander that if he will surrender unconditionally, he and his garrison will be treated as
prisoners of war. He can thus save the effusion of blood
he professes to dread—not otherwise." Then indicating by
a gesture the officer who had had me in charge, he concluded: "Take him off. Let him go the way he came."
It was my dismissal, and joining my guide, we moved away.

This was all I ever saw of Benedict Arnold—and it was
enough. That day saw him blotted from history.

With this safe conduct I had no difficulty in recrossing
20

the river without molestation, and within something less than three hours from the time I started on my mission, I again entered the fort. As I passed the gate I saw the little force had been considerably augmented, and besides, there were now many women and children, who, interested in the preparations, and desirous of being near their loved ones, were waiting for the moment when they must part. There was plenty of movement, and my eye took in the details of the scene as I hurried along in search of the colonel. Gabions were being filled, balls stacked, and ammunition distributed. I finally caught sight of Colonel Ledyard standing on the parapet, scanning the land to the south, while on the level below him were a number of officers. As I neared him, he motioned me to come up, and as I did so, he surprised me by saying :

" 'Twas a fruitless errand, doctor. You might have been saved your trouble, and I knew it as soon as you had left. I would never have asked for, nor made terms with, the enemy, had I been aware that Benedict Arnold was commander ; but I am greatly under obligation to you for the risk you took. What was your experience ? "

I made short work of my story, ending with the ultimatum given me, but to this he made no remark. Descending to the others, he said to an officer :

" Clear the fort of women and children, and stand a guard at the gate, ready for closing. Will there no more come ? "

This last remark was made in a general way to those near him, and was drawn out by the smallness of the force, which should have been at least three times as great. To a question which I did not hear, he answered :

" By the power of God ! we will do our best," and stepping to the embrasure he again mounted the parapet and looked toward the sea. I was standing on the banquette with my hand on a loaded cannon, and my eyes on New London, which had now begun to smoke from a number of points, when the colonel again addressed me :

" You can do yet another service, doctor. Take a man and spike yonder guns. We have no force to spare on them and 'tis too late to mount them here."

He indicated, by pointing, the outwork with its neglected cannon.

" May we work them for a round or two ? " I asked, a quick spirit leaping within me at the chance of firing the first shot.

" Use your judgment, doctor, only render them useless afterward and run no risk. We need every man, and certainly *your* services later "; and stepping down he was soon in earnest conversation with another messenger who came running up at that moment.

The number in the inclosure was rapidly thinning as I turned to find Harry and execute my order. Through the throng there was constant passing to and from the magazine, and over all there brooded a quiet like that of an approaching tempest, which was only broken by loud sobbings, the noise of children in distress, or the rattle of metal against metal.

Then for the first time it came forcibly upon me that this was war, and that I was standing on the edge of a precipice, the depth of which I could not fathom.

I cannot say that I was experiencing a feeling of fear, but it was something akin to it, though it did not hamper my determination to do my duty. I certainly had a quick longing for home ; a wish that the surrounding circumstances did not exist, or that I was safe at the other end of the impending trouble ; but to turn my back on the danger then had no place in my mind.

The necessity for action gave some relief to the nervous tightening in my throat, and I had little difficulty in pulling myself together, singling out Harry, imparting my instructions to him, and recovering my arms ; then together we proceeded to the little battery.

This had been built to prevent the landing of small boats,

and was known as the "water battery," as it lay nearer the stream than the fort itself; for when the works were constructed, its designers looked to an attack by land, and the outwork was afterward added. It was of no value unless backed by a strong force, which to-day it was impossible to collect. The weak defense was rank with grass that grew about the pyramids of balls and the carriages, and seemed to choke the movement of the guns themselves. In the quiet, hot sunshine it looked more like a green bank on which to lie and dream than a menace to an enemy.

As we deposited our rifles against the grassy slope, I found that we had been furnished with but one round of ammunition for each gun. I had called for two, which had been given me, but my companion had received none. Doubting the ability of two men to twice load and fire two guns in the face of an oncoming force, I was content enough, and with little trouble we rammed home the charges, lighted our matches, and waited.

On the other side of the river all opposition to the British had ceased, and wanton conflagration had begun. Beyond the crackling and falling of burning timbers and the roar of flames, which could be plainly heard, a holy calm seemed resting over the earth. The smoke from the consuming town sailed across the river in heavy, graceful masses. The grass bent under the west wind which spread wide the flag on the fort, and the sky was flecked with the light, fleecy clouds of a perfect day in the early fall.

On the hills hard by was still a crowd of people who were awaiting the scene of the onset at a safe distance, and, to their shame be it said, there were among them plenty of men who withheld their services that day, when they were most needed. On the top of Avery's Knoll were a number from the fort watching for the approach of the British, and on them, for the most part, I kept my anxious eyes.

CHAPTER XXXIII.

THE BATTLE OF GROTON HEIGHTS.

How the time passed I know not ; but I had gotten used to the suppressed excitement and felt quite calm ; a calmness soon to be dispelled. It was nearly noon, as I guessed by the sun, when I heard the first distant rattle of the drums of the oncoming British, and noted the hurried breaking up of the group on Avery's Knoll.

The enemy came on our sight shortly after; a mass of scarlet and glitter ; a solid, formidable body, which split by maneuvering into smaller columns, and finally deployed into what I supposed was a line of attack, and then there came a halt. They seemed great in numbers, but what we saw I guessed could not be all their strength, and my rising pulses kept me from fairly counting the odds against us, for my eye and brain were taken up in both admiration of their appearance and regularity of movement, and in watchfulness for our own safety. As yet, we had an open line of retreat to the fort, but as I lay against the bank, my head sheltered by the long grass through which I peered, I saw a detachment separate itself from the rest, and march as though to cross our range. It advanced at first almost parallel with the river, and I was wondering at its object when it suddenly wheeled and came up the hill on a run, in a manner that showed me at once they were attempting to get in our rear, while a body of others from the main line started pointblank for us. We had made no display of ourselves, and I think we were unnoticed, but the battery, which was in no way masked, was in full view and was no doubt the object of their attention. The time had come for quick action unless we were to fall into their hands, and springing into plain sight I cried to my companion :

"Now or never, Hal !   Are you ready ?"

"Aye !" was the hoarse reply.

From that instant I worked for myself, and in the excitement of the moment thought of naught but my own line of action.   Taking a fair sight, I stepped back and laid the match on the vent.

There was a roar as the gun leaped back, but not waiting to see the effect of this, the opening shot of the battle of Fort Griswold, I hastily inserted a spike into the vent, and with a cannon ball drove it home.

As I threw down the ball and grasped my rifle, I shouted :

"For your life, man—we must run for it !" and started at full speed.

I thought Harry had fired with me, but another report close in my rear showed me that he had delayed, and thinking that now he was just behind, I tore on, with my leg movement quickened by the sound of musket shots at my back.   The gate was open and I sprang through into the fort, and in an instant I heard the clang of its closing. Having no thought but that Harry had closely followed me, I ran to an embrasure to see what had been the result of the fire, and to my horror saw him running for the gate. He was something more than halfway to the fort, but already the red-coats held possession of the battery and were swarming in and over it as though surprised to find it empty, while a squad of half a dozen were in hot pursuit of the fugitive.   However, as they came nearly within musket shot of the fort, one after another stopped, though two of them knelt and fired at him before turning back.

Leaving my look-out, I ran to the gate to meet him, and for the first time realized that it was closed and Harry shut out.   It had been deserted as soon as securely fastened,

every soul having gone to the side facing the enemy, and
it was impossible for me to open the barrier alone, though
I heard my friend calling and knocking repeatedly. For
a few moments I tugged desperately at the beams that
barred the portal, but it was hopeless to think of moving
them without help, so with a yell to him to run for his life,
I scrambled to the parapet and looked over.

He was out of sight. My heart beat thickly enough
then as I thought that a musket ball might already have
found him and he had dropped. My anxiety was almost
instantly relieved as I saw him crawling from the eastern
end of the foss, or ditch, into which he had jumped to
shield himself, and in a moment he was out and running
across the open in front of the whole British force. Stooping like an Indian, he sped along with his rifle at trail, and
disappeared into a field of standing corn, the nearest
shelter.

Not a shot was fired as he ran, and my fear was turned
to thanksgiving. As he scrambled through the fence into
the field, and I realized that at least *he* was safe, I turned
around.

At my elevation I commanded the whole interior of the
fort, the enemy beyond, and the ships in the distance, and it
was with a sinking heart that I marked the littleness of our
force as compared with the array in front. There were
only between seven and eight score of men in the inclosure
at my feet, while facing them lay a host nearly a thousand
strong.

The inadequate means of defense, even had the fort
been fully manned, were too apparent. A number of
embrasures were empty of cannon and made a tempting
inlet if, in the assault, the enemy forced themselves as far
as the ditch. The only advantage that lay with us was in
point of position, or the advantage of fighting from behind
shelter as against fighting in an open field. Though I
knew naught of practical warfare, I felt a dread of the

result of this unequal balancing of forces, which was more than the common dread of death in battle.

The walls of Fort Griswold were ten feet high, and on the exterior slope were set closely a row of sharpened stakes projecting for twelve or fourteen feet, at an upward angle, over the foss that surrounded the works. The foss itself was ten feet deep and perhaps fifteen broad, so it was a formidable defense that held us, and might only be taken by swarming numbers against an inferior force. But this was just the condition that beset us, and I was weighing the probabilities when I heard my name called. Looking down, I beheld the squire's man, Matthew, climbing to the top of the gun near which I was standing. As he got within reaching distance he held a paper toward me, and said :

"Hi ! I have ye at last, docther. It's a divil of a hurry I've been in to find ye an' git this intil yer han's, an' the young mistress was in sore distriss that ye rade it to onct. Give me the good word to her,—av there be one,—an' I'll be gittin' out o' this."

So much I recollect hearing, the rest being lost in the tumult of my thoughts as I tore open and read the letter he handed up to me.

It ran thus :

ANTHONY :

Come to me at once. My uncle has known of the expected arrival of the British, and is to return to New York with the ships. I am to be carried off with them, a force coming here for us. I am locked in and cannot escape. The inclosed will give you the details of their intentions. It was given me when I was made a prisoner by my uncle. He has thrown off all disguise. I will try to get this to you through Matthew. Come to me, love ; come at once. You must use force. If I am taken from you by Bromfield, I shall die, for I know it will mean disgrace and ruin.

DOROTHY.

Out of the letter dropped another and larger one, which in a stupor I picked up and put in my pocket. But the stupor did not last. The blood rushed to my head and then out, and I was beset by a whirl of thoughts as I turned to Matthew.

"How—when—where did you get this?" I demanded.

"Arly this mornin', sor," said he, with exasperating slowness. "The lady dropped it from a windy an' 'Whisper' says she, 'Matthew, I'll make yer fortin if ye'll git this to the young docther beyant at onct.' I saw 'twas a quiet thing she was up to, an' wint to ye at home; but the auld naygur towld me ye was here, an' I've been on the lookout for ye intil now, so if ye have a word to say back, say it an' I'll be off."

"Where was the squire then?"

"Divil a bit o' me knows. It's killin' o' me he'll be, for he's that sick-lookin' an' quick wid his tongue, that I hate to cross him. He towld me he was afther goin' away."

"Aye, he is, Matthew—and will leave you in the lurch. Good God! What shall I do?" I cried, as the hopelessness of the situation dawned upon me. My first impulse was to cast myself from the parapet into the ditch and hasten to Dorothy's rescue. Even half reason told me there was yet time for that, as nothing would be done until the fort was reduced; but the following flash of thought showed me that I should lose honor,—perhaps life,—and that naught could justify desertion at such a time as this. My next idea was to get the note through Matthew to Harry, who was outside and free; but that also failed me, as there was no knowing the whereabouts of the latter, and the gates being shut, Matthew would never consent to the leap or the risk. I was beaten. Had I received the note an hour before, I could have slipped away and all might have been well; but now the enemy were preparing to storm us, the gate was closed and my presence had been marked.

I was penned in. In the unreasoning rage of my agony, I turned and cursed the messenger for his delay. He looked at me in stupid wonder for a moment, then, dropping from the gun, disappeared toward the entrance.

I was in an awful quandary. Something must be done, or I stood a chance of having seen my love for the last time ; but I took no action, for the tumult that stirred me showed no loop-hole out of my dilemma. I was brought to myself by Captain Halsey, who commanded me sharply to come down from my elevation.

As I stooped to descend, I noticed a British officer leave the lines, which had been spreading, and advance with a white flag. It gave me a glimmer of hope, as it meant a parley, and the outcome might set me free.

As I reached the ground I mechanically walked to where the colonel was standing, that I might be near when the result of the communication was made known, for an officer from the fort had been at once dispatched to meet the flag of truce.

I believe every man not an officer had found a position either at the guns or on the banquette, and there was the little hum of conversation that always follows a temporary relaxation of the strained senses.

My position of ex-officer and surgeon left me out of the strict laws that were holding just then, and no notice was apparently taken of my presence among those about Colonel Ledyard. The gate which had been opened for the officer who had gone forth was immediately closed and guarded, as much to prevent desertion as for any other reason. As I looked anxiously at it for his return, I saw Matthew and the guard in an excited altercation, the Irishman acting as though in a rage. Presently he came running toward me with tears in his eyes, crying in a whimpering tone :

"Wirrah, wirrah ! docther, they won't lit me out, an' 'tis a dead man I am if I bide here ! Howly Saints ! Why did I iver come to this place ? Till thim to open th' gate, doether. 'Tis not in the foight I am. They'll open fer ye, doether, dear."

" Cease your whining," I said, drawing him aside, " 'tis too late. You would be shot if you went out now. Show your pluck and fight. I fear that is all that is left us," I added, as the officer returned and the gate was once more securely fastened. He threw his arms over his head with a moan and staggered off, and I had too much on my heart to give him further notice.

I knew without asking that it was a summons to surrender, but the consultation was not a short one, and I drew away that I might not appear too forward. My heart was low enough, yet it beat hard with impatience, and half formed plans were whirling through my head, when I remembered the letter inclosed with Dorothy's. It might throw some light on the matter, and drawing it from my pocket, I read the following, which I copy from the original, having always retained it :

My Respected Friend :

The scheme in your letter, which has just reached me, is entirely impracticable. The quarry is too closely watched to permit of its being successful ; nor without undue violence to her, could she be removed without giving an alarm. Were it the last resort, as a desperate one it might be considered ; but I have another plan that is tolerably certain and probable future events make it of little risk. It has lately been determined to invade New London (the reasons not being necessary to explain here). On the night of Sept. fifth, the town will be attacked by a force that will make resistance of little account. The command will be given to Gen. Benedict Arnold, whose knowledge of your section, and whose spirit points him as best fitted for the undertaking. I have already obtained permission to be of the force that is to proceed against Ft. Griswold, which being surprised, will give but little opposition, and I can then turn my attention to you. At the first sound of the guns, if Miss Dorothy is still awake, place her where her escape will be impossible, and where she will be safe from rescue ; then prepare transportation for her sudden removal. If by chance you are interfered with by others, you are armed—do your duty and trust that His Majesty's forces, being at hand, will protect you. Up to that moment your best card is humility. I will shortly join you with a sufficient force to make her removal certain, and once free from the influence of her so-called lover—whom I trust I may meet face to face—I will see to it that she has weighty reasons for reversing her late determination.

I agree with you that your life will not be worth a skewer's value if you remain behind, and I have already completed arrangements for the removal of you and others of the loyal party who wish to accompany us back to New York. Dispose of your valuables as best you can, and be prepared to sail on the instant. We cannot miscarry, though the general outlook south is not bright. You will get this through the usual source.

B——.

I finished with a groan. It was a complete trap, and there had been no hitch, save for the night attack. The squire had played humility well, and I had been a fool. Dorothy was a prisoner, and the force was but waiting the termination of the battle to abduct her.

Still, one thing more might happen : Bromfield was on the field, and—by all the gods of mythology—he might be met with. There was a ray of hope besides this. Were the consultation to end in a decision to surrender, I might scale the walls, and before Bromfield and his squad could arrive at the squire's, I should have rescued Dorothy, and Heaven help the old man if he stood in my way.

On the other hand, if the colonel still determined to fight despite the odds against him (and knowing him, I had little doubt of it), I might meet the villain who was the cause of all my trouble.

I was not in doubt for many minutes after reading and returning the letter to my pocket. There was a movement that indicated decision, and immediately the colonel broke through the throng, and turning to speak so that all could hear, said :

"I will fight them, for I cannot do otherwise ; and, gentlemen, if it be decreed that to-day I lose my honor or my life, you who know me best know which it will be." *

It is fortunate for mankind that the deepest wounds and hardest blows cause the least immediate suffering. As I heard those words that killed all but a forlorn hope, cut me off from my love, and threw my life into hazard, I felt no sense of shrinking, nor was the agony as great as that which I had endured when I first realized the danger to Dorothy, and then it seemed as though there must be a way out of it.

My complete helplessness numbed me, yet let my wits work on the matters in hand. Somehow, the result of the conference was made known to the hosts outside, and somehow I found myself standing on the banquette (or raised step that enables one to fire over a parapet), with my cocked rifle in my hand. With an eager eye I tried to find the one man on whom my present trial hung, that I might single him out and shoot him dead; but the storming party was yet too distant. If we met, he or I would fall ; but the chances were great against such meeting, though I prayed that it might take place.

Men were beside me and men behind me, and now the attention of all was riveted on the red line that started slowly along its whole front, and advanced like an irresistible sea of blood. The order to us had been to hold fire until the word, and as the terrible line in front moved forward at an increasing pace, so did my past and future seem to slip away, and I lived only for the present moment. Danger came to me in a different form than when I was lying under the weight of the water that swept over me on the Long Sand Shoals, and also it came with a different effect. I forgot Dorothy, my father, Charlotte, home, and every-

* His own words.

thing, even death itself, in the fearful determination that was rising within me to stop that steady advance, though I did it alone. In five seconds more I should have pulled the trigger.

They had come to within two hundred feet of us, when like one man, they sprang into a run, and a terrible yell broke from them as they charged.

The battle of Groton Heights had begun. On they came, now resolved into a mass in which one could pick out individual faces, but the face I wanted was not there ; when, clear above the roar of voices rang the word "Fire ! "

There was a crash that jarred every fibre and a corresponding cry of defiance, and the line rolled up like burning paper. I saw men pitch headlong and lie till, while others stumbled over them to rise and fall, mayhap not to rise again. There was an indefinable din, and over it, down the breastworks and through the pall of smoke that blew in on us, came the cry of "Load ! load ! " for others, like myself, had forgotten all but the horrible sight before us.

I was immediately pulled back, and those in waiting sprang into the place of those who had fired. Running to an embrasure I saw through the opening a single spot on the field, where a group of officers were gathered around a fallen man, and ever and anon one would drop under the rifle shots from the fort ; and I rightly guessed that some-one high in rank had fallen, as he was picked up and carried to the rear. I now know it was Colonel Eyre, the commander of the assaulting forces.

The smoke, coming down like a curtain, put an end to further sight, and I loaded my gun with an eye to correctness, as we had been told of the danger of putting in the ball before the charge in the excitement of being under fire. There were cheers now, loud curses, and clinking of ramrods, but through it all was a steady fire from the ramparts. Nothing alive could have withstood the first blast of hell that broke from Fort Griswold that fatal noon, and when I got my head over the parapet, the red line had fallen away and out of range, but its advance was marked by a fringe of prostrate forms that lay still or rolled about in agony.

They had been repulsed. A deadly lull took the place of the pandemonium of a few moments before. It is to be presumed that our fire had been returned from the rear of the assaulting force as well as from the line in front; but to me the only sign of it was that the flag on the southwest corner of the bastion had been shot away by a cannon ball, for not a man within the fort had yet fallen.

Tears of excitement were rolling down my cheeks, and I was trembling like one with palsy. Nor was I alone in this weakness; for tears, blessings, handshaking, and hysterical laughter were on all sides.

The enemy had retired behind the shelter of Avery's Knoll, and for a time I vainly hoped that they were entirely defeated. But presently the cry arose: "They are coming! they are coming!" and it was soon seen that this time they had divided their forces and would attack us on three sides.

Instantly men were called away from the front to strengthen the hitherto undefended sides, and before I had fairly gotten a realizing sense of the new movement, they bore down on us and were met by a withering discharge. Unlike the other, however, our first fire was not re-enforced, and the crimson mass came to the ditch; not in a steady line, but in sections that had been less severely galled.

It was inhuman, the desperation that lit the faces below us. It was inhuman to fire into the crush of humanity that now made the ditch its object. But fine vapors were lost in the riot that took place as they gained the foss. A cry near me called my attention as I fired my rifle for the last time: "Men, men, they are on us!" Casting away my empty gun, I sprang to the rescue, and saw the broad, red faces of several Hessians appear above the level of the embrasure near which I had been stationed, and from which the cannon had been drawn to be reloaded. From the shoulders of those below they must have sprung, else they had scaling ladders which I had not marked, but I had hardly a glimpse before I was violently jostled aside by a man who jumped from behind me and into the breach. Uttering a wild yell he laid about him with a clubbed musket, and the embrasure was cleared in an instant, the Hessians cursing in their jargon as they fell backward, while the gun, again loaded, was run out. But cannon had become of no service against those in the ditch, though it sent death and defiance beyond it, and the hero who had cleared the opening seized a ball and hurled it onto the struggling crowd beneath. His example was immediately followed, and as he shouted : "To hell with the Dutchmen ! We have thim yet ! Hurroo !" he turned, and to my astonishment I recognized Matthew, the embodiment of the wild Irishman, fighting with a zest that has made his countrymen a terror in battle when their blood is up.

There was no attempt at military order now. It was fast becoming a hand to hand encounter. The foss was full of red-coats, and the fort was lost if they got a foothold within it. There was no time to reload. Every man was fighting for himself and in his own way. Following the lead of others, I picked up ball after ball, hurling them over the parapet onto the heads of those beneath, while I shouted like one in a frenzy of madness. They seemed to be clambering through every opening, and a dozen dead bodies of our own side now lay in the thickest of the fight. I had thrown eight or ten balls and then I lost my head. When I regained control of it I found I was struggling at an embrasure with the faithful Rod at my side. There were but three or four with us, and the opening was clogged by fallen men; a mass of yelling Hessians was below, scrambling to get up to us, for something had been thrown into the ditch to aid them in scaling the revetment.

For one instant we would clear the space, but the next would find it again full of faces. I saw an officer whose gold lace showed him to be a major, step to the level of the breach, calling on his men to follow as he snapped his pistol at me. The weapon failed to explode, and on the second, Rod ran him through the throat with his spear. Even in the excitement, I marked the keen blade come out the other side of his neck as he threw up his hands and pitched onto those below, but a maddened throng sprang into the place and I was forced or pulled back.

Cries, groans, and oaths in German and English were mingled with the clashing of steel. With sword in one hand and pistol in the other, I was trying to cut my way forward to where Rod was threatened by a man who had crawled to the crest of the embankment, but before I could get a footing to aim or strike, I saw the negro fall. On the instant, the fellow above had his head nearly severed from his body by a sword stroke.

It was horrible, but it did not seem so. The blood got into my brain again and I laid about me like a madman. It was a rough and tumble fight, and was probably compassed by seconds. In the midst of it, I remember firing a pistol in the face of a man who was about to bring his sword down on me. He was lying along and half over the cannon that served to block the way, the muzzle of my weapon being within six inches of his eyes as I pulled the trigger. He fell forward dead, but the heavy body bore me with it, carrying me off my feet and backward. Something struck me a violent blow across the eyes, a splitting crash on my head turned everything whirling in a crimson sky, and I knew no more.

21

CHAPTER XXXIV.

RETRIBUTIVE JUSTICE.

I COULD not have lain unconscious long, doubtless for a few moments only, but when I came to myself my eyes were full of blood and the body of the man I had shot lay across my chest with his face close to mine. Throwing him from me, I sat up weak and dizzy, but it took me only a little time to regain my strength and find I was not seriously injured. I had been stunned by the fall down the slope, my head coming in contact with a cannon ball at the bottom, while the brass basket-hilt of the dead man's sword had struck me in the face, lacerating my forehead, the blood from which was dripping into my eyes.

The fight had drifted away from me and was at the extreme end of the fort, leaving none but the dead and wounded near me. Taking off my coat I tore the sleeve from my shirt, and binding it about my head, got to my feet. As I did so, I marked four or five British soldiers run across the parade to the gate, and in a moment it was thrown open, a body of the enemy rushing in. The fort had fallen, and desperation seized me. If the man I was after could be found among the victors, I would find him. My sword was gone, but I had one undischarged pistol in my belt, his too, and with his own weapon I would kill him while the fight was on. After, it would be murder.

I drew the pistol and had reached the center of the parade, when Colonel Ledyard appeared, attended by two or three officers.

"Cease firing and surrender!" he shouted, as he ran. "Cease firing and stop this slaughter. The day is lost."

At that instant I saw Bromfield.

With sword in hand and face aflame, he broke through the crush at the gate and came running toward us, followed by some officers and half a dozen Hessians with bayonets at a charge. As they approached, Colonel Ledyard sheathed his sword and lifted his hands in token of surrender, as words could not be heard above the din.

At the other end of the parades shrieks and shots still continued, and men were being bayoneted while unarmed and with hands uplifted. I saw one poor fellow, chased across the upper parade, stabbed in the back by a red-coat just as Bromfield with those behind him drew near us.

"Who commands here?" he demanded ferociously, as the parties halted.

"We surrender, sir," answered the colonel.

"D——n you! Who commands here?" again demanded the major.

"I did, sir, but you do now," was the reply.

"Then give me your sword, you cursed rebel," he yelled, with the blackest look I ever saw on man.

"It is the fortune of war, sir, and I am willing to place it in your hands," said the colonel, drawing his sword and holding it out by the blade. "But let me first say that had it been demanded of me by the traitor who commands you, I would see it buried in my body before I surrendered it to him."

"You rebel dog! you will see it so," thundered Bromfield, as he shifted his own sword from his right hand to his left, and grasping the handle held toward him, he drew it back and plunged the blade into the breast of the gallant officer, then, loosening his hold, stepped back with a diabolical smile.

Colonel Ledyard fell forward without a sound, and the hilt of the sword striking the ground, drove the weapon clear through his body.

This dastardly act, against all precedent in civilized war-

fare, was the signal for massacre the like of which is un-
paralleled in history, but I knew little of that then.

At this deliberate murder (for it was nothing less) my
blood froze, and for a space I was powerless to move, while
even the British who had witnessed the deed remained
motionless as though astounded. But back came my power
with a rush, and stepping forward, I shouted :

"Now, for *you*, you black-hearted devil !"

He turned and saw me, recognizing me in spite of my
bloody countenance. Facing full at me, he parted his lips
over his teeth as in a snarl, and made a rush for me with
bitter hatred blazing in his eyes.

I let him come to within six feet of me, where I had him
fair, then raising the pistol I still held in my hand, I fired.

I did not see him fall, though I saw the sword drop from
his hand, and his knees bend as he pitched forward, but no
more, for I heard at my side the words : "*Gott verdammen
mich!*" and turned in time to see a burly Dutchman making
at me on a run.

His piece was evidently unloaded, for he came on the
charge, and was but a pace or two away when I hurled the
empty pistol at his broad face. The lock took him fairly
between the eyes, and dropping his musket with a howl, he
clapped both hands to his head, while I wheeled about and
fled.

Five minutes before, with my arm made powerless by
the surrender and the enemy victorious, I cared nothing
for life, but the act of Bromfield had changed the face of
matters, and the love of life was revived in me as I dashed
across the level toward the gate. I had started for the
gate instinctively, but had not gotten halfway there when
I saw it was useless to attempt escape in that direction, for
the way was blocked by the soldiers still surging in and
spreading as they entered.

The buildings in Fort Griswold were small and few, but
as I dashed along close to them, they screened me from the

eastern end, and thinking I might possibly have an opening at that point, I turned the corner of the magazine, but a glance showed me that quarter crammed with a struggling crowd which had penned in a number of the fort's late defenders and was in the midst of wholesale massacre.

To attempt to fly that way was suicidal. To turn and go back whence I came, and gain the comparative quiet of the south side, was to run into the arms of my pursuers. No time was left me to think. There was but one thing possible and that my last chance. Doubling around the colonel's quarters, I dove through the open door, slamming it behind me, and ran across the room to the window in the rear. The way lay clear before me, and as I leaped out, I heard the crash of the panels of the door as the red devils rushed in. They evidently jammed themselves in the casement and at first could neither follow nor fire. But I was soon shot at, for I heard the hiss of the bullets as they sped by me, which but served to quicken my pace, and on I flew.

The danger was still great ; for though no man could then catch me on a straight-away run, a shot might, or I might still be headed. So far I was uninjured, and I pointed myself toward the nearest embrasure, with the hope of springing through it and into the ditch. About the gun was a heap of bodies, and one man stood leaning against it bleeding in streams, but sank to the ground as I drew near.

Body and brain were working at full speed as I approached the spot, and my glance took in the details of what I saw ; details that burned so deep that I remember all and shudder as I write.

As I leaped up the slope I saw Amasa Rose with both hands to his throat, and between his fingers were squirting great jets of blood. Agony was on his face as he turned his eyes on me in mute appeal. Across his knees as he sat, lay the dead body of his brother, with his jaw torn away, and around him was a ghastly heap of slain—mostly

British ; but though I saw it all, 'twas no more than a second before I was on the parapet.

Again I was blocked. In front of me was a squad of marching red-coats ; to go down there meant death—and death lay behind me. Turning to the left before they fairly saw me, or a gun could be brought to bear, I sped along the level top of the parapet toward its eastern end.

Now I thanked God, as never before, for the strength he had put into my legs, for I minded me of the fearful leap ahead. At the point where I must now jump the stakes were set close, rising above the edge, and the ditch was wide and far beneath. It was a leap of at least four feet upward, twenty outward, and fifteen down, and I gathered myself for the spring, where a fall meant for me the end of all things.

It was none too long a start,—a hundred feet, perhaps,— and, with a wild feeling coursing through me, I rushed at it, came to the brink, and launched myself into the air.

I never met but one man who saw that leap (and he, Harry), and he told me that I cleared the stakes like a bird, striking fairly with both feet on the counterscarp, or opposite side of the ditch, and then disappeared into it. I think likely ; for I mind me of landing on its edge, but the earth was soft and broken in and gave beneath me, letting me roll to the bottom. I know I struck bottom on my side, falling across my sword scabbard, which I still wore, breaking the metal in two. As it was, nothing more important was broken, and I scrambled to my feet, somewhat shaken by the shock of the jump and the fall, but not really injured.

I was a little winded, but there was no time to rest and recover. Fearing to climb out where I had gone down, I ran along the bottom of the ditch, leaping the dead bodies that lay in my way, to the spot where Harry had clambered up. There was shouting above me as though I had been marked ; shrieks for mercy, and curses, that showed the bloody work was still going on ; but the stakes over me, where they had not been torn away, protected me somewhat and I reached the end unmolested, crawling up to the level ground of the field.

My first glance showed me that I was far from safe, for I was at once seen. There were scattered groups of soldiers moving irregularly toward the gate, and a number among them raised a shout as I appeared from below. I noticed one near me making ready to fire, and as he did so, I threw myself on the ground, the shot going harmlessly over me ; then knowing I was lost if I lay there (for I was not two rods from the parapet and presented an easy mark), I jumped to my feet. But one man, whom I had not seen before, was running along the edge of the ditch behind me, and as I looked around I saw him,—a fine athletic figure, but hampered with gun and trappings,— coming at full speed. As I turned and ran again, he stopped and fired, the ball striking a little ahead of me, as I saw by the puff of dry earth that spurted up. He then threw down his gun, making after me, and it became a race for life. Not another shot was fired by the rest as they watched the upshot of the coursing.

The run was a long one, and though I had fifty feet the start of him, I was out of breath and my legs dragged horribly, as they will in a dream when all power seems abortive. The only possible point of safety was the corn field ahead. Weakened by exertion, excitement, and loss of blood, I was no match for the man behind me in my present condition ; for as I flung a glance over my shoulder I saw him gaining on me. My limbs grew numb and I was rapidly becoming breathless, nevertheless, there might yet be time to gain the wilderness of standing stalks and there be lost to him. With this last hope I put all my remaining strength into a final burst of speed.

I was well-nigh spent, but the fence was close at hand, when my foot missed and I stumbled and fell. I half raised myself to meet him, and could hear his heavy panting as he was about to cast himself upon me, when out from the corn came a flash and a report. Simultaneously with the shot my pursuer doubled up and pitched forward onto me, knocking me flat; the shock driving the last of the wind out of my body.

I have only an indistinct recollection of the minutes that followed; a misty memory of being dragged through the fence rails and falling, but when I had recovered my breath and senses I was lying on the ground with the corn all about, and Harry was standing by me loading his rifle and looking anxiously around, while praying me to pull myself together. I got to my feet at once as the whole thing came back to me, and though partly dazed, I realized the narrowness of my escape.

"Thank God for that shot! Was it you, Harry?" I panted. "Where did you come from?"

"Aye, 'twas no other, and I have been here the whole time, a witness to all the bloody business. I saw you from the minute you got atop of the works; and thank the Almighty! you ran this way else you had no chance. I felt safe for you when you drew that fellow within shot. Come, let us get out; they may fire the field and burn us. Are you hurt, Tony? You look as though just out of the shambles."

"Aye, I will," said I, as I felt my breath coming sound again, "and we have work yet to do. As for me, I am unhurt, but I humbly give thanks that I have gotten out of that hell with no more than a mark on my forehead. 'Tis a modern miracle. We have both been delivered to be the instruments for foiling the devil this day."

I then told him of the message from Dorothy, the murder of Colonel Ledyard, and how I had shot Bromfield.

"Pray God you have killed him!" he exclaimed, when I had finished and we were pushing through the rows of corn ; "but perhaps his orders have been given, and the kidnaping will still go forward."

" 'Tis the one thing I fear ; but they will move quickly to get the better of us, for we have horses, so they be where we left them."

And leaning heavily on him, for my knees shook and had little strength, we, keeping in the shelter of the corn, made our way to the woods. Like a baby I depended on him now, for a child might have taken me single-handed, so exhausted I was; but our way proved clear, and we found the horses whisking their tails violently at the flies ; nagging and stamping at being left so long without food.

By the end of the walk I felt I had regained something of my strength, though I was still shaky ; but I had tasted neither food nor water since the night before, and the strain under which I had been might well have sapped a stronger frame than mine.

There was a spring hard by, and while Hal cared for the animals, I drank deeply of its sweet water and washed some of the blood from my face and hands, though I dared not shift the bandage on my head. I had no mind to appear suddenly before Dorothy looking like a butcher, or worse, like one butchered, and thought the sight of me, hatless and coatless, in a torn and bloody shirt and with a bound-up head, would be shock enough without being plastered with the gore of another man. Therefore I took the time, though time was precious, resolving that the horses should amend the loss.

I had no arms, so Harry gave me his pistol, loaded and primed ; but for the matter of that, I would have bearded the squire, empty-handed and alone, though he was armed to the teeth. If fears had beset me on other occasions, I had none on this, and I wish I felt as certain of happiness in the world beyond as I felt certain of bringing the old villain to book within the hour, were he never so lusty.

My strained muscles knit up of themselves when I was

once more in the saddle and the weight of my body off my
knees, and there was a fierce joy in me as we turned into
the road and set the horses going.

Smoke was all about us, for a change of wind had
swung it low. Not a soul was in sight, for all who could
flee had long since fled. I gave no thought to those I had
left behind—they were past praying for ; all of moment to
me lay in the next sixty minutes, while beyond were visions
of home and Dorothy. Then let what might, come after ;
but I felt that God had not carried me thus far unscathed
through the fiery furnace, to withdraw His hand just as
coolness and hope and almost certainty were before me.

The way we tore along was almost a cruelty, but the
horses, with their noses set toward home and fodder, and
their lean bellies, made urging hardly necessary ; but
that they got, and had anyone seen us (for there might
have been some peeping eye in the woods on the watch
for red-coats), no doubt they would have thought that
nothing short of being chased by the whole British army,
freshly mounted, could have made men ride like that.

Faster than the smoke we sped, and got into clear air,
and when we came to the squire's we entered the home-
lot with a rush, reining up with a jerk that made the
animals slide. Before the door stood two horses, one
saddled, the other put to the chaise—and well I knew
their import; but they were a fair sign, as it proved we
were not too late.

We were out of saddle and at the door in a twinkling ;
though quick as we were, the squire was quicker, for he
had seen us coming, doubtless looking for men with clothes
of another color. He opened only the top half of the door,
showing little more than his head and shoulders, but he
was eating no humble pie just then. His usually white
face was red, and his voice had lost its late smoothness as
he shouted :

"Be off, you villains, be off ! 'Tis my turn now, you

upstart," he said, addressing me. "Be off, else you are lost; the tables are turned and my friends are on the road. Be off now, while you've time! I have the charity to warn you. Your bird has flown. Did you think in your folly I would let her mate with one of your breed? Leave on the instant, or by Saint George! I will settle scores now."

"Settle and be d——d!" I cried, as I put my hand in to unfasten the lower half of the door.

At this he stepped aside and, picking up a gun that was leaning against the wall, said in a threatening tone:

"Beware! I am armed, and will do my duty in the king's name."

Before he had fairly finished his threat the door flew inward from the pressure of Hal's knee as I slid the bolt, and jumping ahead of me, he grasped the muzzle of the squire's weapon before he could shoulder it, and held it aloft while I quickly slipped my arms about the old man, tripped him up, and threw him sharply to the floor, where I held him.

"Now, Hal, cut me a bed-cord and we will bind this villain before we do aught else."

Without answering, he put down his rifle and drawing a knife ran up the stairs.

"You'll suffer for this, you rebel scoundrel!" yelled the squire, as he twisted in his efforts to throw me; for I sat astride him as I would a horse. "By all the furies! you are lost! Will they not hurry? Let me up, I say."

"Never! There is no hurry in them, and no hurry for me. If you pray for hurry it will bring your own end the sooner. Look you, you hoary sinner!" I continued, as he squirmed under me, yelling for help, while I poured forth upon him all my pent-up spleen. "Look you—and stop your noise, else I'll jam the major's letter down your throat. Listen to me, you ancient liar! I have your vile plan at my tongue's end, and less than an hour ago I shot

that devil Bromfield—your master ; shot him dead. Do
you hear? And he lies, toes up, on the parade at Fort
Griswold.   God be thanked ! there is one black heart the
less on earth, and 'twill soon be joined by another."

For though I had no notion of killing him, I was willing
he should think it was my intention ; and as for Bromfield being dead, I was not so sure about it.

At that, he gave a mighty shout and lay still, looking at
me with widely distended eyes.

Just then I heard a great overthrow of furniture upstairs, and Harry came running down with a length of
bed-cord.

"Who sleeps in that bed to-night, sleeps low," he said
with a laugh as he handed me the cord and we proceeded
to bind the old man hand and foot. When we got him
well fastened we laid him on the settle in the kitchen with
a roll of rag carpet under his head, and then together went
in search of Dorothy.

There was nothing living in any of the rooms or closets
on the floor above, and I was beginning to have fearful
misgivings that the squire had not lied to me about her
having flown, when I thought of the garret. The door
leading to it was locked or bolted, I knew not which, but
the fact gave me hope.   Placing my ear against it, I
motioned for Hal to be quiet, and then in the stillness I
heard a muffled cry which I would have known in another
world.   With no feeling of weakness left in me, I rushed
to the hall (for we were in a little room off it) and, seizing
a heavy mahogany chair, I went back and with one blow
shivered chair and panel into pieces.   Two or three blows
with what remained in my hands opened the whole affair
and we bounded upstairs.

There in the dim light, against the smoke-house door,
stood the spinster aunt with her back to it, and her arms
stretched widely out, as though to prevent entry or egress.

Like one crucified, she looked,—or as Hal afterward said,

"more like a strange sort of gigantic, black bug pinned to the wood."

"You cannot enter, sir," she said slowly and evenly, as though it was an every-day affair ; "you *dare* not lay hands on a woman ! "

"*Cannot* and *dare* are large words, madam," said I, as I took one thin arm and Harry the other, and drew her away, her resistance being much like picking up a light thing when you think it is going to be heavy, she moved off so easily.

It took but a second to draw the catch and open the door, and the next moment I had my darling in my arms, weeping as though her poor, bruised heart would break.

CHAPTER XXXV.

CONCLUSION.

THERE was no time to lose, for I feared that a party of the victorious enemy might be on the march to complete the programme laid out by Bromfield; therefore I hurried my love away and down the stairs.

As we reached the light, Dorothy turned, and seeing the plight I was in, gave a shriek as she held me off and looked at me; then woman-like, threw herself into my arms again, crying out that I was killed; to which I answered, I was not—nor likely to be by the look of things.

"What about the old witch?" asked Harry, as we reached the hall. "She may set the squire free and raise the devil."

"Lock her in and let her think," I answered; so we closed the door of the little room at the foot of the garret stairs, piling a mass of furniture against it, as there was no fastening, and hurried away.

"We'll not wait to bid your uncle good-by," said I to Dorothy, as we reached the lower hall. "He has a pressing engagement just now, and is under bonds to keep the peace; so let's be off at once."

When we left the house, not greatly to my surprise both our horses were found to be gone. The knowledge that they had probably run straight home and would appear with empty saddles made me in unusual haste to follow, as I knew what consternation the sight would create. However, the squire's two horses were there, so telling Hal to take the saddled one and ride ahead to announce our coming, I placed Dorothy in the chaise without hat or mantle as she was, and drove after him.

It was a good animal I had, and well used to harness, so off we bowled ; I, with my brain playing on the chances of being followed and having our house burned about our ears if the red-coats came and unloosed the squire, and Dorothy, with moisture in her sweet, brown eyes and traces of dried tears over her smooth cheeks, holding onto me as though to be sure I was real.

In the wide privacy of the moor I bent and kissed her a dozen times, trying to make firm the little, trembling under lip, telling her that from then on, nothing should part us again, and that nothing was before us but life and light and love.

I have had many a drive since that day, but none in which the bitter and sweet were so closely mingled in my heart as on that quiet afternoon. Now no sound of warfare jarred the air, and there was nothing about to suggest the inferno lying so near us, excepting, perhaps, my own appearance.

The effect of the beauty of the land about, and the still river; the nodding of the dusty growth by the wayside, the sweep of the moor and the yet lusty green of the woods, the starting of birds, their quick, clear notes, and the play of the slanting sunlight, was like the relief of waking from delirium.

That was the bright side of the picture, made the more brilliant by the girl so close to me. The shadows lay behind, and from them I tried to turn.

Ere long Dorothy got heart to tell me her story of the day. It was one of brutality and mental agony. Knowing that I must be at the fort, each sound of cannon shook her, and as the day wore on without my coming she had given me up as lost. She had been told a dozen times that I was dead, and was locked in her room until the squire sighted us in the distance, when she had been taken to the smoke-room, to give color to the report that she had gone.

Had the old fool kept his horses in the barn and allowed

me free access to the house, or removed Dorothy therefrom, he might have beaten me for a time, but he doubtless had perfect faith in the coming of Bromfield, and had not the kind of wit that provides for the "slip 'twixt the cup and the lip."

However, I had her now, but told her nothing of the day (not wishing to give her more of a shock) except that I had shot Bromfield, so that she might have nothing to fear from him.

When we passed Farmer Bailey's house, every door and window stood wide open, as if to proclaim its emptiness, and little doubting that they had gone to Hardscrabble, I urged the horse along.

It was a brave home-coming that, for everyone had gathered at the gate to meet us, with more tears and excitement than I cared to have. There was too much talk, inasmuch as the end might not have yet come, and I wanted to put things in shape to meet the worst, should it happen.

Bailey's parents were there (as I had surmised), and the joy of all, except the negroes, was unalloyed. At the foot of the "Ratlines," as I always called the road leading up the heights (the name suggested by old Moon on the night of his first arrival), we were met by Uncle Freeman, who had a large interrogation point in his bleary eyes, but I knew the heart-ache in store for him, and only shook my head when he asked for his boys, for of George I knew nothing and Rod I could not swear was dead, though I had small hopes of aught else.

Now from the elevation of Hardscrabble we could see the smoke of New London, but none of us might guess what was taking place beneath it. It was a fearful thing to know that the old town was destroyed, and both sides of the river in the hands of the red-coats. There was not much to do at home, for the plate and smaller valuables, with what ready money the house had contained, were buried under a muck heap in the barnyard, and all the cattle and horses were turned loose in the forest, save such of the latter as were needed to transport the family in case of necessity. I think there was more thanksgiving at our safe return than mourning over the disasters in town, which was natural, perhaps, for every heart knoweth its own joy as well as sorrow.

I know the first thing I did, after being caressed like a schoolboy, was to demand food and regulate my wound, which was a nasty one, though not serious or even very painful; then we put a look-out in the orchard and called a council of war.

I was forced to make a short story of the attack on the fort and what had come under my observation therein, saving of course, the fall of Rod, for I could not bear the eye of Aunt Freeman. At last it was decided that Uncle Freeman should go to the battle-field and find out what he could. It was a wise decision, for he doubtless would have gone, with or without permission, and afoot if need be, for both the old couple and Nance were getting beyond their own control through fear and suspense.

I felt that there would be little danger for the old man, believing his saying: "Deys nebber teeh a ol' niggah like me. Deys see I's mos' daid an' aint got no harm in me." And so he went, taking the chaise too, because it appeared more peaceful, and he might need it to fetch home his sons.

Though they made a hero of me, and Dorothy was petted to the last degree, it was my father, crippled as he was, upon whom we all leaned and to whom we all looked for advice. He spoke calmly, never for an instant losing control of himself, though fears still beset him that worse than had yet happened might be in store for us.

All that afternoon a watch was kept from the orchard, which overlooked the road for half a mile, and another on the wall that commanded the sea, then, as it drew near
22

sunset, nothing having been seen of Uncle Freeman and there having been no alarm, we made arrangements for the night.

It was decided that Harry was to go down the road as far as his own house, I was to approach him only near enough to be within sound of his rifle, and his father should be the same distance behind me, while Charlotte, Dorothy, and Nance should mount guard in the orchard within earshot of Farmer Bailey's gun. This arrangement was to continue during the night, the girls changing their watch as suited themselves. Thus we had a chain extending nearly two miles, and if the enemy approached by land, as they probably would if at all, the signal would be passed to the house in time to enable my father and the women to escape, and then all would break to the agreed upon rendezvous in the forest. I had no gun, and a pistol might not make noise enough, so I armed myself with the dinner horn, and we sallied forth.

There is little to say of that night. It was a fine, moonless one, with hardly a breath of wind, and a heavy dew. I dared not sit—though much I needed rest—for fear of the sleep that might overcome me, and it lay heavily on my eyelids even as I walked the beat of two hundred feet that I had selected. The hours dragged by in a complexity of physical misery and mental happiness, the chill of early morning becoming penetrating as the sun gave the first hints of its coming. While it was still dark, though there was a livid look to the sky in the east, I heard the clatter of the chaise, the music of which I knew as I knew my own voice, and presently it came up, and I was hailed by Harry, who was in it with a woman from New London. She had been sent for me and bore news. The British were gone. They had sailed away just after sunset the evening before, thus making our long night's vigil unnecessary, had we but known it. There had been no certainty of finding me, as I was known to have been in the fight, but the old negro had told of my escape, and now my services as a surgeon were required.

We hastened back to the house, relieving the sleepy fears of all by the news we brought, and then Harry and I saddled up again, starting once more for the town, but this time freighted with my instruments instead of arms.

I think I slept in my saddle, only coming to myself when we crossed the Mystic bridge near the squire's, and then methought I would see if he had been released. The heavens were broad with light when we arrived there, and the house looked as when we left it, with the doors still open. The gun which had been wrested from the old man's hands lay where it had fallen, and, believing that no one had been there, I advanced boldly into the kitchen.

The squire still lay on the hard settle, bound as we had left him, and I thought him asleep until I found he was unconscious from another cause, and knew that he had reaped the harvest of fear, chagrin, and his own intemperate brain. He was alive, but paralyzed, as was shown by the down-pull of one side of his face, and his insensibility to pain when prodded with a fork—the only instrument that stood handy.

There was a duty to be done here, and we carried him upstairs. The old lady, hearing footsteps, called loudly for help from behind her prison door. We released her, placing her brother in her charge after unbinding and putting him in his bed. I gave her no hope of his life, and no explanation of what had occurred between us; barely speaking to her directly, in fact, so great was my resentment toward her. In as few words as possible I gave her to understand that I should come or send for the effects of her niece, and that later I would give the paralytic what attention I could; though I foresaw he would ere long need nothing but decent burial.

I cannot go into the details of that day. My indigna-

tion, my abounding wrath, swallowed up the horrors of
them then, but now the horror stands paramount.

New London was still smoking when we got to the
fort, and the dead lay thickly scattered within the ruined
inclosure. The wail of women and children was heard
before we reached it; a wail that must have shaken the
heavens and made the angels weep. The enemy had done
their work in a way that made the efforts of those in my
profession well-nigh useless. There had been a semblance
of war in the beginning, but it had ended in murder, and
they had even shown their spite on the dead.

History tells of the brutality of the British; of the load
of wounded men piled into a wagon, like logs, and rushed
down the hill toward the river; of the hellish ingenuity
displayed in cutting off the water supply; in the wanton
destruction of private property, the outrages perpetrated
on defenseless women, and in mutilation by the sword after
the bullet and bayonet had done their work. Of the one
hundred and odd souls that had manned the fort in the
morning, over eighty had been mercilessly butchered after
the surrender. There were but few prisoners, and fewer
escapes. Perhaps a dozen or fifteen had died in fair
fight—not more; the rest fell in a manner to make the
descent on New London forever a shame to its perpe-
trators.

It has been urged in extenuation that the leader of this
famous raid (which utterly failed in its main purpose)
was an American renegade; that the sword that killed
Colonel Ledyard was surrendered to an American, and that
the force behind them was made up of men not English in
any sentiment—a foreign element for whose actions the
English nation was not accountable.

I grant the facts, but in return: the artisan knows the
use and character of his tools; the executioner feels the
edge of his ax; the bullet flies where it is sent, and it was
not the crucifix and spikes that were responsible for the

sufferings of our Saviour. There is no palliation of the monstrous deed in the fact that Benedict Arnold dragged out a long life of remorse and poverty in a strange land, or that Bromfield met with his deserts. As the dregs of a nation sink, the scum rises to the top, and it is a striking commentary on the authorities of the times that they hastened to make use of the latter.

.   .   .   .   .

My story has drawn its length. With the drifting away of the smoke of the battle there had drifted away the adverse fate that had hung over me so long and threateningly—making my tale worth the telling.

With the rising sun was rising an era of peace, though I knew it not ; peace for both my country and the remainder of my days, and little now remains to relate.

George was killed—killed in a dozen places, I might say ; and Matthew (over whose mutilated body I asked forgiveness for my unreasonable outburst) was hacked almost apart. Rod was found fearfully wounded, but recovered and lived to be the progenitor of what bids fair to be a long line of dusky Freemans. Strangely enough, the coat I had taken off in order to tear out my shirt sleeve for the purpose of binding up my head, lay undisturbed just where I had dropped it near him, with the papers in its pockets all intact.

Whether or not my shot proved fatal to Bromfield I can only surmise, for from then till now I never heard of him. His ally, the squire, lived but two days after his stroke, and almost immediately his sister quit our section and disappeared.

But all that seems long ago and I hasten over it, for the days darken as they pass, like the shadow that falls on the zenith and follows the sun as it drops away.

The tumult, or the result of it, kept my darling from my arms but little longer, for when the news of Yorktown came to us in October, and we knew the war was over, we were married—quietly, as became us in the great sorrow around ; and it was a double wedding, for Charlotte and Harry joined hands at the same time.

My father—God bless his memory !—lived to enjoy the childhood of his grandchildren, and to be their adviser in youth. Never failing in resource and wisdom, he stood among us all until the great weight of his years broke him, and he passed away, dying of no disease.

And the dear face that still lies close to mine, bears yet the sweetness of girlhood, though no eye but mine can see it, and we still love—ah, you with hope and passion and youth yet with you—not with a chill in the love because, forsooth, it is the love of age, but one so closely welded that it will always abide ; even until the last trumpet sounds and the heavens roll together like a scroll.

THE END.

APPLETONS' TOWN AND COUNTRY LIBRARY.

PUBLISHED SEMIMONTHLY.

Each, 12mo, paper cover, 50 cents; cloth, $1.00.

For sale by all booksellers; or sent by mail on receipt of price by the publishers.

New York: D. APPLETON & CO., 72 Fifth Avenue.

S. R. CROCKETT'S LATEST BOOKS.

UNIFORM EDITION. EACH, 12MO. CLOTH, $1.50.

BOG-MYRTLE AND PEAT.

"Here are idyls, epics, dramas of human life, written in words that thrill and burn. . . . Each is a poem that has an immortal flavor. They are fragments of the author's early dreams, too bright, too gorgeous, too full of the blood of rubies and the life of diamonds to be caught and held palpitating in expression's grasp."—*Boston Courier.*

"Contains some of the most dramatic pieces Mr. Crockett has yet written, and in these picturesque sketches he is altogether delightful. . . . The volume is well worth reading—all of it." –*Philadelphia Press.*

"Hardly a sketch among them all that will not afford pleasure to the reader for its genial humor, artistic local coloring, and admirable portrayal of character."—*Boston Home Journal.*

"One dips into the book anywhere and reads on and on, fascinated by the writer's charm of manner."—*Minneapolis Tribune.*

"These stories are lively and vigorous, and have many touches of human nature in them—such touches as we are used to from having read ' The Stickit Minister ' and ' The Lilac Sunbonnet.'"–*New Haven Register.*

" ' Bog-Myrtle and Peat ' contains stories which could only have been written by a man of genius."—*London Chronicle.*

THE LILAC SUNBONNET. *A Love Story.*

"A love story pure and simple, one of the old-fashioned, wholesome, sunshiny kind, with a pure-minded, sound-hearted hero, and a heroine who is merely a good and beautiful woman; and if any other love story half so sweet has been written this year, it has escaped our notice." –*New York Times.*

"A solid novel with an old-time flavor, as refreshing when compared to the average modern story as is a whiff of air from the hills to one just come from a hothouse."—*Boston Beacon.*

"The general conception of the story, the motive of which is the growth of love between the young chief and heroine, is delineated with a sweetness and a freshness, a naturalness and a certainty, which places 'The Lilac Sunbonnet' among the best stories of the time "—*New York Mail and Express.*

"In its own line this little love story can hardly be excelled. It is a pastoral, an idyl -the story of love and courtship and marriage of a fine young man and a lovely girl no more. But it is told in so thoroughly delightful a manner, with such playful humor, such delicate fancy, such true and sympathetic feeling, that nothing more could be desired." *Boston Traveller.*

"A charming love story, redolent of the banks and braes and lochs and pines, healthy to the core, the love that God made for man and woman's first glimpse of paradise, and a constant reminder of it." –*San Francisco Call.*

New York: D. APPLETON & CO., 72 Fifth Avenue.

A STREET IN SUBURBIA. By EDWIN PUGH. 12mo. Cloth, $1.00.

"Simplicity of style, strength, and delicacy of character study will mark this book as one of the most significant of the year."—*New York Press.*

"Thoroughly entertaining, and more - it shows traces of a creative genius something akin to Dickens."—*Boston Traveller.*

"In many respects the best of all the books of lighter literature brought out this season."—*Providence News.*

"A clever series of character sketches."—*Elmira Telegram.*

"Rippling over from end to end with fun and humor."—*London Academy.*

MAJESTY. A Novel. By LOUIS COUPERUS. Translated by A. TEIXEIRA DE METTOS and ERNEST DOWSON. 12mo. Cloth, $1.00.

"No novelist whom we can call to mind has ever given the world such a masterpiece of royal portraiture as Louis Couperus's striking romance entitled 'Majesty.'"—*Philadelphia Record.*

"A very powerful and cleverly written romance."—*New York Times.*

"There is not an uninteresting page in the book, and it ought to be read by all who desire to keep in line with the best that is published in modern fiction."—*Buffalo Commercial.*

THE NEW MOON. By C. E. RAIMOND, author of "George Mandeville's Husband," etc. 12mo. Cloth, $1.00.

"A delicate pathos makes itself felt as the narrative progresses, whose cadences fall on the spirit's consciousness with a sweet and soothing influence not to be measured in words."—*Boston Courier.*

"One of the most impressive of recent works of fiction, both for its matter and especially for its presentation."—*Milwaukee Journal.*

"The story is most graphically told, the characters are admirably drawn, and the moral of the whole thing is very desirable as inculcating an important lesson."—*Chicago Journal.*

"A surprisingly clever book in its way, being direct and simple, and true on every page to the author's purpose."—*New York Times.*

THE WISH. A Novel. By HERMANN SUDERMANN. With a Biographical Introduction by ELIZABETH LEE. 12mo. Cloth, $1.00.

"Contains some superb specimens of original thought."—*New York World.*

"The style is direct and incisive, and holds the unflagging attention of the reader."—*Boston Journal.*

"A powerful story, very simple, very direct."—*Chicago Evening Post.*

New York: D. APPLETON & CO., 72 Fifth Avenue.

By A. CONAN DOYLE.

THE STARK MUNRO LETTERS. Being a Series of Twelve Letters written by J. STARK MUNRO, M. B., to his friend and former fellow-student, Herbert Swanborough, of Lowell, Massachusetts, during the years 1881–1884. Illustrated. 12mo. Buckram, $1.50.

This original and dramatic story presents fresh types, extraordinary situations, and novel suggestions with a freshness and vigor which show that the romancer's heart was in his work. How far certain incidents of the story are based upon personal experiences it is impossible to say, but the unflagging interest and unexpected phases of the romance are no less in evidence than the close personal relations established between author and reader. In the "Stark Munro Letters" the author has achieved another success which will add to the number of his American friends and readers.

"Any one who has read any of the fascinating stories in which the shrewd detective, Sherlock Holmes, figures as the very personification of detective logic applied to the detection of crime, knows that Conan Doyle is a story-teller of the very first order of merit. Like his own character, Sherlock Holmes, he possesses the power of getting out of everything all there is in it."—*Philadelphia Item.*

"Dr. Doyle's stories are so well known for their strong dramatic style, for the elegance of expression, that anything new from his pen is sure to be warmly welcomed. His readers are sure of getting a literary treat from anything he writes. He is broadminded and liberal, and the man who could write two such books as 'The White Company' and 'The Refugees' has a future which the shades of Scott and Dickens might envy."—*Albany Times-Union.*

SEVENTH EDITION.

ROUND THE RED LAMP. 12mo. Cloth, $1.50.

The "Red Lamp," the trade-mark, as it were, of the English country practitioner's office, is the central point of these dramatic stories of professional life. There are no secrets for the surgeon, and, a surgeon himself as well as a novelist, the author has made a most artistic use of the motives and springs of action revealed to him in a field of which he is the master.

"Too much can not be said in praise of these strong productions, that, to read, keep one's heart leaping to the throat and the mind in a tumult of anticipation to the end. . . . No series of short stories in modern literature can approach them."—*Hartford Times.*

"If Mr. A. Conan Doyle had not already placed himself in the front rank of living English writers by 'The Refugees,' and other of his larger stories, he would surely do so by these fifteen short tales."—*New York Mail and Express.*

"The reading of these choice stories will prove an exciting pleasure to all who may linger on the pages that present them."—*Boston Courier.*

"A strikingly realistic and decidedly original contribution to modern literature."—*Boston Saturday Evening Gazette.*

"Every page reveals the literary artist, the keen observer, the trained delineator of human nature, its weal and its woe. . . . Dr. Doyle has a rich note-book or, we should say, a golden memory."—*London Freeman's Journal.*

SOME STANDARD FICTION.

THE GODS, SOME MORTALS, AND LORD WICKENHAM. By JOHN OLIVER HOBBES. With Portrait. 12mo. Cloth, $1.50.

"Mrs. Craigie has taken her place among the novelists of the day. It is a high place and a place apart. Her method is her own, and she stands not exactly on the threshold of a great career, but already within the temple of fame."—G. W. SMALLEY, in *The Tribune.*

"One of the most refreshing novels of the period, full of grace, spirit, force, feeling, and literary charm."—*Chicago Evening Post.*

"Clever and cynical, full of epigrams and wit, bright with keen delineations of character, and with a shrewd insight into life."—*Newark Advertiser.*

A FLASH OF SUMMER. By Mrs. W. K. CLIFFORD, author of "Love Letters of a Worldly Woman," "Aunt Anne," etc. 12mo. Cloth, $1.50.

"The story is well written and interesting, the style is limpid and pure as fresh water, and is so artistically done that it is only a second thought that notices it."—*San Francisco Call.*

"Will attract a wide circle of admirers. It is a charming novel in every way. The characters are living ones, and the incidents are so cleverly worked out that one recognizes the hand of a master in the work."—*Columbus Dispatch.*

MAELCHO. By the Hon. EMILY LAWLESS, author of "Grania," "Hurrish," etc. 12mo. Cloth, $1.50.

"A paradox of literary genius. It is not a history, and yet has more of the stuff of history in it, more of the true national character and fate, than any historical monograph we know. It is not a novel, and yet fascinates us more than any novel."—*London Spectator.*

"Abounds in thrilling incidents. . . . Above and beyond all, the book charms by reason of the breadth of view, the magnanimity, and the tenderness which animate the author."—*London Athenæum.*

IN THE FIRE OF THE FORGE. A Romance of Old Nuremberg By GEORG EBERS, author of "Cleopatra," "An Egyptian Princess," etc. In 2 vols. 16mo. Paper, 80 cents; cloth, $1.50.

"A delightful and stirring romance of that wonderful old city of Nuremberg in the time of Emperor Rudolph. . . . A romance that needs no startling *dénoûment* to commend it or to sustain its even measure of interest."—*Boston Herald.*

"A quiet, refined story. Though the incidents are never startling, they are strong enough to hold the reader's attention throughout."—*New York Times.*